SMOCKING and F
19th Century

Near the end of the 19th century, when costume reached absurd proportions with the enormous bustle and mutton sleeve, smocking, primarily as dress ornamentation for women's garments, established a vogue for both casual and formal wear as well as for decorative items around the home.

The making of garments became a practical pastime with the latest published patterns easily available and the understanding that every detail could be mastered by the home sewer. Before the term *French Hand Sewing* became today's "in" term, all sewing of this period was simply denoted as *Plain Needlework* and covered all the knowledge required for the careful workmanship and detailing of these elaborate costumes.

This volume includes several of the lessons from Weldon's, the premier women's handwork magazine from England, published during the 1880's and 1890's which focused on late Victorian needlework. From this rich source, the related subjects of Smocking, Plain Needlework, Jeweled Embroidery—focusing on exquisite embellishment ideas; and Knick-Knacks—showing how the same sewing techniques were applied to decorative household items; were selected.

CON

LACIS
PUBLICATIONS
3163 Adeline Street, Berkeley, CA 94703

© 1998, LACIS

ISBN 1-891656-04-X

WELDON'S PRACTICAL SMOCKING.
(SECOND SERIES.)
How to Work Smocking, and Make Useful Articles and Garments for Ladies and Children.

SMOCKING.

SMOCKING is more than ever in vogue this season, and is applied to every conceivable article of dress, for not only are children's artistic costumes smocked round the neck, or in a yoke across the chest, but the fashion is arising for ladies' blouses, and Garibaldi jackets, which are elaborately smocked, and the fulness confined round the waist by a band and a buckle; these are really comfortable for every-day wear, and are most useful, as any skirt can be worn with them. Panels for tea-gowns are smocked across the bust, and again at the waist, the intermediate space being left loose and baggy. Some new skirts are made with a breadth of material smocked on each side to the depth of about a quarter of a yard from the waist. A piece of smocking looks well let into the front of a bodice like a vest, or as a waistcoat. Sleeves are smocked at the back below the shoulder, or midway between the shoulder and the elbow, and again at the wrist. Hats and poke bonnets for little children are smocked to match their costumes. Even sunshades are smocked, and it is wonderful how readily, owing to its extreme elasticity, the work adapts itself to any and every purpose.

Although essentially a dress ornamentation, smocking can be used for various articles of household decoration; it makes a pretty covering for drawing-room work-baskets, cushions for the drawing-room, footstools, also glove and handkerchief cases, bags, &c., and odd pieces of silks and satins may be employed, joining them with due regard to colour, and when gathering it can be managed that the joins come at the back of the pleats, where they will be quite invisible.

Smocking may be worked upon almost any material, the Liberty silks, Pongee silks, and Umritza cachemire being especially suitable. White or coloured embroidery silk of fast colour should be employed for the work, unless the smocking is to be done upon linen, when ingrain cotton may be used.

We here present a variety of lovely and perfectly original designs both of new smocking stitches and of smocking as applied to ladies' and children's garments. The favourite honeycomb smocking, and other useful fancy stitches, will be found in No. 19 of this Work Series, together with full explanations for working the same, and instructions for preparing and gathering the material.

It is impossible to work good smocking unless the gathering threads are run perfectly straight, and at equal distances from each other, and each stitch taken exactly the same length, so that when drawn up tightly the pleats lie even and regular. Briggs' Transfer Designs, No. 400 and No. 401, dotted for honeycomb, are a great con-

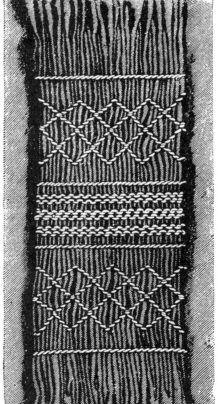

The Montague Pattern.

venience to ladies' working. Otherwise, we strongly recommend the plan of **ruling lines** straight across from right to left on the *wrong* side of the material, measuring the distances by a tape measure, three-eighths of an inch or half an inch apart, as may be desired, and crossing these lines by others drawn perpendicularly half an inch apart for gauging the size of the stitches; these lines can be drawn with a yellow lead pencil on dark material; then thread a needle with cotton, white for gathering on dark material, and black for gathering on light fabrics, make a good knot at the end, and run straight from right to left upon each parallel line, inserting the needle where the perpendicular lines cross, and bringing it out midway between these latter. When all are done, draw up and secure each gathering thread by passing round a pin. The advantage of gathering with thread of opposite colour to the material is that it makes a more visible guide, as you can at a glance distinctly perceive it between the pleats. Of course, the smocking is worked on the right side of the material, and every row begins on the left-hand side. No stitches whatever should show at the back of the work. When the smocking is finished the gathering threads are taken out, and the work should be elastic, expanding or contracting, as may be desired.

MONTAGUE PATTERN.

THIS is a combination of the diamond pattern with utline stitch, rope stitch, and cable stitch; it is simple of execution, and quickly worked, yet very pretty and effective. It measures 4½ inches in depth. Prepare the material by drawing seventeen parallel lines straight across from right to left, a quarter of an inch apart, to ensure perfect regularity of the gathering threads, and cross these by perpendicular lines, three-eighths of an inch apart, for gauging the size of the pleats. Gather the seventeen lines according to previous instructions, and when all are done draw up the threads as tight as required, and fix each with a pin at the end. Then, having the needle threaded with silk for working, hold the material the right side towards you, and bring the needle up from the back in the first pleat on the left-hand side, exactly over the first gathering thread, insert the needle from right to left to take up this first pleat only, keep the silk well over the needle, and draw the needle out: take up the second pleat in the same way, then the third pleat, and so on, one pleat at a time, always exactly over the gathering thread, and always bringing the needle out below the stitch; this is known as outline stitch. Work the same upon the seventh gathering thread; also on the eleventh and on the seventeenth gathering threads. Next, for the diamond pattern, bring the needle up in the first pleat on the second gathering thread, make a stitch on the second pleat on the same gathering thread, bringing out the point of the needle below the stitch just formed, work a stitch successively on the third, fourth, and fifth pleats each a little lower than the preceding, and so that the stitch upon the fifth pleat comes exactly upon the third gathering thread, make a stitch upon the sixth pleat on the same gathering thread, bringing the needle out above the stitch just formed, work a stitch successively on the seventh, eighth, and ninth pleats, each a little higher than the foregoing, and so that the stitch upon the ninth pleat comes upon the second gathering thread, work a stitch on the tenth pleat on the same gathering thread, bringing out the point of the needle below the stitch just formed, and continue thus up and down to the end of the row. For the second row, commence in the first pleat on the fourth gathering thread, take up the second pleat on the same gathering thread, bringing out the point of the needle above the stitch just formed, take up in succession the third, fourth, and fifth pleats, each a little higher than the preceding, and so that the stitch upon the fifth pleat comes upon the third gathering thread close by the stitch that already is worked there in the course of the first row, take up the sixth pleat on the same gathering thread, bringing out the needle below the stitch just formed, take up successively the seventh, eighth, and ninth pleats, each a little lower than the foregoing, and so that the stitch upon the ninth pleat comes upon the fourth gathering thread, take up the tenth pleat on the same gathering thread, bringing the needle out above the stitch just formed, and continue. The third row of the diamond pattern begins on the fourth gathering thread, close to the commencement of the second row, and is worked first down and then up, as directed for the first row: and the fourth row begins on the sixth gathering thread, and is worked like the second row, first up and then down. This same diamond pattern is repeated from the twelfth to the sixteenth gathering threads. This done, there remains the rope stitch and the cable stitch to be worked in the central space of the material. The rope stitch is placed just above and just below the eighth gathering thread, and is carried out in this manner,—bring up the needle in the first pleat, take up the second pleat, bringing out the needle below the stitch, take up the third pleat, bringing out the needle above the stitch, take up the fourth pleat and bring the needle out below the stitch, take up the fifth pleat, and bring the needle out above the stitch, and so on, working only one pleat at a time, and keeping the stitches perfectly straight; by the method of bringing out the silk first below the stitch and then above, it appears as if every two pleats were coupled together. Repeat the two lines of rope stitch on both sides of the tenth gathering thread. There now remains the ninth gathering thread, along each side of which a row has to be worked in a similar manner to that described for rope stitch, but insomuch as by a slight variation in working the lower row, where the needle is brought out *above* the stitch in doing the *second* pleat, and *below* the stitch in doing the *third* pleat, and so on, making every alternate stitch meet in the centre with the corresponding stitch of the first row, it much resembles the links of a cable.

No. 3719.—SMOCKED TEA-GOWN.

A CHARMING model for a tea-gown, suitable for reproduction in all soft materials, the front being of silk if preferred, or all one material can be used. It is cut *en princesse* with a lining front, on to which the full silk front is arranged, this being gauged at the neck, then smocked in any design one may prefer, the fulness beneath the smocking falling in pouf form, turned under just below waist, where moiré ribbon is arranged in loops and ends. From here the fulness of the front is pressed in pleats to the extreme edge of the skirt. The material front then meets this full front, and the French back cut to a little below waist has the full skirt part gathered on to it and turned over, which has a pretty effect. The sleeve consists of a lining foundation cut in coat shape, on to which a full upper is arranged, this being gathered into the armhole, also smocked just below the shoulder and at wrist. Numerous new suggestions for smocking are shown by the several pretty combinations of stitches illustrated in this issue. Quantity of cachemire for entire gown, 6 yards. Flat pattern, 1s.; untrimmed, 2s.; trimmed, 5s. 6d.

No. 3709.—SMOCKED PINAFORE, WITH ROUND NECK AND SLEEVE CARRIED INTO NECK.

A PRETTY little pinafore or overall for children of 2 to 10 years, or it can even be converted into a dress by cutting the skirt part longer, and encircling the waist with a soft silk sash. The sleeve is cut into the shoulder just as

No. 3719.—Smocked Tea-Gown.

countrymen's smocks are done, then the smocking is arranged to form a round yoke, leaving a tiny frill to stand up round the neck, the sleeve being gathered in just above the elbow, also just below it, where it is smocked in cuff form, leaving a frill round the wrist. The edge of pinafore is hemmed and ornamented with a row of fancy stitching. The smocking consists of two rows of honeycomb stitch, divided by two rows of outline or rope stitch, see illustrations 4 and 5 in "Weldon's Practical Smocking," 1st series; or any other pretty stitch could be employed. Quantity of 36-inch material, 2¾, 3, 3½, and 4 yards. Flat pattern, 6d.; untrimmed, 1s. 4d.; trimmed, 2s.

No. 3727.—SMOCKED PRINCESS DRESS.

FOR children 6 to 12 years this dress is exceedingly becoming, while it is capable of reproduction in all soft goods. The smocked front and outside of sleeve could even be of soft silk, and the rest of the dress of cachemire. It is cut quite *en princesse*, the extra fulness of the front being smocked at the neck in yoke form, from whence the fulness is pressed into pleats and taped at the waist, also midway down the skirt part to prevent getting out of order.
The French back is cut with a short basque, on to which the full skirt part is gathered and turned over, then the neck is finished with a band collar. The sleeve is cut sufficiently full to permit of its being smocked on the outside at the shoulder, elbow, and wrist. It would be an extremely pretty pattern for washing materials, and those not desiring to work the smocking could very well gauge the neck and sleeve. Honeycomb, outline, and rope stitches are shown in the illustration, or basket stitch No. 8. Feather stitch and chevron No. 11, Feather stitch and zigzag, No. 10, Spanish pattern, No. 12, Empress pattern No. 15, are all suitable designs, and these are fully detailed and clearly illustrated in "Weldon's Practical Smocking," 1st series. Quantity of 27-inch material, 4, 4½, and 5 yards. Flat pattern, 9d.; untrimmed, 1s. 6d.; trimmed, 3s. 6d.

No. 3654.—SMOCKED PRINCESS PINAFORE WITH FULL SLEEVE.

THIS would equally well serve as a dress, and if not wished to hang straight from the smocking, it could be gathered again at the waist, and even have a sash tied in loops and ends over the back. It is a pretty arrangement for all soft goods such as cambric, plain and checked linens, alpaca, brown or grey holland, smocked with coloured embroidery cotton, &c., as may suit one's ideas and fancies. The extra width of the fronts is smocked to a few inches below the neck in honeycomb, Spanish, diamond, herring-bone, or diamond lattice stitches, all of which are fully detailed and described in "Weldon's Practical Smocking," 1st series, or there are many pretty designs in this issue. The smocking draws the fulness in to the width of the chest, the back being quite plain and *en princesse*, joined at the shoulders and under arms by a run and felled seam, when the edge of each back is hemmed, then buttons sewn on and buttonholes worked to correspond, the neck being finished with a turn-down collar, which, however, may be replaced by a frill of lace, or the neck merely piped if preferred. The full sleeve gathers to the size of the armhole, then is stitched in, while the wrist part is smocked in honeycomb stitch to draw it in to the wrist size, leaving a tiny frill to fall over the hand. The inferior edge of the pinafore is finished by a hem, which can be headed with a fancy stitching, if desired, or tucks could even be added. This pattern is arranged in sizes 2 to 10 years. Quantity of 36-inch material, 1¾, 2¼, 3, and 3½ yards. Flat pattern, 6d.; untrimmed, 1s. 4d.; trimmed 2s.

No. 3710.—POINTED SMOCKED PINAFORE WITH FULL SLEEVE TO NECK.

THIS little smocked pinafore has the full sleeve cut into the shoulder just as country smocks are made, and our illustration is suitable for print, alpaca, holland, &c., while cut a little longer, and with a sash round the waist, it would form a pretty dress for cambric, cachemire, veiling, tussore silk, &c. The pattern can be had in ages 2 to 10 years. It consists of four pieces—front, back, sleeve, yoke—the sleeves after being joined to the back and front being gathered up and smocked with the pinafore to form a point yoke like effect, back and front, an inch or so being left round the neck as a frill. Nearly all the stitches shown in this issue, as well as those in "Weldon's Practical Smocking," 1st series, can be employed, and the smocking is strengthened by being sewn on to a fitted yoke, then the full sleeve is smocked in honeycomb stitch round the wrist in cuff form, leaving a tiny frill over the hand. The seam under the arm should be run and felled, and the lower edge hemmed up, above which two or three narrow tucks should be run in. Quantity of 36-inch material, 3, 3½, 4 and 4½ yards. Flat pattern, 6d.; untrimmed, 1s. 4d.; trimmed, 2s.

No. 3705.—SMOCKED PRINCESS DRESS.

FOR girls of 6 to 10 years this is a most becoming dress, and looks well in such soft materials as tussore, art silks, cachemire, veiling, zephyrs, or any of the pretty cambrics now manufactured. It is cut as a princess dress, the lining of which is fitted to the figure, and on to which the material front is arranged, this being cut sufficiently full in the centre to permit of gathering up, and it is then smocked as a square yoke. The fulness from here is pressed in pleats. The back has the superfluous fulness in the centre placed in pleats which fan out nicely under the sash, this being of soft silk, folded round the waist, and tied behind. The neck has a roll collar. The full sleeve gathered into the armhole is gathered or smocked with rope stitch about midway between shoulder and elbow, and just below here it is smocked in cuff form, with the same stitch, leaving an inch or so to form a frill over the hand. The yoke part is smocked in honeycomb and rope stitches, or the various new stitches shown in this issue can be employed. Quantity of 36-inch material, 5 and 6 yards. Flat pattern, 9d.; untrimmed, 1s. 8d.; trimmed, 4s.

No. 3653.—SMOCKED YOKE PINAFORE WITH SMOCKED SLEEVE.

THIS becoming little overall or pinafore is suitable for children of 2 to 10 years; it would serve nicely for a dress, as the waist could be encircled by a soft silk sash tied in loops and ends behind. The pattern consists of a princess front and back which must be gathered round the neck to the required size, then finished a roll collar, or a tiny piece of the material may be left as a frill all round the throat, as shown by illustration 3710, or it can be piped or finished with a quilling or turn down frill of lace or embroidery. From the neck, back and front, as far as the dotted line marked across the pattern, it is smocked in diamond lattice pattern, or any fancy stitch preferred, for which see "Weldon's Practical Smocking," 1st series, or the numerous stitches here illustrated. The smocking, when done, is made firm by the plain fitted yoke which is attached on the wrong side, then from this smocking the pinafore hangs full, with the hem headed with a fancy stitching which has a pretty effect. The sleeve is full on the outside only, and is smocked at the top and wrist to match the yoke-like smocking of the front and back. Quantity of 32-inch material, 2¼, 3, 3½ and 4¼ yards. Flat pattern, 6d.; untrimmed, 1s. 4d.; trimmed, 2s.

No. 3706.—SMOCKED BLOUSE DRESS WITH FULL SLEEVE.

EXTREMELY becoming to children of 4 to 10 years, while it is a style suited to all soft fabrics, and is especially pretty in silk, veiling, cachemire, or zephyr cottons. It consists of a sailor blouse, with the full sleeve cut into the neck just as the country smocks are done, then it is gauged or smocked to form a round yoke, leaving an inch or so round the neck for the tiny frill. Rope or outline stitches, see "Weldon's Practical Smocking," 1st series, or a pretty and quickly-worked design is offered by Pointed Honeycomb on our centre pages. The fulness from the yoke is turned under at the waist and gathered on to the lining foundation bodice, thus forming a blouse or Garibaldi effect, from under which the full skirt is pleated, this being finished with a deep hem and tucks. The fulness of the sleeve is gathered in above and below the elbow, at the last-named the gauging or smocking being continued to correspond with the yoke, and a tiny frill is left to fall over the hand. Quantity of 32-inch material, 4½, 5 and 5½ yards. Flat pattern, 9d.; untrimmed, 1s. 8d.; trimmed, 3s. 6d.

SMOCKED WAISTCOAT.

THOUGH appearing rather elaborate in the engraving, this piece of work is not at all difficult to accomplish, and is a very pretty addition to the front of a dress. It may also be employed as a panel for an afternoon tea-gown. For a waistcoat, procure a piece of Pongee or Indian silk, 24 inches long and 24 inches wide. Prepare for smocking by drawing parallel lines on the wrong side thereof, the first line to be four and a half inches from the top, followed by twenty-six other lines at intervals of a quarter of an inch apart; cross them with perpendicular lines three-eighths of an inch apart for gauging the size of the pleats. Leave seven inches for fulness to hang loose. Then draw six more parallel lines for smocking at the waist. Gather. Now, just above and just below the first gathering thread work a double row of cable stitch, and the same just above and just below the tenth gathering thread. Work simple cable stitch upon the second, third, and fourth, and upon the seventh, eighth, and ninth gathering threads. Work five rows of outline stitch in the space between the fifth and sixth gathering threads. Begin the diamond pattern upon the eleventh gathering thread, working six rows to make three complete diamonds, after the manner detailed in the Montague pattern; this will bring you to the seventeenth gathering thread. For the waist, you repeat the five rows of outline stitch, with two rows of cable stitch above and below. When finished draw the smocking to the required width, and tack it upon a stiff lining. It may be set into the bodice with revers or in any other way according to taste.

No. 3709.—Smocked Pinafore, with Round Neck and Sleeve carried into the Neck.

No. 3699.—THE VALERIE DRESS.

THIS charming dress is particularly suited to soft materials, our illustration showing for the beautiful art silks and cachemire, or veiling. The foundation skirt is of lining, faced up a few inches with material, then trimmed on the right side with a couple of widths of silk, the fulness of which is smocked over the hip, with any of the pretty designs shown in this issue. The drapery of cachemire, or some material of an equally soft nature, is pleated five times into the waist on the right side and four times on the left, the fifth pleat here being made into the side seam of the skirt, where the tunic side joins its entire length. The back drapery pleats or gathers into the same waistband as the skirt back, and on either side it goes into one downward pleat; then just below the waist each set of two holes should be placed to the corresponding holes in the skirt and secured, and the same with the single holes, each of which should be sewn to the corresponding holes in skirt, thus arranging a graceful pouf, while the fulness is equally regulated to the skirt edge. The bodice is smocked back and front in yoke form, on to a fitted lining front and back, which are cut to a little below the waist, so that when the skirt is put over it there is no fear of riding up. The full front and back are marked by a dotted line for gathering up the neck, for the depth of the smocking, and for the waist line, any of the smocking designs illustrated in this issue or in "Weldon's Practical Smocking," 1st series, being suitable. The sleeve is cut full on the outside and smocked at the shoulder and wrist to correspond with bodice. In ages 12 to 18 years. Quantity of cachemire, 5, 5½ and 6 yards; silk, 2½ and 3 yards. Flat pattern, 9d.; untrimmed, 1s. 9d.; trimmed, 4s. 6d.

BELVIDERE PATTERN.

THIS pattern measures 3½ inches in depth, and seventeen parallel lines should be drawn on the material from right to left for the proper disposal of the gathering threads, the first and second lines are only one-eighth of an inch apart, the third and fourth, and fifth and sixth lines are each respectively a quarter of an inch below, the seventh line again is one-eighth of an inch from the sixth line, and the same distances are repeated till the requisite depth is attained. The perpendicular lines for gauging the size of the pleats require to be three-eighths of an inch apart. When the gathers are duly in order, work first of all the cable stitch which occupies the two first gathering threads, begin on the first gathering thread by bringing the needle out in the first pleat, take up the second pleat only bringing out the needle below the stitch, take up the third pleat only bringing out the needle above the stitch, next the fourth pleat only bringing out the needle below the stitch, then the fifth pleat only bringing out the needle above the stitch, and continue thus alternately to the end of the row. The next row is worked in the same manner, but reversely, thus you commence on the first pleat upon the second gathering thread, take up the second pleat only bringing out the needle above the stitch, take up the third pleat only bringing out the needle below the stitch, and so on, and by this procedure every alternate stitch comes nearly close to the approximate stitch in the former row, and the two rows together bear a resemblance to the links of a cable. Work a similar cable stitch on the sixth and seventh, the eleventh and twelfth, and the sixteenth and seventeenth gathering threads. Then for the upper insertion, which is chevron stitch, commence on the third gathering thread, bringing up the needle in the first pleat, take up the second pleat on the same gathering thread and bringing the needle out below the stitch, take up the third, fourth, fifth, and sixth pleats each in rotation, and just so much lower than each other as to take the sixth pleat exactly over the fourth gathering thread, take the seventh pleat just a trifle lower, take the eighth pleat on the same level as the stitch last formed and let the needle come out above the stitch, take up the ninth pleat precisely over the fourth gathering thread, and then take the tenth, eleventh, twelfth, and thirteenth pleats, each in succession upwards, and so that the thirteenth pleat is taken exactly over the third gathering thread, then take up the fourteenth pleat on the same gathering thread but bring the needle out below the stitch, and proceed downwards, and then upwards, keeping precisely on the same level to the end of the row. Three more rows of chevron stitch are to be worked successively under this row, each quite close together; as in the row just worked the sixth pleat is taken on the fourth gathering thread, so in the second row the fifth pleat is taken there; in the third row the fourth pleat is taken there; and in the fourth and last row the third pleat is taken on the fourth gathering thread, and the seventh pleat and the eighth pleat will both be taken on the fifth gathering thread; thus the whole four lines of chevron stitch occupy the material from the third to the fifth gathering threads. When this is done work together the fifth and sixth pleats in a honeycomb dot on the gathering thread between each chevron. The same stitch is repeated for the lower insertion from the thirteenth to the fifteenth gathering threads. The centre insertion forms a series of lozenges worked in feather stitch. Hold the material so that the pleats run from right to left instead of up and down, and bring the needle out in the first pleat just a trifle to the right of the ninth (the central) gathering thread, make a stitch on this first pleat, then secure the silk under your left thumb while you take the second pleat on the needle a little further to the right of the preceding stitch, draw the needle through the pleat and over

No. 3727.—Smocked Princess Dress.

No. 3654.—Smocked Princess Pinafore with full Sleeve.

No. 3710.—Pointed Smocked Pinafore with full Sleeve to Neck.

No. 3705.—Smocked Princess Dress.

No. 3653.—Smocked Yoke Pinafore with Smocked Sleeve.

No. 3706.—Smocked Blouse Dress with full Sleeve.

the loop of silk, take the third pleat yet a little more to the right, looping the silk in the same manner, take the fourth pleat exactly over the eighth gathering thread, and take the fifth pleat yet a trifle more to the right, then take the sixth pleat over the eighth gathering thread, looping the silk round the needle from right to left, work on the seventh, eighth, and ninth pleats each a little further towards the left hand and with each stitch looping the silk round the point of the needle; the stitch on the first pleat should come level with the stitch on the first pleat; now turn again towards the right, then to the left, four stitches each way, to the end of the row. Re-commence by bringing the needle out in the first pleat a very little to the left of the ninth gathering thread, make a stitch on the first pleat, then work four feather stitches towards the left, four towards the right, and so on, to correspond exactly with the stitches of the first row. Finish by working a honeycomb dot in the centre of each lozenge.

SMOCKED SLEEVE.

OUR engraving shows a sleeve cut in one piece and smocked to the depth of three inches midway between the top and the elbow, and again above the wrist, upon just that portion of material which, when in wear, comes at the back of the arm. About 22 inches in width of material will be required for a full-sized sleeve. Draw the first parallel line four inches from the top of the material, and then draw three more lines each one inch apart further below; the cross-lines for gauging the size of the pleats are three-eighths of an inch apart. Work a row of cable stitches on each of the gathering threads. Fill the space between the first and second gathering threads with feather stitch, doing six stitches up and six stitches down in vandyke. Work the same between the third and fourth gathering threads; and along the centre of the space between the second and third gathering threads work five lines of outline stitch closely together. Finish with a row of feather stitching worked perpendicularly close to the first and last pleats. When arranged upon the sleeve lining the smocking should be drawn out to occupy three square inches. A similar square of smocking is worked just above the wrist.

GOTHIC PATTERN.

THIS is a bold, handsome pattern, quite easy to work, and only requires a little practice to get the stitches perfectly even. It measures 4½ inches in depth. Draw thirteen parallel lines from right to left across the material, three-eighths of an inch apart, on which to run gathering threads, and cross these with perpendicular lines half an inch apart for gauging the size of the pleats. Gather in the usual manner. On the first, second, third and, fourth, and on the tenth, eleventh, twelfth, and thirteenth gathering threads, work rows of outline stitch. Then for the first row of insertion, bring out the needle in the first pleat just below the top row of outline stitch, and sew the second and first pleats together twice, insert the needle in the same place in the second pleat only bringing the point of the needle out under the stitch just made, take up on the needle the third pleat only just above the second row of outline stitch, and then sew the fourth and third pleats together twice, insert the needle in the same place in the fourth pleat only bringing the point out above the stitch just made; then work first the fifth and then the sixth and fifth pleats together, and afterwards the sixth pleat only just below the top row of outline stitch, and then first the seventh, and then the eighth and seventh pleats together, and afterwards the eighth pleat only just above the second row of outline stitch, and continue. Work in the same manner in the space between the third and fourth rows of outline stitch, and this completes the upper insertion. The lower insertion is worked similarly between the corresponding rows of outline stitch. The Gothic portion of the design extends over three inches of material, and the *centre* of the pattern comes precisely upon the seventh (the middle) gathering thread. The stitches are formed in the same way as the up and down stitches of the insertion, but now four dots are worked in an

Smocked Waistcoat.

upward direction, then three dots downward, three up, three down, and so on. To begin, bring up the needle in the first pleat on the seventh gathering thread and work the second and first pleats together twice, then the second pleat only in the same place and bringing the needle out above the stitch; the next dot is formed on the third and fourth pleats midway between the sixth and seventh gathering threads, the third dot on the fifth and sixth pleats on the sixth gathering thread, the fourth dot on the seventh and eighth pleats midway between the fifth and sixth gathering threads; then working downwards make a dot on the ninth and tenth pleats on the sixth gathering thread, a dot on the eleventh and twelfth pleats midway between the sixth and seventh gathering threads, and a dot on the thirteenth and fourteenth pleats on the seventh (the middle) gathering thread, and this constitutes one Gothic point; proceed in the same manner to the end of the row. The next row is worked *above* this row, and commences midway between the sixth and seventh gathering threads with the first dot upon the first and second pleats, and the point is carried upwards till the highest or fourth dot comes upon the fifth gathering thread, and the stitches then turn downwards to the same level upon which the row commenced. The third row begins on the sixth gathering thread and extends thence upwards to midway between the fourth and fifth gathering threads. Then to form the lower portion of the Gothic points you re-commence upon the seventh gathering thread, working one stitch only upon the dot which already is worked there, and proceed downwards as far as midway between the eighth and ninth gathering threads, and continue for all three rows exactly as the upper portion is worked, only in reverse position, as will be seen by reference to the illustration. The little dots in the centre of each Gothic pattern are made separately afterwards, and are worked simply as a honeycomb dot, the ends of the silk being brought into the same pleat at the back and tied together for security.

No. 3694.—THE AMIENS DRESS.

No more desirable style can possibly be shown than the one here illustrated, and which is suitable for children of 4 to 12 years. It is made *en princesse*, and trimmed with pinking, the front having a fitted plastron, on to which the silk plastron is honeycombed at the neck and waist, or it can be merely gauged if desired. The illustrations in this issue offer pretty ideas for smocking this dress. It is cut with a princess front, French back, to a little below waist, on to which the pleated skirt part is arranged, from the side-seam being brought a sash of ribbon, which ties over the full back in loops and ends. Quantity of 24-inch cloth, 3, 3½, 4, and 5 yards; silk, 1½ and 2 yards. Flat pattern, 9d.; untrimmed, 1s. 6d.; trimmed, 3s. 6d.

POINTED HONEYCOMB FOR THE FRONT OF CHILD'S DRESS.

REQUIRED, a piece of material from 12 inches to 14 inches long to reach from the neck to the waist, and about 68 inches wide to allow for the front and the backs to be worked in one piece. Hem the top in a hem half an inch deep to form a frill, or put a strip of coloured material inside for a false hem of that depth. Then prepare lines for the smocking; let the first line be drawn close under the hem, five eighths of an inch from the top of the material, and draw five more lines below this line, half an inch apart, and cross them with other lines also half an inch apart. Mark the width of the material with a bit of coloured cotton at halves, quarters, and eighths, so that you may arrange the fulness accurately upon the body lining. Then commence the smocking by doing a row of outline stitch on the first gathering thread. Begin honeycombing midway on the space between this line and the next gathering thread, working a dot here, then a dot on the second gathering thread, and so on, up and down, to the end of the row. Begin the next row

No. 3299.—The Valerie Dress.

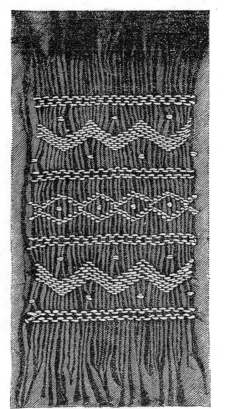

The Belvidere Pattern.

Smoc

Pointed Honeycomb for the Front of Child's Dress.

No. 3652.—Yoke Pinafore with Blouse Sleeves.

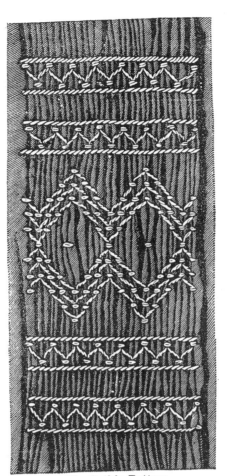

The Gothic Pattern.

No. 3694.—Amiens Dress.

eeve

o. 3711.—Smocked Garibaldi Blouse.

No. 3634.—Smocked Yoke Dress with Full Sleeves.

Smocked Front for a Child's Bodice.

of honeycombing in the space midway between the second and third gathering threads, and work a dot in the space alternately with a dot on the third gathering thread, till you have done eight dots in the top line, and seven dots below, when fasten off. Now bring the honeycomb dots gradually to a point, by working six dots and five dots respectively below the row last worked. Then four dots and three dots again below; and end with two dots and one dot. Commence the next point on the next two pleats of the third line of honeycomb dots, and work it in the same manner. And so on till all the points are complete. Have the lining cut to shape to fit the child, and sew up the shoulder seams, but not the seams under the arms at present. Divide the lining in halves and quarters, and arrange the smocking thereupon to correspond, placing the pleats rather closely round the neck, and gradually expanding to the shape of the shoulders. Place the fulling nicely, and tack it in place on the top of the arm, and cut away as much of the material as is necessary to shape the armholes. Then join up the body seams in the usual way, and pleat the fulness to the waist.

No. 3652.—YOKE PINAFORE WITH BLOUSE SLEEVE.

A SWEETLY pretty little pinafore, for holland, gingham, alpaca, and such soft materials, made with a plain yoke back and front to which the full front and back of the pinafore are smocked in honeycomb stitch, then gathered into the armhole is a full sleeve which, at the wrist, has its fulness honeycombed to match front, leaving an inch frill to fall over the hand. Avoid a seam down yoke front and pinafore front by placing these parts of the pattern to a fold in the material, adding gores at the sides of the back and front of pinafore to gain the desired width. The edge is hemmed, and above this three narrow tucks are run in, and which are allowed for in the pattern. The neck is finished with a roll over collar, or it can be merely piped and a piece of lace or embroidery sewn on. In ages 2 to 10 years. Honeycomb smocking is shown on page 5 of "Weldon's Practical Smocking," 1st series. This pinafore arranged as a dress is shown by illustration 3652, centre top figure on page 11. Quantity of 32-inch cambric, 3¼, 3½, 4, and 4½ yards. Flat pattern, 6d.; untrimmed, 1s. 4d.; trimmed, 2s.

No. 3711.—SMOCKED GARIBALDI BLOUSE.

THIS design is an extremely pretty one, smocked as a pointed yoke, and yet the easy blouse or Garibaldi effect is retained. It reproduces well in soft silk, flannel, sateen, cambric, veiling or cachemire, its neck being smocked in V-shape back and front, with the neck secured by a band collar, over which a frill is gathered. There is a lining back and front given, which fits the figure, and on to which the smocking is secured, then the pattern of the two side pieces serve for cutting out the material and lining. The fulness from the smocking at back is brought down to the waist, and gathered on to the lining, while the front fulness is gathered so as to droop over a trifle in Garibaldi form, round the waist being a belt. The sleeve is smocked on the outside a trifle below the shoulder, while the wrist part, cut wider than in an ordinary sleeve, is smocked all round to draw it up to the required size, forming a frill over the hand. Open Diamond pattern is shown in our illustration, No. 13, see "Weldon's Practical Smocking," 1st series. Quantity of 36-inch silk, 4 yards. Flat pattern, 6d.; untrimmed, 1s. 6d.; trimmed, 3s. 6d.

No. 3634.—SMOCKED YOKE DRESS WITH FULL SLEEVES.

THIS quaint little dress is suitable for merino, cachemire, fine serge, flannel, or washing goods, made *en princesse* back and front, fitted with a yoke, above which is a turn down collar, then the sleeve is full on the outside, smocked at the shoulder and wrist. The front of the dress is gathered at the neck, then smocked, this being repeated at the waist, and from each side is a full sash tied behind in loops and ends. The full back is smocked under the yoke to correspond with the front, but the waist need only be gathered, or even left quite loose, as the sash which is stitched on each side of the waist smocking in front, will confine the back fulness sufficiently. The skirt part is finished with a deep hem, above which are three narrow tucks, each of which is headed with a fancy stitching worked in silk, this stitching being repeated on the collar. For children of 2 to 10 years this is as pretty a little dress as could be desired, and those not wishing to smock it can gauge the fulness, which would look very well. Full particulars, as well as numerous illustrations showing and describing the various stitches in smocking, are given in "Weldon's Practical Smocking," 1st series, price 2d., post free 2½d.; or there are suitable designs in this issue. Quantity of 27-inch material, 4½, 5½, 6¼, and 7 yards. Flat pattern, 9d.; untrimmed, 1s. 6d.; trimmed, 3s. 6d.

SMOCKED FRONT FOR A CHILD'S BODICE.

THIS bodice is smocked in separate pieces, forming a front and two backs. The material used for the front of our example is 14 inches long and 40 inches wide. The work consists of an insertion of Diamond pattern flanked by five straight rows on each side, the top row and the lower row being worked in cable stitch, the three centre rows in rope stitch (for description of working these stitches see Montague pattern), these rows are at a distance of a quarter of an inch apart. The Diamond insertion is worked in three rows, and occupies the depth of one and a quarter inches, a quarter of an inch being left vacant between it and the straight lines of cable stitches. When the smocking is finished pin the centre of it to the centre of the shaped lining, arranging the pleats in equal fulness on each side. Work the backs similarly. The bands on the shoulders are feather-stitched along each edge, and worked in the centre with three lines of fancy stitching. The collar is arranged to turn down over a neck band, and is edged with feather stitching and arrows embroidered at each corner. The waistband is feather-stitched to match.

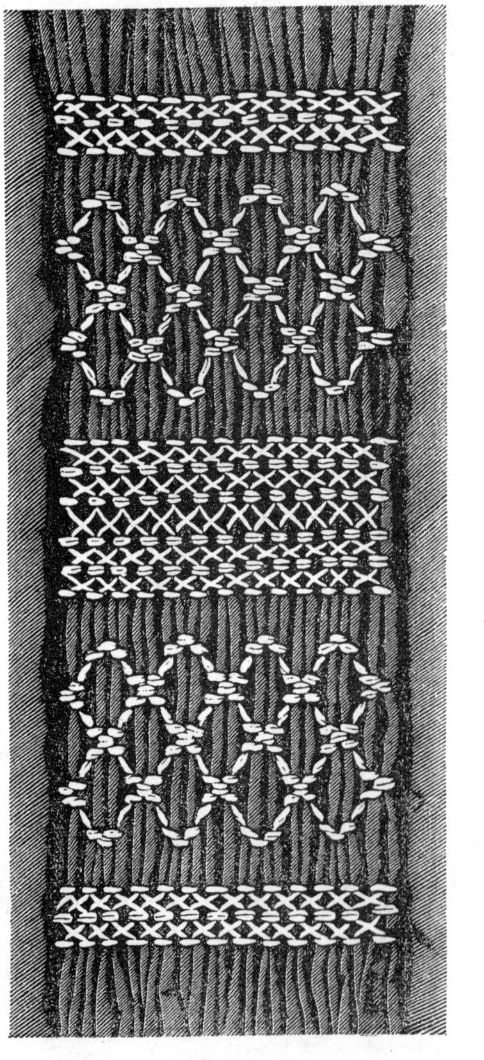

The Victoria Pattern.

VICTORIA PATTERN.

THIS is a wide elaborate pattern measuring 8½ inches in depth. Draw eighteen gathering lines from right to left at the distance of half an inch apart, crossed by perpendicular lines also half-an-inch apart, so forming a series of perfect squares. Then, having the pleats in order, begin smocking on the left-hand side, bring up the needle in the first pleat on the first gathering thread, take up the second pleat on the same gathering thread bringing out the needle below the stitch, take up the third pleat midway between the first and second gathering threads keeping the silk above the needle, take up the fourth pleat on the same level bringing the needle out above the stitch, take up the fifth pleat on the first gathering thread, take up the sixth pleat on the same gathering thread, bringing out the needle below the stitch, take up the seventh pleat midway between the first and second gathering threads keeping the silk above the needle, take up the eighth pleat on the same level bringing the needle out above the stitch and continue to the end of the row. The stitches of this row now have to be crossed, to accomplish which recommence midway between the first and second gathering threads bringing the needle up in the first pleat, take up the second pleat on the same level, then the third pleat and next the fourth pleat both on the first gathering thread, and so on, working exactly as in the first row, and taking up always the pleats intermediate between those already worked upon. Next do another line of crossed stitches to extend from the line just completed to the second gathering thread. Now to work the oval insertion, begin by bringing up the needle in the first pleat on the fourth gathering thread, take up the second pleat on the same level, take up the third pleat a tiny bit higher, take up the same (the third) pleat again just below the third gathering thread, take up the fourth pleat upon the third gathering thread, in all these stitches bringing out the needle above the stitch, take up the fifth pleat on the third gathering thread, bringing the needle out below the stitch, take up the sixth pleat a trifle below the third gathering thread, then the same (the sixth) pleat again a little above the fourth gathering thread, and take up the seventh pleat level with the first pleat, that is, just upon the fourth gathering thread, take the eighth pleat on the same level, but bringing the needle out above the stitch, and proceed in the same manner up and down to the end of the row. Recommence in the first pleat close to the first stitch of last row, take up the second pleat on the same level, take up the third pleat a tiny bit lower, take up the same pleat again just above the fifth gathering thread, take up the fourth pleat exactly upon the fifth gathering thread, then take the fifth pleat on the same gathering thread, with the needle brought out above the stitch, and work on in completion of the ovals to the end of the row. The next two rows form a continuation of the oval pattern, and are executed in precisely the same manner, commencing upon the sixth gathering thread. Work from the eighth to the ninth gathering thread in crossed stitches similar to the upper insertion; the same is done from the tenth to the eleventh gathering thread; then the space from the ninth to the tenth gathering thread is filled with stitches worked in the same manner, but *longer*, so as to occupy the half inch, as will be seen by referring to the engraving. Work a repetition of the oval pattern from the twelfth to the sixteenth gathering threads. Then fill up the space between the seventeenth and eighteenth gathering threads with rows of crossed stitches to correspond with the first portion of the pattern.

No. 3715.—Norfolk Bodice with Smocked
Yoke.

No. 3852.—Girl's Smocked Dress
or Pinafore.

No. 3712.—Bodice with Smocked
Front and Sleeves.

No. 3716.—The Alexandra Smocked Dress.

No. 3636.—Smocked Dress with
Short Sleeves.

No. 3707.—Confirmation Dress with
Smocked Waist Bodice.

No. 3715.—NORFOLK BODICE WITH SMOCKED YOKE.

THIS is a novelty 'n Norfolk bodices, the smocked yoke having an extremely pretty effect above the box-pleats, or those not desiring to smock it, can arrange same in tiny lengthway pleats to the size of the fitted lining given, and stitch each down lengthways, or the fulness can be gauged with excellent effect. Again, those not desiring a full yoke can use only the lining yoke, which is fitted over the shoulders, and to which the full front and back are set in box-pleats, these being stitched round the waist to keep them in place, over which a material belt is worn. The neck, after being smocked and tacke l round to the neck of the yoke, is put into a band collar. The smocking must be carefully tacked round the armhole of yoke, then the sleeve is gathered up to the size of armhole and sewn in. The wrist part is smocked to correspond with the yoke, leaving a frill to fall over the hand. Any of the varieties of stitches shown in this, or "Weldon's Practical Smocking," 1st series, can be employed. Quantity of 27-inch material, 5½ yards. Flat pattern, id.; untrimmed, 1s. 6d.; trimmed, 3s. 6d.

No. 712.—BODICE WITH SMOCKED FRONT AND SLEEVES.

A PARTICULARLY pretty style of bodice, with smocked front and sleeves, although if preferred the fulness can be merely gauged at the neck and waist. The lining front fitted to the figure joins in with the shoulder and under-arm seam, and hooks down the front after the full front is smocked on to it. The smocking is done to form a yoke at neck, while the waist is smocked to shape it in nicely to the figure, then the basque is rounded over the hips and formed into box-pleats at the back; the neck being finished with a roll collar. The sleeve, full on the outside only, is smoc'-ed at the shoulder and wrist. All soft materials can be employed for this style of bodice, and any of the ne.. stitches shown in this issue, as well as those in the 1st series of "Weldon's Practical Smocking," price 2d., post free 2½d., can well be employed. Quantity of 36-inch material, 3 yards. Flat pattern, 6d.; made-up, untrimmed, 1s. 6d.; trimmed, 3s. 6d.

No. 3716.—THE ALEXANDRA SMOCKED DRESS.

THIS design is suited to simple or elaborate material, it reproducing most perfectly as a morning dress in any of the pretty zephyrs, while for afternoon wear it would look charming in merino, or veiling opening upon a skirt of soft silk. The foundation-skirt is of lining faced up a few inches with material, then the entire side filled in with material smocked over the hip in any stitch desired, full description as well as numerous illustrations for this artistic needlework being given in "Weldon's Practical Smocking," 1st series, price 2d., post free 2½d., or this issue contains many new and practical designs The drapery, which needs to be of some soft material, pleats 6 times on the right side into the waist, while the reverse side pleats 10 times into waist, the 4 last pleats being pressed down their entire length, forming a kilted panel on the left side. The pattern of the tunic front is given in 2 pieces, owing to the paper not being sufficiently large to cut it all in one, and the width of material would first be joined until the desired length is obtained, the seams requiring to be well pressed. The back drapery gathers into the waist with the skirt back, then each side there is a downward pleat, the centre of the back being raised by two leats. Across the tunic back, a few inches below waist, will be seen two holes, which have to be placed over the corresponding holes in the skirt, then lower down each single hole has to be placed over the corresponding single hole in skirt back and secured, thus forming a dainty little pouf. The tunic on the right side falls a little over where the smocked silk part of the skirt comes, and which joins between the side seam and front of the skirt, while on the left side the tunic joins into between the side seam and back of skirt. The bodice is extremely becoming and charming with its smocked neck, which back and front forms a yoke, the fulness beneath being evenly gathered into the waist, where it is secured on to the fitted lining front and back, a belt of material surrounds the waist, and the neck is finished with a roll collar. The sleeve has a fitted lining upper, on to which the full upper is smocked at the shoulder and wrist, or

those not desiring to do the smocking could well gauge this sleeve, also bodice neck, which is simple enough to do, and very effective. Any of the attractive stitches shown in this, or the 1st series of "Weldon's Practical Smocking," can be employed. Quantity of 24-inch material, 17 yards. Flat pattern, 1s.; untrimmed, 2s. 3d.; trimmed, 6s.

No. 3636.—SMOCKED DRESS WITH SHORT SLEEVES.

A PRETTY arrangement for smocking suitable for flannel, cambric, merino, silk, &c., cut as a dress fitted with a plain yoke and princess, full, short sleeve, in sizes suitable for children of 1 to 8 years. To the yoke back and front, the princess front and back are gathered, then smocked to the depth of 2 or 2½ inches in honeycomb stitch, which is again repeated at waist, this confining the fulness nicely into the figure, while the skirt part is finished with a deep hem, about which are three narrow tucks, each headed with a fancy stitching worked in silk to correspond with that employed for the smocking. The neck is simply corded, or else put into a narrow band, over which a piece of lace is turned. The full sleeve is gathered over a fitted lining sleeve, and the edge is smocked to correspond with the rest of the dress. Quantity of 24-inch material, 3¼, 3¾, 4¼, and 5 yards. Flat pattern, 9d.; made-up, untrimmed, 1s. 6d.; trimmed, 3s. 6d.

No. 3707. — CONFIRMATION DRESS WITH SMOCKED WAIST BODICE.

GRACEFUL and becoming is the design here shown for young ladies of 12 to 18 years, and which, if intended for confirmation wear, would be made of white cachemire, veiling, fine serge, or flannel, muslin, zephyr, embroidered cambric or sateen. For ordinary wear this style of dress would make up splendidly in all soft materials in such shades as cream, mauve, pink, blue, &c., or soft navy blue serge would smock splendidly with red silk. The foundation-skirt of lining consists of a ored front, side gore, and back breadth, faced up a few inches with material, then the right side filled in with a width of material, smocked over the hips in any pattern desired. The outer edge of the smocked piece joins between the side-seam and back of skirt, while the inner side is hemmed down on to the skirt, carried sufficiently under the tunic not to show the foundation-skirt. The drapery is exceeding graceful, and has five pleats on the left side carried into the waist, then the tunic joins down between the side seam and back of skirt. The fulness on the right side goes into five pleats at the waist, then the skirt-back is arranged with a dainty little pouf, and the side is hemmed. Gather or pleat the tunic back at waist into the same band as the skirt back, and each side make a downward loop. The fulness is then arranged by placing the sets of two holes over the corresponding holes in the skirt, and securing same. I eneath these will be seen a row of single holes, each of which has to be placed over the corresponding holes in the skirt and secured; thus regulating the fulness nicely to the skirt edge, while each side of the tunic back joins between the side-seam and back of skirt, so that all may be put into one waistband. The bodice made full back and front can be smocked in any style or stitch preferred, full directions for which,

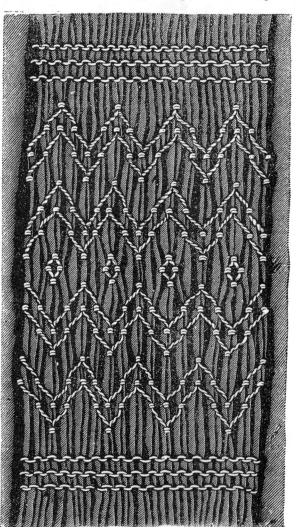

The Vandyke Pattern.

together with numerous illustrations, will be found in this issue, also in "Weldon's Practical Smocking," 1st series, price 2d., post free 2½d. The smocking is done across the neck in yoke form, and from this the fulness is gathered into waist, on to a lining foundation, the waist being encircled with a material belt. The neck is finished with a roll collar, and the sleeve arranged full on the outside is smocked at the shoulder and wrist. Quantity of cachemire, 5½, 6, and 8½ yards. Flat pattern, 9d.; made-up, untrimmed, 1s. 9d.; trimmed, 4s. 6d.

VANDYKE PATTERN.

THIS is an exceedingly pretty design for working across the whole front of a Garibaldi bodice, or it may be adapted for a waistcoat by smocking to the extent of forty-two or fifty pleats across the bust, then leaving five or six inches in depth for fulness, and repeating the smocking at the waist, where of course you work the same number of pleats; but draw them in rather more tightly. Prepare the material for working by drawing eighteen parallel lines from right to left, three-eighths of an inch apart, for gathering threads, and cross them with perpendicular lines, half an inch apart, for gauging the size of the pleats. Run the gathering threads in the usual manner. Work a row of rope stitch along the first gathering thread, also along the second gathering thread, and the same in the space midway between. Then commence for the Vandyke by bringing up the needle in the first pleat upon the fifth gathering thread, sew the second and first pleats together twice, insert the needle in the second pleat only bringing it out above the stitch just made, take up the third pleat only on the fourth gathering thread, then sew the fourth and third pleats together twice, insert the needle in the fourth pleat only bringing it out above the stitch, take up the fifth pleat on the third gathering thread, and sew the sixth and fifth pleats together twice, insert the needle in the sixth pleat only bringing it out below the stitch just made, take up the seventh pleat on the fourth gathering thread, sew the eighth and seventh pleats together twice, insert the needle in the eighth pleat only by bringing it out below the stitch, take up the ninth pleat on the fifth gathering thread, sew the tenth and ninth pleats together twice, insert the needle in the tenth pleat only bringing it out above the stitch just made, and continue thus, up and down, to the end of the row. Re-commence on the sixth gathering thread and work another Vandyke line in the same manner. Then work two more Vandyke lines beginning respectively on the eighth and on the ninth gathering threads. Thus half the Vandyke pattern is accomplished. For the remaining half you commence a line on the tenth and a line on the

smocked to correspond with the yoke, or it can be gathered into a velvet band to button round the wrist, while the neck is put into a band collar of same material. Quantity of 27-inch material, 5, 5½, and 6½ yards; velvet, ¾ of a yard. Flat pattern, 9d.; untrimmed, 1s. 6d.; trimmed 3s. 6d.

No. 3633.—DRESS SMOCKED WITH POINTED YOKE AND SWISS WAIST.

THIS pretty dress is smocked in a most becoming style, forming a pointed yoke and Swiss belt arrangement in front, as far as the under-arm part, from here being a sash which confines the fulness of the waist behind, tied in loops and ends. The dress is cut *en princesse* with a front and back, the neck part of which is smocked as a point and secured on to a fitted lining for support, after which the neck is finished with a band collar. The sleeve is joined in right from the neck, as shown by two and three notches, then after the neck-part is smocked, the fulness from the shoulder forms the sleeve, which has one seam only on the under part of arm, and the wrist is gathered and smocked to match the rest of the dress. The skirt part is finished with a deep hem, above which are 4 rows of fancy stitching, headed at intervals with French knots, worked in silk, or rows of braid can be thus arranged, twisted into loops at equal distances. Soft serge, flannel, merino, or cambric, would form this

No. 3635.—Smocked Sailor Dress.

No. 3633.—Dress Smocked with Pointed Yoke and Swiss Waist.

No. 3564 —The Athole Dress.

eleventh gathering threads, and work each in the same stitch but reversely, going first down and then up, as will be seen by a glance at the engraving. Two more lines, the one beginning on the thirteenth, and the other beginning on the fourteenth gathering threads, will complete the Vandyke. The tiny diamonds in the centre of each Vandyke are worked from the ninth to the tenth gathering threads, and consist of four dotted stitches with the silk carried on from one dot to the other as in the Vandykes. Three rows of rope stitch from the seventeenth to the eighteenth gathering threads will complete the pattern.

———

No. 3635.—SMOCKED SAILOR DRESS.

FOR girls of 4 to 10 years, this style of dress is always admired, and the smocked yoke effect gives a pleasing change to the becoming sailor blouse. It consists of a lining back and front, on which the full sailor blouse is arranged, the neck of this both back and front being smocked in honeycomb stitch, for which see "Weldon's Practical Smocking," 1st series. The fulness below the smocking is arranged in blouse form, turned under at the waist, and gathered on to the lining, to which the skirt is sewn, this consisting of single box-pleats, finished with a velvet band of about three inches cut on the cross. The full sleeve gathers into the arm-hole, and again at wrist, where it is

pretty dress, which is suitable for children of 6 to 14 years. The smocking, although shown in honeycomb stitch, can be varied as fancy suggests, numerous suitable designs being given in this issue. Quantity of 27-inch material, 6½, 7, 8, and 8½ yards. Flat pattern, 9d.; untrimmed, 1s. 6d.; trimmed, 3s. 6d.

———

No. 3564.—THE ATHOLE DRESS.

ALL materials of a soft nature reproduce in this style very successfully, which consists of a yoke blouse bodice, made upon a fitted foundation bodice of lining, fastened down the back, while across the edge of yoke a row of fancy stitching is arranged as a heading to the honeycomb work of the full front and back. This forms its sole trimming, the waist of the blouse being gathered and turned under so that it may be joined into a waistband, which takes also the lining bodice. To this waistband is secured the kilted skirt, which would consist of 5 or 6 widths of 24-inch material, put into broad pleats, which will require thoroughly pressing, and a tape put across the centre on the wrong side to keep them from getting displaced. The kilt is bordered with a deep hem, and on the right side is a row of fancy stitching, to correspond with the yoke. A folded silk or velvet sash encircles the waist, tied in loops and ends behind. The sleeve is cut full so that it can be gathered into the shoulder and again at wrist, where it is honeycombed to match the bodice, then put into a narrow velvet cuff. In sizes 6 to 12 years. Quantity of 24-inch material, 7½, 8½, 9½ yards. Flat pattern, 9d.; untrimmed, 1s. 8d.; trimmed, 3s. 6d.

No. 3662.—SMOCKED TEA-GOWN.

HERE is offered a very stylish and becoming tea-gown, composed of moss-green cachemire, pale pink, or blue satin, or soft silk front, and moss-green velvet revers, but it can be reproduced in other colours and materials as may suit one's fancy. It consists of a princess lining front, on to which the full silk front is smocked at the neck and waist, the fulness above the smocking being just a trifle loose, and from the waist the silk is pressed in pleats, which can be taped across on the inside to keep them nicely in place. The cachemire fronts are loose fitting, and from the waist these are trimmed with a velvet revers tapered off to a mere nothing just below the waist. Then the French back, just reaching a few inches below waist, has the full back, which would consist of a width and a half of cachemire, or three widths of 24-inch material,

armhole to armhole, back and front, thus finishing off the yoke. From the yoke the fulness falls unconfined as the belt draws it closely into the waist, and in front the fulness is a trifle raised in blouse or Garibaldi form to droop over the waistband. The under arm part of this blouse is fitted with two side pieces, so as to shape it in nicely to the figure. The full sleeve, cut all in one piece, gathers into the armhole, and is again gathered in just below the elbow with rope and outline stitch, beneath which is another small pouf, then the fulness is honeycombed in cuff form, to fit the wrist, leaving just an inch or so to fall over the hand as a tiny frill. The collar rolls over a band collar, so as to set it well and closely round the neck. Quantity of 36-inch material, 5 yards. Flat pattern, 6d.; untrimmed, 1s. 6d.; trimmed, 3s. 6d.

No. 3672.—SMOCKED TEA-GOWN.

A CHARMING model is here shown for cachemire and silk, the arrangement being a princess lining front made close fitting, and on to which a full silk

No. 3662.—Smocked Tea-Gown.

No. 3713.—Bodice with Smocked Yoke and Sleeve.

No. 3672.—Smocked Tea-Gown.

gathered on to it and turned over. The sleeve in bell form is faced up with material matching the smocked front, and which also forms the cuff and band collar. This design would make a pretty home-gown, and can be reproduced in any material one may desire. Almost any variety of smocking can be here employed, and of which there are numerous new designs in this issue. Quantity of 24-inch satin, 6 yards; cachemire, 5½ yards; velvet, ½ a yard. Flat pattern, 1s.; untrimmed, 2s.; trimmed, 5s. 6d.

No. 3713.—BODICE WITH SMOCKED YOKE AND SLEEVE.

THIS bodice is smocked back and front in honeycomb stitch, each two diamonds of the honeycomb being divided by an outline and rope stitch, see illustrations 4 and 5 in "Weldon's Practical Smocking," 1st series, and to thoroughly secure the last row a row of machine stitching can be done from

front is smocked in a point at the neck, with honeycomb stitch, or after the style shown by the bottom left-hand cut in the centre pages, the waist also being honeycombed to fit it closely, while the silk between this and the pointed neck part droops a little in pouch form. From the waist smocking the silk is pressed down in broad pleats, or it may fall unconfined, the soft China silks being admirably adapted to this style. The cachemire fronts are semi-fitting, but the back made tight fitting, and in French shape, has the full skirt part gathered on to it a little below waist, and turned over, thus giving a graceful fulness to the skirt part. Down the entire length of the front and round neck is a ruche of silk, made by cutting it on the cross, fraying out the edge, then closely pleating up. The cachemire sleeve in bell shape is lined with silk, and opened over a full silk sleeve, which gathers into the armhole, while the wrist part is gathered and smocked, leaving a frill to fall over the hand. Quantity of cachemire 6 yards; silk, 24-inch wide, 8 yards. Flat pattern, 1s.; untrimmed, 2s.; trimmed, 6s.

WELDON'S
PRACTICAL SMOCKING

(THIRD SERIES.)

NEW DESIGNS FOR LADIES' & CHILDREN'S DRESSES, PINAFORES, MANTLES, VESTS, &c.

TWENTY-SIX ILLUSTRATIONS.

SMOCKING.

SMOCKING still continues greatly in fashion as a decorative embellishment for dresses, and certainly in the shape of nothing is prettier or more universally becoming, the variety of the fancy stitches and the folds of the pleats imparting a softness and grace to the figure which is not attainable by any other style of dress. A yoke of smocking, or an insertion carried the whole way across the chest from armhole to armhole, is immensely becoming to slender busts, the folds falling straight down, and being confined under the waistband, while the innumerable ways in which the ever useful jersey and blouse can be shaped and ornamented, and the great popularity of these fashionable garments, are proof positive that the ART OF SMOCKING will never again be suffered to fall into disuse as far as ladies' attire is concerned. It also is particularly pretty and comfortable for children's little dresses. True it is that a great deal of machine-stitched smocking is now to be seen on the jerseys and dresses and pinafores manufactured at a cheap rate for the million, but the difference between machine work and hand work can very easily be detected, and while the machine can do only simple Honeycomb and a few of the very easy stitches, there is a vast range of fancy patterns and elaborate designs quite within the reach of a fairly painstaking worker, and these can never become common, in fact, they give an air of refinement and ladylike style to even an inexpensive material. Smocking is quite as suitable for winter costumes as for summer dresses, as there is, of course, a degree of warmth in the pleated material, and it is always advisable, even if the whole of the bodice be not lined, to place a piece of shaped lining underneath the smocking, to keep it from stretching beyond the space it is intended to occupy.

All the preliminary details of smocking, the process of regulating the gathers by means of straight lines drawn upon the material, or a vest or a waistcoat

No. 4171.—Smocked Silk Bodice.

by the use of Briggs' Transfer Dots, the method of gathering drawing up the threads to form pleats, and other working details, with full instructions for working Honeycomb smocking, Diamond smocking, Lattice smocking, Feather stitch and Chevron, and many other fancy stitches, and combinations of stitches, have been explained and fully illustrated in No. 19 of "Weldon's Practical Needlework Series," and still further detailed in No. 29 of the same series, where also will be found a great variety of new designs in Fancy smocking, and many illustrations of fully worked patterns for vests and waistcoats, yokes of dresses, fronts of jerseys, costumes, bodices for little girls, and children's pinafores and blouses.

In bringing forth a third number upon SMOCKING, we desire once again to impress upon the minds of our readers the necessity of taking the greatest care in the preparation of the material, for no good smocking can be worked unless the gathering is first of all done in perfectly straight lines, and every stitch of the gathering exactly the same size, so that the pleats may be perfectly even, each pleat having its own allotted proportion of depth. The preparation for the gathering, and the gathering itself, is really the most tedious part of the work, for when once the pleats are drawn up, the smocking, though needing a true eye, is not so very difficult of accomplishment, and a competent worker will feel pleasure in seeing the dainty stitches grow as it were upon the pleated material. The Honeycomb stitch always looks neat and pretty either in straight rows or in points. Diamond smocking is much used, and the patterns that have the silk worked entirely upon the surface of the pleats are very effective, forming vandykes and zigzags. In many patterns silk of two colours or even three colours may be employed for the smocking.

We have had a variety of handsome new patterns expressly designed for the present issue to still further promote the use of smocking as applied to the ornamentation of dress for ladies and children ; many of these designs are illustrated in almost full working size, with every stitch easily discernible, and are thus almost sufficiently clear for reproduction even without the copious instructions which accompany each, and which will be found invaluable as a guide to correct working, and others are represented in the form of made-up vests and waist-coats, jerseys, and costumes, with details of the manner of working and making up, and the quantity of material required for each.

This issue, together with the two previous issues, No. 19 and No. 29 of "Weldon's Practical Needlework Series," comprises a large and valuable collection of examples, stitches, patterns, and designs for smocking, which cannot fail to be useful to beginners in the art as well as to experienced workers.

No. 4171.—SMOCKED SILK BLOUSE.

THE lady's blouse shown in our illustration is particularly elegant and stylish, and may be worn either indoors or out of doors, at pleasure. Our model is of red China silk, of which 5 yards will be required, or the blouse can be made with cachemire, merino, or cambric, if preferred. A dozen skeins of embroidery silk of the same colour as the material, or a good contrasting colour, will be needed for the smocking. The two fronts and the back are smocked separately, and the work extends 7½ inches downwards from the neck. A yoke is cut in lining to fit across the shoulders from the neck to the armpits to lay the smocking upon. The collar turns down, and is of China silk, double, cut in the shape of an ordinary round collar, and embroidered along the margin with a simple row of Feather stitch. Having cut out the blouse from our pattern, which may be had for a small, medium, or large figure, arrange for the gathering by drawing lines from left to right on the wrong side of the material, the first line 1½ inches from the top. The second and third lines each half an inch below, then a space of 1¾ inches and a fourth line, followed by a fifth line half an inch below, a space of one inch and a sixth line, and another line half an inch below, then a space of 1¾ inches and the eighth line, which completes the depth required ; cross these by perpendicular lines half an inch apart for gauging the size of the stitches ; gather, and draw the material up in pleats. Now, having the needle threaded with silk for smocking, hold the material the right side towards you, and work a row of Rope stitch (see No. 5 "Weldon's Practical Smocking," 1st Series) straight along upon the first line of gathering thread, and do the same also upon the third, fourth, seventh, and eighth lines of gathering threads. Work a row of simple Herringbone between the two first rows of Rope stitches, for which the second gathering thread will be a guide, but the stitches must be taken regularly and alternately one-eighth of an inch above and one-eighth of an inch below the gathering thread, so as to occupy a quarter of an inch space, and insert the needle in only *one* pleat at a time, and there will be one pleat left at top, and one at bottom between each stitch of herringbone. Now, the space between the third and fourth gathering threads is to be worked in a Diamond pattern, thus, bring up the needle in the first pleat a quarter of an inch below the third gathering thread, make a stitch on the second pleat on the same level, bringing out the point of the needle below the stitch just formed, work a stitch successively on the third, fourth, and fifth pleats, each a little lower than the preceding, and so that

the stitch upon the fifth pleat comes exactly in the middle of the space between the two gathering threads, make a stitch upon the sixth pleat on the same level bringing out the needle above the stitch just formed, work a stitch successively on the seventh, eighth, and ninth pleats, each a little higher than the foregoing, and so that the stitch upon the ninth pleat comes on the same level as the stitch upon the first and second pleats, work a stitch on the tenth pleat on the same level, bringing out the needle below the stitch, and continue working down and up to the end of the row, which should finish exactly as it begun ; then for the completion of the diamond, bring up the needle in the first pleat a quarter of an inch above the fourth gathering thread, take up the second pleat on the same level, bringing out the point of the needle above the stitch just formed, take up in succession the third, fourth, and fifth pleats, each a little higher than the preceding, and so that the stitch upon the fifth pleat comes close by the stitch that already is worked there in the course of the first row, take up the sixth pleat on the same level, bringing out the needle below the stitch just formed, take up the seventh, eighth, and ninth pleats successively each a little lower than the other, and so that the stitch upon the ninth pleat comes level with the stitch on the first and second pleats, take up the tenth pleat on the same level, bringing out the needle above the stitch just formed, and proceed to the end, so forming a line or row of perfect diamonds. The same Diamond Pattern is to be worked in the space between the seventh and eighth gathering threads, and the points of these diamonds should come evenly below the points of the diamonds worked above. Now you have to work along the fifth and sixth gathering threads, and this is to be done in Herringbone stitch, yet bringing the pleats somewhat in resemblance of honeycomb ; Herringbone stitch is illustrated on page 6, "Weldon's Practical Smocking," 1st Series, and this Honeycomb Herringbone is executed in the same manner, inserting the needle in the material two pleats at a time alternately, one-eighth of an inch above and one-eighth of an inch below the fifth gathering thread, so that the stitches occupy a quarter of an inch space ; when the first row is thus worked, a second row is done along the sixth gathering thread in the same manner

Honeycombing in Stripes alternated with Beaded Feather Stitch.

exactly, not forming the top stitch under the bottom stitch of the preceding row as is shown in the engraving referred to, but working the top stitch of the second row on the same pleats as the top stitch of the first row, with the result that the pleats instead of standing perpendicularly, are drawn right and left as in honeycombing. This will complete the smocking for the back of the blouse, and you now have to smock the two fronts to correspond, while the full sleeve, after being gathered into the shoulder, is smocked round the wrist, leaving a tiny frill over the hand. Quantity of 24-inch silk, 5 yards. Flat pattern, 6d. ; untrimmed, 1s. 6d. ; trimmed, 3s. 6d.

HONEYCOMBING IN STRIPES ALTERNATED WITH BEADED FEATHER STITCH.

THIS is a new variety of Honeycombing that is very pretty and effective for jerseys, blouses, the fronts of dresses, and other purposes. The material is spaced and gathered exactly as detailed for the Honeycomb smocking illustrated on page 5, "Weldon's Practical Smocking," 1st Series, and when the pleats are prepared ready for working you proceed as there instructed, and do four Honeycomb dots on the first gathering thread, and three dots on the second thread, four dots on the third gathering thread, three on the fourth thread, and so on, downwards, for the depth required. Then miss one pleat, and repeat the Honeycomb dots, and continue thus in stripes of Honeycomb as far as your material will permit. Take out the gathering threads, and you will find a vacant space of material between each stripe of Honeycomb, and down this you may embroider either of the patterns shown in the accompanying illustration, securing the beads by an additional small stitch. The silk with which the Feather stitch is worked is of a different colour to that used in the smocking, and the beads may be either white or coloured, gold, steel, or jet, of a size just sufficiently large to slip over the needle. Be careful to keep the fancy stitching in a straight perpendicular line, just as far from the Honey-combing on one side as on the other side.

———

No. 4163.—SMOCKED BLOUSE.

HERE is shown a particularly smart style of blouse, suitable for washing materials, pongée silks, tussore, white cambric, &c. The

smocking in either the trimmed or untrimmed pattern, but full directions as well as numerous illustrations will be found in Nos. 19 and 29 of "Weldon's Practical Needlework Series," price 2d., post free 2½d. Quantity of 24-inch silk, 5 yards. Flat pattern, 9d.; untrimmed, 1s. 6d.; trimmed, 3s. 6d.

———

No. 3787.—THE NAPTHORNE DRESS.

A SMART dress is here shown for young ladies of 12 to 16 years the skirt being of striped material cut on the cross, while the bodice is of creamy white flannel or silk. It is made with a fitted front, to which is hooked in a full plastron arranged on a fitted lining front, so that it may be smocked at the neck in Honeycomb stitch to form a pointed yoke, from whence the fulness falls unconfined to the waist, where it goes in one small downward pleat each side to allow it to droop over the belt. The back is cut all in one piece, which gives a little fulness at the waist, which is retained by the belt. The neck is fitted with a band collar, while on to the front is a sailor

No. 4163.—Smocked Blouse.

No. 3787.—The Napthorne Dress.

No. 4176.—Smocked Pinafore.

pattern is arranged with a fitted lining front and front side piece, shaped into the figure by means of two darts, to form a foundation for smocking the full front on to. This is shaped by one dart only, and it has the neck smocked in Honeycomb stitch to form four decided points, as clearly illustrated, from whence the fulness is brought down to the waist and gathered on to the lining as narrow as possible, while surrounding the waist is a broad ribbon tied in loops and ends in front. The back is arranged to fit the shoulders, but there is a little fulness at the waist, then the basque is simply turned up and hemmed. The full sleeve is gathered into the arm-hole and mounted upon a fitted lining foundation, cut with a coat-shaped upper and under, the full sleeve being smocked at the wrist in Honeycomb stitch, to correspond with the yoke, and from beneath the smocking a tiny frill is allowed to fall over the hand. Owing to the brittleness of the paper, it is impossible to do the

collar, the ends of which come partly down each side in *revers* form. The sleeve is cut full in the upper part, which gathers into the shoulder, where it is smocked, and again at wrist, then fixed on to the fitted lining upper. The skirt has a lining foundation, cut with a gored front, side gore, and back breadth, faced a few inches with material, then the deep drapery is arranged, this forming a complete second skirt, the front of which goes into ten small pleats into the waist, the five front ones pleating towards the waist centre, and the other five falling towards the side of skirt, these being pressed down their entire length to form kilts on either side. The back drapery pleats or gathers into the waist with the skirt back, then goes in one pleat each side and one in the immediate centre just below waist, the *pouf* being formed by placing the two holes in the drapery over the two corresponding holes in skirt, both of which have to be here stitched together, then place each single hole in tunic over the

6

corresponding single hole in skirt, and stitch them together, thus regulating the fulness and length of the back nicely, while the sides join between the side seam and back of skirt. Both the tunic front and back are marked for one stripe, and if this stripe be placed accurately to a stripe in the material, all the other stripes will follow on correctly. Quantity of 27-inch stripe, 6 and 7 yards; plain, 3½ yards. Flat pattern, 9d.; untrimmed, 1s. 9d.; trimmed, 4s.

No. 4176.—SMOCKED PINAFORE.

A PRETTY little design for pale pink, blue, grey, or cream zephyr, while it would also make up nicely in muslin, soft silk, nun's-veiling, or cachemire as a little dress, encircling the waist with a soft silk sash. The pattern consists of the full front and back, smocked round the neck in pointed Honeycomb stitch, and which was fully illustrated on page 8 of No. 29 of "Weldon's Practical Needlework Series," and also described in the same issue. Care must be taken to run the draw-threads in evenly, and it can be smocked with white or coloured crochet cotton or silk. The lower edge is turned up, then hemmed, and above which narrow tucks are run in. The full sleeve gathers in to the armhole, while the wrist is finished with Honeycomb stitch to correspond with the neck, leaving a tiny frill to fall over the hand. Quantity of 27-inch material, 5 and 5½ yards. Flat pattern, 6d.; untrimmed, 1s. 4d.; trimmed, 2s.

No. 4153.—GIRL'S SMOCKED DRESS.

THIS dressy little frock is suitable for pongée silk or coloured cambrics, zephyrs, sateens, &c., while it makes up nicely in cachemire, nun's-veiling, and beige. The pattern can be had for children of 2 to 8 years, and is arranged with a fitted lining front and back, cut to a little below the waist, then the neck is covered with a yoke back and front, beneath which the full back and front are smocked in Diamond shape in any stitch one may desire. Our illustration shows for Honeycomb smocking, and this, as well as a variety of other stitches, are fully illustrated and described in No. 19 of "Weldon's Practical Needlework Series," price 2d., post free 2½d. The full front and back are again gathered at the waist, and here is joined on a box pleating to form the skirt. This would consist of about four breadths of single-width material joined together, and the seams opened and pressed, then the lower edge hemmed up, when it can be put into box pleats, kilts, or gathers, as fancy may dictate. To render it still more dressy, narrow tucks would form a pretty finish to the box pleated skirt, or two or three rows of fancy stitching. Surrounding the waist is a soft silk sash tied in loops and ends behind, while the neck is finished with a roll collar ornamented with Coral stitching, working this in silk the same colour as that used for the smocking. The full sleeve gathers into the armhole, while the wrist part is smocked in Honeycomb stitch, leaving a tiny frill to fall over the hand, and over which, just above the smocking previous to joining it, a small pleat is made to give the drooping effect. This dress would look extremely pretty in old rose silk smocked white and with a sash of white silk, while it would repeat nicely in white pongée silk, with the smocking worked in grass-green silk, with which the sash would match. Quantity of 24-inch material, 4, 4¼, and 5 yards. Flat pattern, 9d.; made-up, untrimmed, 1s. 6d.; trimmed, 3s. 6d.

No. 4087.—SMOCKED DOROTHY MANTLE.

THIS attractive little cloak, which may be had in ages 4 to 16 years, is copied in cachemire as well as soft materials usually employed for mantles, while it affords a good opportunity for the display of smocking, or the neck can be simply gauged if desired. It would also make up well in beige as a dust or travelling cloak for children. The pattern consists of the fitted lining front and back cut to a little below the waist, then there is the full front, long sleeves, full back, collar, and upper and under coat sleeve, and this last-named need not be used if not desired, in which case the armholes would be bound for neatness and durability. In making up this mantle the first thing to know is how to cut it out, therefore place the front edge of sleeve to the exact straight or selvedge of the cloth, while the centre of the fronts must also come to the straight. The full back consists exactly of a width of 27-inch cloth, therefore place the centre of the pattern to a fold in the cloth and thus avoid a seam. Having cut out all the parts place the lining front *under* the full front and tack them

together along the shoulder round armhole and down side to a little below waist, which is as far as lining extends, then join the lining back on along the shoulder. Next join the sleeve and back together as clearly denoted by the three notches, after which join the front part of the sleeve from the neck to a few inches down between the slit made just beyond the shoulder of the full front, as denoted by two notches. The neck is then ready for smocking any depth desired, or in any pattern one may prefer, and after running in the threads they must be drawn up to the size of the fitted lining, therefore it is essential to see that the lining fits the child nicely about the shoulders. This done, pin up the under-arm gore, then join the lining back to the round side piece which is cut on the front as far as it will join, which is to a little below the waist. Next run in three or four rows of gaugings across the full back at the waist and draw same up as closely as possible on to the fitted lining, or, if preferred, the waist could be smocked, from whence the fulness would fall unconfined to the skirt edge. The extreme edge of the sleeve is secured to the extreme edge of the front, as shown by four notches, then from each side of the fronts, just below where the fitted lining ends, would be sewn an elastic to go across the back on the inside to keep them in place. The fulness of the fronts at the waist is gathered on to the fitted lining fronts, and joined in with the under-arm gore is a strap of velvet fastened in the centre of the waist with a clasp or fancy buckle. The neck is put into a band collar of velvet, while the coat sleeves could be simply finished with a row of machine-stitching, then sewn into the armhole in the ordinary manner, or if they are not needed, then bind the armhole for neatness. The long full over sleeve should be turned in down its front and lower edges, then either invisibly hemmed or a piece of binding felled on, while it would also add much to the beauty of the mantle to line the sleeve entirely with a pretty shade of satin or merv or cheap silk. This style can also be had in ladies' sizes, for which see No. 3963, illustration 5. Quantity of 27-inch tweed, 5, 5¾, 6½, 8¼, and 9½ yards. Flat pattern, 9d.; made-up, untrimmed, 1s. 6d.; trimmed, 3s.

No. 4092.—LILIAN FROCK.

A PRETTY arrangement for a smocked dress is here shown for children from 2 to 8 years, while it is suited to such materials as beige, cachemire, veiling, zephyr, and other materials of a soft nature. The pattern is cut with a lining front and back, which reaches to a little below the waist, this being a guide for drawing up the smocking. The material front and back are cut *en princesse*, and extra full to permit of smocking at the neck and waist, where they are ornamented in Honeycomb stitch divided by Rope, or any other pretty stitch may be employed as fancy may dictate; while full directions and illustrations of all that is novel and artistic in the art of smocking are given in Nos. 19 and 29 of "Weldon's Practical Needlework Series," which can be had of all booksellers, price 2d. each, or post free 2½d. each from this office. The neck, both back and front, is smocked to form a square yoke, the fulness of which descends to the waist, where it is again smocked to lend the effect of a band, and from whence the fulness descends to form the skirt, which would be finished with a hem, upon which three rows of narrow braid or velvet are run, or by cutting the material a little longer it would permit of it being set in tiny tucks, which are always desirable for children's dresses, since they not only look pretty, but permit of letting down as the child grows. The neck is put into a band collar of material, which can be ornamented if desired with a piece of lace, then the short sleeve is arranged with a fitted lining, upon which the material is gathered at the armhole and again on the end of the lining, where it is finished with a pleating of lace. At the seam of the puff sleeve a pleat is made, as shown by the two notches, and which brings it to the depth of the lining sleeve. Owing to the brittleness of the paper, it is quite impossible to do the smocking in either the trimmed or untrimmed pattern. Quantity of cachemire, 2, 2¼, and 3 yards. Flat pattern, 9d.; made-up, untrimmed, 1s. 8d.; trimmed, 3s. 6d.

SMOCKED VEST.

THIS is a useful and pretty vest to place in the front of a dress bodice. It can be made of Surah or Pongée silk, or of material to match the dress, half-a-yard of thirty-two inch width material is required, and half-a-dozen skeins of embroidery silk for the smocking. Prepare by drawing eleven parallel lines from left to right on the wrong side of the material, the first line to be three inches from the top, followed by four more lines, each one inch apart from the other, then leave four inches and a-half of space, and draw seven more lines each one inch apart, these are to ensure regularity of the gathering threads; cross them by perpendicular lines, half an inch apart, for gauging the size of the pleats. Fifty-six pleats will take the pattern. Gather in the usual manner, and draw up the threads as tight as required, fixing each with a pin at the end. On the first line of gathering thread work a row of Cable stitch, as instructed in the Trellis Pattern Smocking, page 13 in the present issue. Work the same on the second, fourth, and fifth lines of gathering threads. Then in the space between the first and second lines do two rows of Feather stitch, and work similarly between the fourth and fifth lines. Proceed next with the working of the Diamond Pattern, which occupies the space between the second and fourth gathering threads; by reference to the engraving you will see six pleats are occupied in the formation of each diamond, and the pattern extends three whole diamonds in depth; for the method of working the Diamond Pattern see Montague Pattern, page 3, in No. 29 of

needle on the left-hand side in the first pleat, midway between the first and second gathering threads, take the second and first pleats together twice, insert the needle in the same place in the second pleat and slipping it downwards at the back bring it out in the same pleat but upon the second gathering thread, where take the third and second pleats together twice, insert the needle in the same place in the third pleat and bring it out in the same pleat midway between the second and third gathering threads; take the fourth and third pleats together twice, insert the needle in the same place in the fourth pleat, and slipping it upwards at the back bring it out in the same pleat but upon the second gathering thread, where sew the fifth and fourth pleats together twice; insert the needle in the same place in the fifth pleat and bring it out in the same pleat midway between the first and second gathering threads, where work as at first, and continue the three rows of Honeycomb dots up and down to the end of the row. Now begin again on the left-hand side in the first pleat a tiny bit above the second gathering thread, so as to have the silk level with the *top* of the *middle* row of dots. Pass the needle downwards under the first of these dots (not through the

No. 4153.—Girl's Smocked Dress.

No. 4087.—Smocked Dorothy Mantle.

No. 4092.—Lilian Frock.

"Weldon's Practical Needlework Series." This completes the upper portion of the smocking. Repeat the pattern of the first insertion, and also the Diamond Pattern, upon the lower gathering threads, and when the depth of four diamonds is accomplished continue the pattern, sloping it on each side, till you bring the work to a point of one diamond in the centre. The vest may be set into a bodice with *revers*, or in any other way, according to taste.

———

OSTEND PATTERN.

This elegant pattern measures 5 inches in depth. Prepare the material by drawing nine parallel lines straight across from right to left, five-eighths of an inch apart, for the gathering threads, and cross them with perpendicular lines half-an-inch apart, for gauging the size of the pleats. Run the nine gathering lines, and draw the material in close even pleats, securing the threads with pins. On the first and third, and on the seventh and ninth gathering threads, work rows of Outline stitches. For the first insertion, bring up the

material at all), upwards under the second dot, downwards under the third dot, upwards under the fourth, and so on; turn at the end of the row, and work up and down in reverse position, so that a thread of silk appears to pass like a chain from dot to dot, as see illustration. The top and bottom line of dots remain without this addition, and in the space between these dots and the row of Outline stitches on each side you embroider a row of Feather stitch, doing one stitch on each of the first three pleats sloping to the left, then one stitch on each of two pleats to the right, one stitch on each of two pleats to the left, and so on. This done, re-commence midway between the fourth and fifth gathering threads, and work Honeycomb dots the same as are worked in the top insertion, elaborating the middle row of these dots also with the chain-like band. You next proceed to work the Chevron, bring the needle out in the first pleat, just above the upper row of Honeycomb dots, take up the second, third, fourth, fifth, sixth, and seventh pleats, each in succession, making one stitch on each gradually upwards, then one stitch on the eighth pleat on a level with the last stitch, bringing out the needle below

Smocked Vest.

Ostend Pattern.

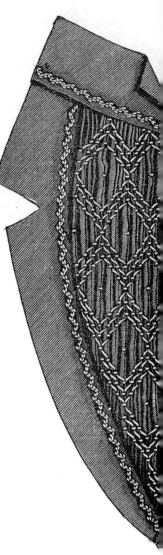

Diamond Pattern Smockin

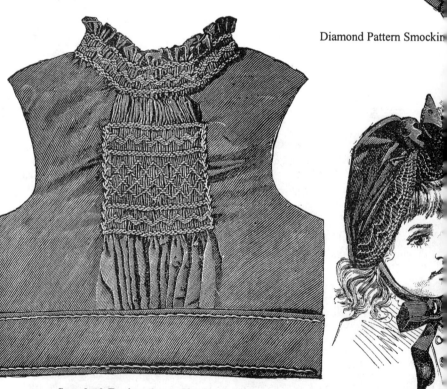

No. 4147.—Frock or Pinafore for a Little Girl.

Smocked Design for a Child's Bodice.

No. 964.—Smocked Grann

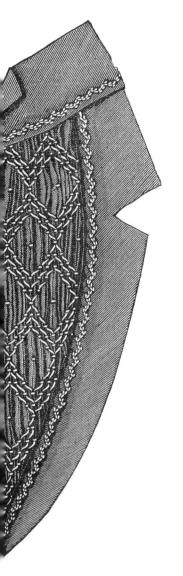

Savoy Pattern.

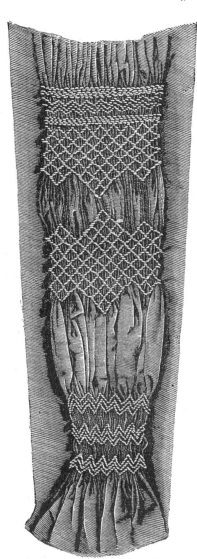

Smocked Front of a Dress.

a Plastron

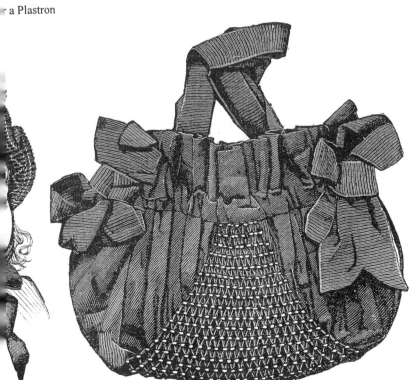

Bonnet.

Smocked Hand Bag.

[19]

No. 4148.—Ploughboy's Blouse.

the stitch, then one stitch in succession on the ninth, tenth, eleventh, twelfth, and thirteenth pleats gradually downwards, then one stitch on the fourteenth pleat, level with the last stitch, and level also with the stitch with which you began the row, and proceed in the same manner up and down to the end. Work another row of Chevron stitches closely above this row. Then go to the opposite side of the series of Honeycomb dots, and work a double row of Chevron stitches to correspond. The space between the seventh and ninth gathering threads is occupied with a repetition of the first insertion. This completes the pattern.

DIAMOND PATTERN SMOCKING FOR A PLASTRON.

FOR working this vest, which is extremely handsome, yet not by any means difficult of accomplishment, procure a piece of pongée silk or other material 13 inches in length and 32 inches wide, and 4 skeins of embroidery silk, either a perfect match in colour or else a good contrast. Prepare for smocking by drawing nineteen parallel lines from right to left upon the wrong side of the material, leaving 3 inches margin at the top, and each line at equal distances of half an inch apart, and cross these with perpendicular lines also half an inch apart for gauging the size of the pleats; there will be fifty pleats required for the exact working of the pattern. When the gathering threads are run, turn the material the right side uppermost, and commence by drawing up the needle in the first pleat on the fourth gathering thread, sew the second and first pleats together twice, then take the second pleat only and bring the needle out close above the stitch just made, take up the third pleat midway between the third and fourth gathering threads, sew the fourth and third pleats together twice, then take the fourth pleat only and bring the needle out close above the stitch, take up the fifth pleat on the third gathering thread and there sew the sixth and fifth pleats together twice, insert the needle in the fifth pleat only and bring it out close above the stitch, take up the seventh pleat midway between the second and third gathering threads and sew the eighth and seventh pleats together twice, insert the needle in the eighth pleat only and bring it out close under the stitch just made, take up the ninth pleat upon the third gathering thread and there sew the tenth and ninth pleats together twice, take up the tenth pleat only and bring the needle out close under the stitch, take up the eleventh pleat midway between the third and fourth gathering threads and sew the twelfth and eleventh pleats together twice, insert the needle in the twelfth pleat only and bring it out under the stitch, take up the thirteenth pleat upon the fourth gathering thread and there sew the fourteenth and thirteenth pleats together twice, insert the needle in the fourteenth pleat only and bring it out above the stitch just made, and repeat the vandyke up and down three more times, and fasten off the last stitch upon the same gathering thread as you commenced upon. You next work two more rows in exactly the same manner at equal distances above this row, beginning the one midway between the third and fourth gathering threads, and carrying it up to the second gathering thread, and beginning the other on the third gathering thread, and working upwards to midway between the first and second gathering threads. Thus the three top rows of the first vandyke are accomplished. The three next rows of the vandyke are commenced respectively upon the fourth gathering thread (working on the stitch that is already there), midway between the fourth and fifth gathering thread, and upon the fifth gathering thread, and they are worked first down and then up to correspond with the three rows already done, as will be clearly seen by referring to the engraving. Next begin the seventh row upon the eighth gathering thread, and work for the seventh, eighth, ninth, tenth, eleventh, and twelfth rows, as the previous six rows are worked; all these rows cover the entire width of the fifty pleats. The narrowing is commenced in the thirteenth row, where you begin by bringing the needle up in the seventh pleat *on the stitch* which you made in the twelfth row for the point of the vandyke, and the vandyke is carried on up and down in the same manner and terminates on the corresponding pleat at the end of the row; two similar rows are worked below this row. The sixteenth row commences in the thirteenth pleat, and consists of two vandykes only, and the nineteenth row commences in the nineteenth pleat, and forms but one vandyke, and with the two rows below it brings the vest to a point. The tiny Honeycomb dots are now worked sepa-

rately in the centre of each vandyke, tying the silk firmly at the back so that they do not come undone. The smocking is now placed upon a lining and cut to shape. The *revers* of the dress material and the neckband are ornamented with an edging of Feather stitch, or the smocking may be made up in any other fashion according to taste.

SAVOY PATTERN.

THIS is a particularly handsome pattern measuring nearly six inches in depth. Our example is executed upon dark material with silk of two good contrasting colours, white and pale blue being in this instance selected, though any two colours may be chosen according to taste, or the work may be carried out entirely with one colour if preferred. Draw ten gathering lines from left to right at the distance of five-eighths of an inch apart, and cross them by perpendicular lines also five-eighths of an inch apart for gauging the size of the stitches. Gather according to previous instructions. Then having the pleats in order, work upon the first, second, ninth, and tenth pleats, with white silk, a double line of Outline stitch; and in between the spaces thus formed at the top and bottom of the design work two rows of Rope stitch with blue silk double. Now for the centre of the design use double silk throughout. Thread the needle with white silk and bring it up in the first pleat on the fourth gathering thread, sew the second and first pleats together twice, and then in the same place sew the second pleat only, bringing out the needle above the stitch; take up the third pleat only on the third gathering thread, sew the fourth and third pleats together twice, sew the fourth pleat only in the same place and bring out the needle below the stitch; take up the fifth pleat on the fourth gathering thread, sew the sixth and fifth pleats together twice, sew the sixth pleat only and bring out the needle above the stitch; and repeat to the end. Do another line in the same manner commencing on the fifth gathering thread and working up to the fourth; another the same beginning on the sixth gathering thread and working down to the seventh; and another beginning on the seventh gathering thread and working down to the eighth; all with white silk. Then in the same way work with blue silk intermediate between the first and second, and between the third and fourth of these indented rows. For the middle row of the pattern, with blue silk double, bring up the needle in the first pleat in the space between the fifth and sixth gathering threads, work a stitch on the second pleat on the same level bringing out the needle above the stitch, work a stitch on the third pleat on the fifth gathering thread, work a stitch on the fourth pleat on the same level bringing out the needle below the stitch; work a stitch in the centre on the fifth pleat and a stitch on the sixth pleat on the same level bringing out the needle above the stitch, and continue to the end; and turn the work upside down, and work the same again, so that the middle stitches of the two rows meet together in the centre of the pattern.

SMOCKED FRONT OF A DRESS.

THIS handsome piece of work will require 20 inches of silk, satin, or other material, 36 inches in width. The smocking may be worked with embroidery silk of a colour to match, or a good contrasting colour. Draw seven lines for gathering threads upon the wrong side of the material, from left to right, the first line three inches from the top, the second line one inch below, the third line one inch and three-quarters below that, the fourth line three inches below, the fifth line four inches and a-half below that, and the sixth line and the seventh line each one inch below the other; draw perpendicular lines across, half an inch apart, to denote the size of the gathering stitches. Gather, and draw up; there should be fifty pleats to take in the pattern. Now thread the needle with silk for smocking, and begin directly upon the first gathering thread to do a row of Rope stitch, and close above and close below this work another row of Rope stitch, so that there are three rows of Rope stitch worked close together, the lower stitch of the top row and the upper stitch of the second row meet together, and the lower stitch of the second row and the upper stitch of the third row meet, and so form, as it were, a double set of Cable-like stitches. Do the same pattern along the second gathering thread. Now between these rows of Cable-like stitches work three rows of Chevron. Begin Diamond stitch just below the last row of cable, and get the depth of three complete diamonds to reach to the third gathering thread, six pleats making a diamond; proceed to a point of four diamonds in depth on each side, and to a point of five diamonds in the centre; the mode of doing this is clearly seen in the engraving. When this portion is finished, the pattern of Pointed Diamonds that goes across the middle of the vest is begun in the centre, leaving half an inch of space from the centre point of the diamonds just completed, this part of the smocking extends to the depth of seven complete diamonds in the centre, and to the depth of five complete diamonds on each side, the fourth gathering thread is the guide for keeping these diamonds straight. Along the fifth, sixth, and seventh gathering threads you work as in the upper insertion three rows of Chevron stitch, arranging so that the points of the chevrons come nearly together; this confines the fulness in place for the waist. The material is hemmed at the bottom, and hangs full. Make up the smocking on a stiff foundation, and make loops or eyelets on each side in which to secure the hooks that will be attached to the dress bodice.

too tightly, but just so much so as to contract the material to the size of the child's body. In the space between the first and second rows, and also between the third and fourth rows of Rope stitch, work three rows of Feather stitch close together in zigzag, doing four stitches on consecutive pleats to the right to begin, then three stitches to the left, three stitches to the right, and so on. When the Feather stitch is all complete proceed to fill in the space between the second and third rows of Rope stitch with a Diamond Pattern, six pleats in a diamond, and one and a-half diamonds in depth, as shown in the illustration of a Smocked Frock for a Child's Bodice, page 9 "Weldon's Practical Needlework Series," No. 29. The entire width of the smocking is 4 inches from the top, including the hem, and front and backs are alike. A piece of thin lining may be placed at the back of the smocking if liked, or a narrow band of material, about 11 inches long for the front and 5½ inches for each back, may be hemmed on behind the top row of Rope stitching to hold the dress in to the size of the child's chest. Cut two pieces of material for shoulder-straps, 6 inches long and 5 inches wide, fold each double

No. 4091.—Winifred Frock.

No. 3955.—Smocked Dress.

No. 4097.—Smocked Dress with Long Sleeves.

No. 4147.—FROCK OR PINAFORE FOR A LITTLE GIRL.

THIS pretty little design is suited to children of 2 to 8 years, and which can be copied in washing material, beige, nun's-veiling, cachemire, and pongée silk. It consists of a full front and back, smocked across the neck to lend the effect of a yoke, from whence the fulness falls unconfined, and the lower edge is turned up and hemmed, above which three narrow tucks are run in. The shoulder-straps turn back in a half diamond, and this forms the upper part of the armhole for gathering in the sleeve, the wrist part of which is smocked to correspond with the front and back. For SMOCKING this little garment draw four guiding lines on the wrong side of the material from left to right, the first line one inch below the hem and the other lines one inch apart from each other; cross them by perpendicular lines ¾ inch apart to gauge the size of the pleats, and gather in the usual manner, draw up, and turn the material the right side out. Having your needle threaded with blue cotton, proceed on each of the four gathering threads to work a row of Rope stitch, not

and sew across upon the narrow band or lining to form shoulder-straps, embroider the straps with Feather stitch and French knots, as in the engraving. One width of material 16 inches long, cut in half, will be sufficient for sleeves, hem the wrist, and smock round in the same pattern as used for the front, and the same depth; shape the top of the sleeves, join up, and set the sleeves in straight under the arm, and the fulness gathered at the top. Cover six tiny linen buttons with material, make a cross on each with a double thread of blue cotton, so, +, and sew three down the smocking on each side of the back, and from the buttons on the right-hand side work a loop of buttonhole stitches to secure to the buttons on the left-hand side. Quantity of 24-inch material, 4, 4½, and 5 yards. Flat pattern, 6d.; untrimmed 1s. 4d.; trimmed, 2s. 6d.

SMOCKED DESIGN FOR A CHILD'S BODICE.

THIS bodice is made in separate pieces, forming a front and two backs; the backs are intended to be plain, on a lining, and the front is smocked in the shape of a square, as shown in the engraving. The material can be cachemire, merino, fine serge, or any soft fabric. A piece 12 inches long and 30 inches wide is required for the front of the bodice. Leave five clear inches on each side, and in the centre of the material, on the wrong side, draw lines from left to right to guide the gathering, the first line two inches and a-half from the top, followed by four more lines each one inch and a quarter below the other, and cross these with perpendicular lines half an inch apart to gauge the size of the pleats; gather with cotton of different colour from your material that the thread may be easily discernible. Turn the material the right side uppermost, and having at hand a supply of embroidery silk of good contrasting colour, begin SMOCKING by working a row of Cable stitch along the first and second, and the fourth and fifth gathering threads; the mode of doing this Cable stitch will be found in the description of the Trellis Pattern Smocking, page 14 in the present issue. This done, work three rows of Chevron in zigzag in the space between the first and second and also between the third and fourth rows of Cable stitch, doing the three rows closely together, as is clearly represented in the engraving. Next, work the Diamond Pattern in the exact centre of the design, making it extend two diamonds in depth, one diamond being above and one diamond below the centre gathering thread, as see instructions in the Montague Pattern, page 3 in No. 29 "Weldon's Practical Needlework Series." Finish with a row of Feather stitching worked perpendicularly close to the first and last pleats. Arrange the material upon a shaped lining, fixing the middle of the smocking securely to the middle of the lining, also secure the first and last pleats upon the lining at just sufficient distance to nicely expand the pleats. Cut a long straight strip of material for the neck-band, a hem is made at the top to form a frill, and the smocking is worked to correspond with that already done upon the first to the third gathering threads. Stitch the neck-band upon the bodice with the pleats well extended at the bottom, and let them contract at the top to draw the band in to the size of the neck. The waist-band is a straight piece of material machine-stitched upon the bodice.

No. 964.—SMOCKED GRANNY BONNET FOR CHILD OF TWO OR THREE.

PROCURE or make a shape similar to the one shown in the engraving, with a large high crown; the brim, which narrows to nothing at the back, is about three inches wide in front, and is arranged in three "pokes" over the forehead. The material used for the bonnet may be China silk, satin, or cachemire, and the smocking is worked on both sides of the brim with embroidery silk to match; for this two straight strips of material, about 4½ inches wide and 90 inches long, will be required. Turn down half an inch along the strip of material, and draw the first gathering line along the centre of this turn-down piece. The next gathering line will be on the single material, at the distance of a quarter of an inch space; another gathering line at half an inch space, and another also at half an inch from the last, which makes in all four gathering lines for working the outside smocking for the brim. Only the first three of these lines will be required for smocking the inside of the brim. On both these pieces the perpendicular lines for gauging the size of the gathering stitches need only be a quarter of an inch apart, as the pleats are not needed to be very deep. Gather in the usual manner. Then on the first gathering thread work a row of Outline stitch, picking up each pleat through both thicknesses of material. Work on the second line a row of Rope stitch. Then re-commence in the first pleat, close by the line of Rope stitch, and work in Feather stitch, taking up the second, third, fourth, fifth, and sixth pleats each in succession to the left, and so that the stitch on the sixth pleat comes upon the third gathering thread; then work Feather stitches on five successive pleats to the right, and continue. The precise method of working Feather stitch is fully explained in the Belvidere Pattern, for which see No. 29 of "Weldon's Practical Needlework Series." Work another vandyke of Feather stitch to extend from the third to the fourth gathering threads. The smocking for the under-part of the brim is worked in similar manner, but omitting the last row of Feather stitch. Arrange the smocked pieces on the brim, and catch the edges together just over the margin of the shape, expanding the pleats here and drawing them closer together the nearer they approach the crown, where tack them evenly round. The crown is covered with a piece of material laid lengthways in box pleats; the trimming in front consists of a bow of ribbon and a small feather. Put in a head lining, and add strings to tie under the chin.

SMOCKED HAND-BAG.

REQUIRED, a piece of peacock-blue satin 25 inches long and 32 inches in width, 2 skeins of coral-pink embroidery silk, 2 yards of inch-wide ribbon, and a little pink sarcenet or satinette for lining. Cut off 12 inches of the satin, to be afterwards run on and used as a frill with double hem in which to run a tape to draw the mouth of the bag to shape. This will leave 13 inches of satin for the formation of the bag, or the hem can be allowed for on the piece, if preferred, 6 inches at the top and 6 inches at the bottom. Prepare for smocking by drawing 34 parallel lines three-eighths of an inch apart from right to left across the centre of the satin *width-ways;* cross these with perpendicular lines half-an-inch apart, whereon to run gathering threads. The bag is smocked in Honey-comb stitch, beginning with a row of nine dots in the exact centre of the first gathering thread, and increasing one dot in each row till in the seventeenth row you work as many as twenty-five dots, and you then decrease gradually to eight dots. Honeycomb smocking is worked thus: having the needle threaded with silk, bring it up over the second gathering thread in the pleat on which you intend to begin working, catch the next pleat to the right to this pleat by a stitch from right to left through each, work another stitch through both pleats, then insert the needle in the same place but in the second pleat only, and slip it upwards at the back, keeping it in the second pleat till you bring it out over the first gathering thread, catch the third pleat to this by a stitch through each, work another stitch through both pleats, then insert the needle in the same place but in the third pleat only, and slip it downwards in the cavity of the same pleat till you bring it out over the second gathering thread, and proceed, working a stitch on each of the two gathering threads alternately till nine dots are worked on the first and ten dots on the second gathering thread, always slipping the needle up and down invisibly at the back of the work and taking in front two pleats together in every stitch, so the last pleat of one stitch becomes the first pleat of the next stitch. When the piece of smocking is accomplished, fold it in half widthways, round the two sides a little, and join them together in bag-shape. Cut the lining similarly and tack it in place, letting the satin be a little loose; now divide it into two pieces each 6 inches wide and run one piece on the front and one piece on the back of the bag, leaving the ends open; turn it down and hem it on the lining, and above the hem run a row of stitches to allow a place for a tape to be run in, and this tape is secured to the size you wish for the mouth of the bag. Put on ribbon for handles, and finish with a bow at each corner of the bag.

No. 4148.—PLOUGHBOY'S BLOUSE.

THIS little smocked pinafore or blouse is made exactly after the style of the smocks worn by country people, and it is exceptionally pretty for boys in petticoats, as well as for those wearing suits, as it forms a thorough protection, and at the same time is very dressy. The pattern can be had in ages 2 to 10 years, while such material as blue linen, brown holland, or any of the fancy linens now sold can be employed. The smock is cut with a full front and back which are gathered in the immediate centre, and smocked with a variety of pretty stitches, on either side of which Feather stitching is arranged, and any fancy embroidery stitches can ornament it as may be desired, and which would be worked in the same coloured cotton as that used for the smocking. The back and front are joined on the shoulders by embroidered straps, which forms the upper part of the armhole for the insertion of the sleeves, and which are then gathered into the armholes, while the wrists are smocked to correspond with the front, leaving a tiny frill to fall over the hands. For the SMOCKING, prepare the material by drawing lines on the wrong side of it, the first line from right to left three inches from the top, and five more parallel lines each one inch below the other; cross these by perpendicular lines half an inch apart for gauging the size of the pleats; gather, and draw up, and turn the work the right side out. Thread your needle with blue cotton and commence for the first row on the first gathering thread, working Cable stitch, which is two rows of Rope stitch linked in resemblance of a cable. For full-sized engraving and description of this stitch see the Belvidere Pattern, page 8 in No. 29 of "Weldon's Practical Needlework Series," also the Trellis Pattern smocking for the front of a dress, page 14, in the present issue. Work the same Cable stitch along the second gathering thread, and also along the fifth and sixth gathering threads, and do it besides *above* the third gathering thread and *below* the fourth gathering thread, with the object to leave here in the middle of the design a wider space in which to work a Diamond Pattern. When you have the six lines of Cable stitch completed, work three rows of Chevron in zigzag in the space between the first and second lines of the Cable stitches, and also in the space between the fifth and sixth lines of cable, this Chevron stitch is represented clearly in the Design for the Front of a Dress, page 9 in this issue. Next, do three rows of Outline stitch quite straight and close together in the centre of the space between the second and third lines of Cable stitch, and also between the fourth and fifth lines of Cable stitch. Now there remains the Diamond Pattern to work across the middle of the design, and here there are six pleats in a diamond, and the work is one and a-half diamonds in depth, as may be seen in the illustration of a Smocked Front for a Child's Bodice, page 9 in No. 29 of "Weldon's Practical Needlework Series." Smocking in Diamond Pattern with eight pleats in a diamond is detailed in No. 19 of "Weldon's Practical Needlework Series," where see illustration on page 10. The whole of the smocking for the front of the blouse being now accomplished, you have to decorate 2½ inches width of plain holland on each side of the smocking, by embroidering a scroll in Chain stitch, and further ornamenting with Feather stitch and stars, as shown in the engraving. The BACK OF THE BLOUSE is worked in exactly the same manner, only it is done in two pieces, being slit down the middle and hemmed as an opening and placket hole. The strip of double material for shoulder-pieces is embroidered and ornamented with Feather stitch to match the work on the front and back of the smock. The sleeves are like shirt-sleeves, and gather into the armholes, while the wrists are smocked similarly to rows two, three, four, and five of the front. The collar is cut double in the front and at the back, the embroidery upon it is worked in Feather stitch and it has a Chain stitch wheel at each corner. Cover twelve small linen buttons with holland, cross them with a double thread of blue cotton, so, +, and sew five buttons on one side and five on the opposite side of the back, from the collar to the bottom of the smocking, and work a loop of buttonhole stitch from the right-hand side buttons to secure across. Place the two remaining buttons where the collar opens in front. Quantity of 36-inch linen, 2¼, 2¾, 3, and 3¼ yards. Flat pattern, 6d.; untrimmed, 1s. 6d.; trimmed, 2s. 6d.

No. 4091.—WINIFRED FROCK.

SMOCKED dresses are always becoming to children, and this pattern may be had in ages 2 to 8 years. Materials of a soft nature are naturally to be preferred for this style, and our pattern would make up nicely in cachemire, putting in the full smocked fronts of soft silk, while any of the fine makes of twill flannel, as well as beige, veiling, &c., reproduce this style of dress. It is arranged with a princess front, down the entire length of which is a plastron, this consisting of a fitted lining, upon which a full silk plastron is smocked at the neck and waist, as clearly illustrated, the full plastron being cut a little longer than the lining, as the smocking takes this extra depth up. This plastron would be sewn to the left front, while the right one would hook invisibly over on to it, or for such young children this style of dress can well hook or button down the back. On either front from the shoulder a piece of lace

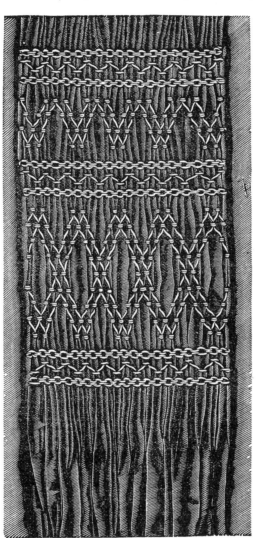

Trellis Pattern Smocking for the Front of a Dress.

is put on and turned back, thus lending the effect of a *revers*, and from under which at the waist a soft silk sash is pleated, this being tied round the body in loops and ends. The back is cut to a little below the waist only, and on to this the full skirt back is pleated or gathered; then the neck is put into a band collar, while the small puff sleeve is arranged with a fitted lining, upon which a full material sleeve is gathered into the armhole and smocked on the outer edge, leaving about half an inch to fall round the arm as a frill, or a narrow piece of lace could be eased on. Owing to the brittleness of the paper, it is impossible to do the smocking in either the trimmed or untrimmed pattern, therefore we refer our readers to Nos. 19 and 29 of "Weldon's Practical Needlework Series," price 2d. each, post free 2½d. each, which are devoted to this interesting needlework, and contains all necessary details, as well as numerous illustrations, of the newest stitches. Quantity of cachemire, 1½, 1¾, and 2 yards; of silk 30, 32, and 36 inches. Flat pattern, 9d.; made-up, untrimmed, 1s. 8d.; trimmed, 3s. 6d.

No. 3955.—SMOCKED DRESS.

A CHARMING little dress is here shown for children from 6 to 10 years, and which is suitable for materials of a soft nature. Cachemire, beige, soft tweed cambric, and China silk, best suit such a style, which is cut *en princesse*, and the neck smocked in Honeycomb stitch, to form a pointed yoke back and front, beneath which the fulness is left unconfined, and drawn into the waist with a soft silk sash tied in loops and ends behind. The lining yoke is given as a guide to draw the smocking up to back and front, while the sleeve gathered into the armhole has the wrist part smocked to correspond with the neck, leaving an inch or so to form a frill over the hand. The edge of the skirt is hemmed, then set into three tucks, or these can be dispensed with if desired, and rows of narrow silver, gold, or self-coloured braid employed, or even fancy stitching. The pattern consists of a full front, full back, sleeve, and yoke, and forms an easy and desirable dress for growing girls. In place of the smocking ordinary gauging could be employed, while the sleeve could be gathered at elbow, as well as wrist, forming two *poufs*. How to work smocking is fully explained and illustrated in No. 19 also in No. 29 of "Weldon's Practical Needlework Series," price 2d. each, or post free, 2½d. each, and to which we refer our readers, as owing to the brittleness of the tissue paper it is impossible to do the smocking in either the trimmed or untrimmed patterns. Quantity of 24-inch material, 6 and 7 yards. Flat pattern, 6d.; untrimmed, 1s. 6d.; trimmed, 3s. 6d.

No. 4097.—SMOCKED DRESS WITH LONG SLEEVES.

A MOST desirable dress is here shown for children of 2 to 10 years, and which would reproduce in any material of a soft nature. It is admirably suited to pongée silk, beige, veiling, cachemire, or the pretty zephyrs now shown, and the only trimming it needs is a soft silk sash, brought from either side and tied over the back in loops and ends. The pattern consists of the princess lining fronts, the neck part of which is covered with a full yoke, smocked to the width of the lining; then beneath this yoke, down the centre of the entire front is a full plastron, this being gathered at the top and smocked at the waist, so as to shape it into the figure and fit it closely to the lining, from whence the remaining fulness is put into pleats. This plastron is met on either side by the material fronts, while the French back has the full skirt part pleated or gathered on, as may be preferred, the join of which is hidden beneath the silk sash, which ties behind as clearly illustrated. The neck is put into a roll collar, and the coat sleeve is gathered into the armhole across the upper part, from whence it is smocked to the depth of about three inches; then the fulness is left unconfined to within three inches of the wrist, where it is again smocked on the outside in any fancy stitch one may desire. Owing to the brittleness of the paper, it is impossible to do the smocking in either the trimmed or untrimmed pattern, but ladies will find all the information they desire in Nos. 19 and 29 of "Weldon's Practical Needle-work Series," price 2d. each, post free 2½d. each. Quantity of 27-inch material, 3¾, 4¼, 5, and 6 yards. Flat pattern, 9d.; made-up, untrimmed, 1s. 8d.; trimmed, 3s. 6d.

TRELLIS PATTERN SMOCKING FOR THE FRONT OF A DRESS.

This design is suitable for a simple or rich material, and is an effective wide pattern for smocking the front of a dress; it measures 7½ inches in depth, and is a little difficult to accomplish, as great care must be observed to make the long stitches of the wide trellis to slant all in the same uniform direction. You may carry on the pattern to any width required, or merely work sufficient to use as a vest or waistcoat, for which a piece of material 14 or 15 inches long, and 23 inches wide will be sufficient. Draw gathering lines, twenty-two in number, from left to right, at the distance of three-eighths of an inch apart, the first line to be one inch and a half from the top of the material; cross these by perpendicular lines half an inch apart for gauging the size of the stitches. Gather the twenty-two lines in the usual manner, and draw up, making thirty-eight pleats. Now thread the needle with the silk you intend to use for the smocking, and commence first of all with the CABLE STITCH, which occupies the 1st, 3rd, 8th, 10th, 20th, and 22nd lines of gathering thread. CABLE STITCH is worked thus— Bring up the needle in the first pleat a trifle above the gathering thread, take up the second pleat only bringing out the needle below the stitch, take up the third pleat only bringing out the needle above the stitch, next the fourth pleat only bringing out the needle below the stitch, then the fifth pleat only bringing out the needle above the stitch, and continue thus alternately to the end of the row, always a trifle, just a mere thread, above the gathering thread; then another row is worked in the same manner, but reversely, as you commence in the first pleat a trifle below the gathering thread, take up the second pleat only bringing out the needle above the stitch, take up the third pleat only bringing out the needle below the stitch, and so on, always a trifle below the gathering thread, and by this procedure every alternate stitch comes nearly close to the approximate stitch in the former row, and the two rows together much resemble the links of a cable. When the six lines of CABLE STITCH are complete, proceed with a SMALL TRELLIS stitch for which the second gathering thread will be a guide, bring up the needle in the first pleat a quarter of an inch above the gathering thread, sew the second and first pleats together, then sew the second pleat only bringing out the needle below the stitch, carry the silk in front and insert the needle in the same pleat a quarter of an inch below the gathering thread, sew the third and second pleats together, then sew the third pleat only bringing out the needle above the stitch, retain the silk in front and take up the same pleat a quarter of an inch above the gathering thread; sew the fourth and third pleats

together, then sew the fourth pleat only bringing out the needle below the stitch, and continue in this way down and up to the end of the row. Work SMALL TRELLIS stitch in the same manner along the ninth and twenty-first gathering threads. Then begin for the WIDE TRELLIS in the first pleat on the twelfth gathering thread, sew the second and first pleats together, sew the second pleat only and bring the needle out above the dot the stitch has just formed, keep the silk in front of the work, insert the needle to take the second pleat on the eleventh gathering thread, sew the third and second pleats together, sew the third pleat only bringing out the needle below the stitch; insert the needle to take the third pleat on the twelfth thread, sew the fourth and third pleats together, sew the fourth pleat only, bringing out the needle below the stitch, insert the needle to take the fourth pleat on the thirteenth thread, sew the fifth and fourth pleats together, sew the fifth pleat only bringing out the needle below the stitch, and continue making dots and long stitches like the last slantingly downwards till on the nineteenth gathering thread you sew the tenth and eleventh pleats together, thence go upwards three dots, and fasten off. Re-commence in the same way as before, on the fourteenth gathering thread, the first and second pleats, and work dots upwards (slipping through where a dot is already made) to the eleventh thread, then slant downwards to the nineteenth thread parallel with the dots already made, do two dots upwards, and fasten off. Now bring up the needle in the centre of the dot on the fourteenth thread, work three dots upwards, then proceed downwards as at first, ending with three dots upwards, and fasten off. Then begin by bringing up the needle in the centre of the dot on the fifteenth thread, work four dots upwards, then make dots downwards to the nineteenth thread, thence go two dots up, and fasten off. Continue to the end as shown in the illustration. The small insertion above, that covers the material from the fourth gathering thread to the seventh gathering thread inclusive, is similar to the work done from the sixteenth thread to the nineteenth thread, therefore work in accordance therewith. This small insertion and the smocking on the three gathering threads above may, if wished, be repeated below the design, as shown in the engraving, but is not necessary for a vest, as the pattern already is of sufficient depth.

No. 4164.—D'Orville Bodice.

No. 4164.—D'ORVILLE BODICE.

SMOCKING forms a pretty trimming for the full bodices now so much worn, and our illustration gives a smart idea to be carried out in silk, or any of the pretty cambrics now shown. It is arranged with a fitted lining, which consists of a front, two side pieces, and a French back to form the foundation for the smocking. The full front and back which are cut in silk, are smocked at the neck to lend the effect of a small pointed yoke, from whence the fulness is brought down nearly to the waist, where it is smocked to lend the effect of a Swiss belt back and front, the basque being merely turned up and hemmed. The neck is put into a band collar, while the full sleeve gathers along the top part of the arm into the armhole, the wrist being smocked all round to correspond with the yoke, leaving a tiny frill to fall over the hand. Quantity of 24-inch silk, 4½ yards. Flat pattern, 9d.; untrimmed, 1s. 6d.; trimmed, 3s. 6d.

WELDON'S
PRACTICAL PLAIN NEEDLEWORK.

(FIRST SERIES.)

How to Sew, Hem, Tuck, Stitch, Gather, Pipe, &c.

FORTY-THREE ILLUSTRATIONS.

PLAIN NEEDLEWORK.

"The ART OF SEWING is exceeding old,
As in the Sacred Text it is enrolled,
And till the world be quite dissolved and past
So long at least the needle's use shall last."—JOHN TAYLOR.

THE accomplishment of **Sewing** is the first recorded act of our first parents. We are told that Adam and Eve sewed in the Garden of Eden ; they sewed fig leaves together and made themselves aprons—rather primitive work, perhaps, but still the best they could do under the circumstances. Next, we hear of a pretty coat of many colours, presumably patchwork pieces, that Jacob made for his son Joseph, the sight of which so excited the envy of Joseph's brothers that they determined to kill Joseph ; but, after much deliberation, they instead sold him to a company of travelling merchantmen who were going down to Egypt, where, in course of time, rising in favour with the king, he was arrayed in robes of fine linen and made ruler over the land.

Later on, but still quite early in the world's history—in fact, in the time of Moses—we read of Aaron's sons wearing " coats girded with girdles," of woollen garments and linen garments for the priest's ordinary attire, and of various " holy robes " made of gold, blue, purple, and scarlet, and fine-twined linen and woven linen, elaborated with magnificent needlework embroidery in colours and jewels. Solomon's Temple was enriched with much choice needlework—the veil was of blue, purple, and crimson, and fine linen, with cherubims wrought thereon, and the priests wore gorgeous vestments of gold embroidery.

The Egyptians, Assyrians, and Babylonians seem to have been particularly partial to decorative needlework, for they used it not only in their temples, houses, and on their clothing, but even for the sails of their boats. It was from these nations that the Jews learnt the art. Then the Greeks and Romans became proficient, and instructed the nations whom they conquered. The Popes of Rome collected the most beautiful known specimens, and ordered that costly presents of needlework should be given by the faithful to all churches and religious houses. Some of these ancient examples are in existence at the present day. A few are preserved in the South Kensington Museum.

So, as the knowledge of the art increased, its varieties became classed under different names, just as we now have different names for different works. Anglo-Saxon ladies were celebrated for their outline embroidery, worked mostly for church purposes, in symbolical design on linen and silk.

After the Roman Conquest, William I. invited foreign weavers into this country, and later on a colony of Flemish weavers were established in England, under the protection of Henry III. In the eleventh century linen was woven in Ireland, and the manufacture of this and the manufacture of cotton in England increased so rapidly that exports began to be made to the same countries from whence imports formerly came.

English needlework attained great celebrity both at home and abroad from the twelfth to the sixteenth century. Katherine of Arragon, wife of Henry VIII., who came from a land celebrated for its embroideries and lace, passed many hours at her needle, and instructed her maids of honour and the poor people at her gates in the art of making lace and doing embroidery. Taylor, in the " Needles Excellency," speaks of Katherine of Arragon as celebrated for her needlework—

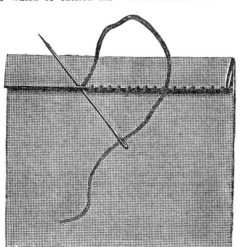

Fig. 1.—Hemming.

' I Read that in the seventh King Henrie's raigne,
Fair Katherine, Daughter of the Castile King,
Came into England with a pompous traine
Of Spanish ladies, which she thence did bring.
She to the eight King Henry married was,
And afterwards divorc'd, where virtuously,
(Although a Queene), yet she her days did passe
In working with the Needle curiously,
As in the Towre, and places more beside,
Her excellent memorialls may be seene ;
Whereby the Needle's prayse is dignifide
By her faire ladies, and herselfe a Queene.
Thus far her paines, here her reward is just,
Her workes proclame her prayse, though she be dust."

Handmade tapestries now came into vogue and wall hangings, and the numerous banners, altar cloths, and church vestments that embellished the gorgeous ritual of the Romish church.

An idea of the various descriptions of needlework practised by English ladies in the sixteenth century may be gleaned from the following poem from the pen of Skelton :—

" With that the tappettes and carpettes were layde,
Wherein these ladyes softely might rest,
The samplers to sowe on, the laces to embroyde.
To weave in the stole some were full prest,
With slaies, with tavels, with nedelles well drest,
The frame was brought forth with his weaving pin ;
God give them good speed their work to begin."

Some to embroider, put them in prease,
Well gydyng their glotten to keep straight their silke ;
Some pyrlyng of golde, their work to encrease,
With fingers small, and handes as whyte as mylke,
With reehe me that skayne of tewly sylke,
And wynde me that batoume of such an hewe—
Grene, red, tawney, whyte, purple, and blewe."

Queen Elizabeth is not known to have been specially industrious, but it is recorded that she, at six years of age, made a shirt to present to her brother on his birthday. Queen Mary II. was devoted to needlework of every description, and a great deal of beautiful work executed under her supervision still

4

remains at Hampton Court Palace. Queen Charlotte was another clever embroideress. Our own gracious Sovereign Queen Victoria finds time to accomplish quantities of needlework and knitting to give to hospitals, and the Royal Princesses have nearly all made their mark as workers in some capacity or other. The Duchess of Teck, the Duchess of York, and the Duchess of Albany work hard for the Needlework Guild, founded by Lady Wolverton in 1882. This Guild has grown to enormous proportions, and by the aid of "branches" and "groups," co-operating under "presidents" and "vice-presidents" in all parts of the country, it was able, in the autumn of last year, to distribute upwards of 250,000 articles of new wearing apparel among the sick and destitute of the many hospitals, missions, homes, refuges, and poverty-stricken districts throughout England, all these being made and contributed by members who undertake to make and give two articles a year to the Guild; of course, no one is limited to *two*, but this is the number stated as necessary to constitute membership.

Now, it is quite necessary that all women should know how to sew. Rich and poor alike are benefited by the knowledge. Needlework is an **Art**, and as such deserves a certain amount of time to be spent upon it—first, in learning the correct method of procedure, then in intelligent and careful practice to acquire skill. The beauty of Plain Needlework depends upon the neatness and regularity of the stitches as well as on the care shown in cutting out the article. Whatever is worth doing is worth doing well, and if it be but

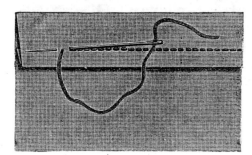

Fig. 2.—A Stitched Hem.

the sewing on of a loop of tape or a button there is a right and a wrong, a tidy and an untidy way of doing both. No one, who has not been a frequent visitor in the houses of the poor, is aware of the extravagance and waste usual among women of a humble class, arising from their ignorance in matters of cutting out and sewing plain needlework, nor how much instruction they need on these points, even to the making of a chemise and a pinafore. The same ignorance and unskilfulness, and the same consequent waste of money, is common among our female servants, who by putting out their clothes to dressmakers, pay about half as much for the making as they pay for the materials. The direct saving of expense upon articles of dress, were they qualified to work for themselves, would with them—and indeed with others, besides servants—be an important annual item. But the indirect benefit would be of infinitely more account. The thrifty disposition, the regular habits and neatness, the ideas of order and management inspired by conscious ability and successful exertion in this *one* leading branch of good housewifery, cannot be too highly prized or too diligently cultivated and pursued, for the effect is *moral*. The orderly house reflects the orderly mind; the wife and mother who quietly executes her daily stitchery in the regular routine of her daily tasks, improves the comforts, the visible respectability of her husband and children, and is the possessor of a secret by which she unites her best and tenderest affections with her everyday employment, and finds no weariness in her labour because it is congenial and for the welfare of those she loves.

"She wrought so well in needle-worke, that shee,
Nor yet her workes, shall ere forgotten be."—J. TAYLOR.

A practical acquaintance with needlework is a qualification absolutely required in every girl and in every woman, whatever may be the position of either of them in society. You may say, "Oh, I shall never have to do a great deal of sewing," or, "I shall use a sewing machine." But, even supposing you are well enough off to employ others to work for you, you should at least know how to distinguish good work from bad; and though machines are very useful, and a great saving of time in long seams and close stitching, there is much that cannot be done by them, and for many purposes handwork must rank first.

Probably the rising generation will be more accomplished sewers than the women of the present day, thanks to the thorough teaching now given in board schools and technical schools, and the multitude of cut-out paper patterns which are to be had at the cost of a few pence. We issue from this office well-shaped cut-out patterns of every description of underclothing for ladies and children, babies' long and short coating sets, variety in pinafores for girls and boys, stylish dresses and cloaks, &c., &c.

MATERIALS FOR PLAIN NEEDLEWORK.

Linen, calico, longcloth, muslin, flannel and flannelette are the materials most generally employed in plain needlework; that is to say, as far as the making of undergarments is concerned; but print, gingham, galatea, holland, chintz, and various other cotton and woollen fabrics have each their respective uses. Whatever is required should be carefully selected of the best quality

procurable, especially if for undergarments, which are in constant wash and wear, and will soon become threadbare if not good and strong. Perhaps more money is wasted in the purchase of bad calico than in any other textile fabric. Calico, of course, is bought in the hope and expectation that its serviceable qualities will permit it to last a reasonable number of years, and therefore durability is one of the primary good qualities it should possess. If this is not obtained, obviously it is a disappointment and a fraud, and the money expended in its purchase is entirely thrown away. Three sets of *good* underlinen will outlast five or six sets of inferior quality, and besides, save a lot of time and trouble in the making.

The best **Linen** is of Irish manufacture. It is not, however, so much used for underclothing as in years gone by, but still is considered quite the right thing for sheeting, pillow-slips, and shirt fronts. The production of linen damask for tablecloths, teacloths, and other napery has risen to the highest excellence, and often possesses considerable beauty of design—floral, antique, and geometrical patterns being introduced in the process of weaving, and consequently the design is actually woven in, and is as durable as the linen itself. Messrs. Robinson and Cleaver, Messrs. Richardson, and Messrs. Murphy and Orr, all of Belfast, are old-established linen factors.

A varied specialité of linen for embroidery purposes deserves to be mentioned, although we are now treating practically of such fabrics as pertain more especially to the requirements of plain needleworkers; this class embraces plain and patterned linen for communion cloths and chalice veils, and also the kinds used for embroidering in crewels, silk, flax-thread, and cotton.

Lawn is a very finely woven linen, and is chiefly employed for surplices, babies' shirts and caps, pocket handkerchiefs, and frillings.

Calico should be free from dress, which is a preparation of lime, employed by some manufacturers to whiten the fabric, but which tends to rot it, and causes it to wear badly; fortunately the adulteration is easily detected—if you take the calico in both hands and rub the surfaces smartly together, the dressing will at once fall out, and you will be able to see the closeness of the threads and thereby judge the real quality of the material. Horrocks' and Crewdson's calicoes and longcloths are standard makes, and may be relied upon. Longcloth is usually considered to be stronger and superior to calico; both these goods run in various widths, some three-quarters, some seven-eights, some a yard, and some one and a quarter yards; the yard width is most generally useful; it should be of smooth substance, soft, without knots or specks, and the threads and selvedges even. Twilled calico is especially soft. Unbleached, or grey calico, is both warmer and stronger than the white; it is, however, but little used nowadays, excepting by the working class and those thrifty people who prefer durability to daintiness; certainly after two or three washings it becomes white and soft, but at first there is a roughness about it that is anything but pleasant. All linen and calico goods should be scalded before cutting out and making up, and not scalded only, but well soaked, soaped, and rubbed just as if dirty, so that all the dressing may come out; it should then be pulled perfectly straight, and ironed or mangled while still damp.

Muslin is much employed for aprons, which are now made in exceedingly dressy style for young ladies' morning wear; it also is used for infants' underclothes and frocks, for servants' caps, for nightcaps, and for frilling; it can be had plain, chequered, and in pretty fancy stripings.

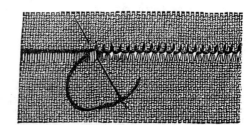

Fig. 3.—Hem Stitching.

Flannel varies in texture according to the district in which it is made. Welsh flannel is generally considered the best; it is mostly bluish grey in colour, with a broad grey selvedge, rather rough looking in its cheaper qualities, but very durable, and less given to shrinking than any other flannel. Many other varieties, however, are now manufactured, which are very nearly, if not quite, as excellent in quality. Yorkshire flannel is white and smooth, has a very narrow selvedge, and is generally satisfactory. Some of the Lancashire flannels have cotton mixed with the wool; those made of pure wool have the surface on one side slightly raised. Saxony flannel is fine, white, and soft, so is well adapted for ladies' under-vests worn next the skin, and for infants' clothing; it is said not to shrink in washing, which, however, entirely depends upon the method by which the washing is accomplished. Flannel gauze is peculiarly thin and cobwebby, and is chiefly used by residents in India and other tropical climates. There is no advantage in purchasing too fine or too closely woven flannels, for they wash hard and thick.

Bath Coating is a description of flannel especially suitable for petticoats; one yard, either white or red, will suffice for a garment, it being from 54 inches wide, and considerably thicker and stronger than flannel.

Lan-ura and **Silcura** are two natural wool flannels, admirably suited to underwear, boating shirts, blouse bodices, &c., and may be had in plain, striped, chequered, and fancy designs of all drapers. They are delightfully soft, warm, and wear well.

Flannelette has of late years risen favourably in public estimation, and the shops are flooded with nightdresses, chemises, drawers, and other things made of this pretty and useful material in self colours and in stripes of colour;

it is soft and pleasant to wear, shrinks very little, if any, and is decidedly cheap. Swansdown flannelette is warm for invalids.

Cosy Cotton Flannel (to be had only of C. Williamson, 91 Edgware Road, London, W.) is a very charming fabric, soft, warm, and durable, delicate in tint and in texture, and excellent for winter underclothing, nightdresses, jackets, dressing gowns and lining purposes. It also is made in a special wide width for sheets.

Prints and **Muslins** often wash badly; if, therefore, you propose buying a doubtful colour it would be advisable to purchase a piece as pattern, and wash half of it, which, when compared with the other half, will show at once whether the colours are fast or not. Lilac and pink are generally safe; also such as carry the pattern almost as clear on the wrong side as on the surface.

White **Holland** is used for window blinds; brown holland for boys' pinafores and smocks, and for covering chairs and sofas.

Chintz and **Cretonne** are both extensively employed for upholstery purposes.

Single thread **Canvas** is desirable for samplers.

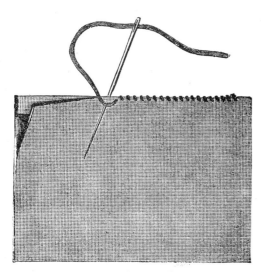

Fig. 4.—Seaming or Sewing.

REQUISITES FOR PLAIN NEEDLEWORK.

A WORK-BOX, or work-basket, is indispensable to keep the requisites together; formerly mahogany or fancy wood boxes were considered quite the thing, and people prided themselves upon the daintiness of the fittings, and were particular to have the tray lined with silk or satin and a pocket padded and quilted within the lid. But time brings changes, and elegant work-baskets, in all manner of shapes and sizes, are now appealing to cultivated tastes and find great favour. Whether you have a box or a basket, it should

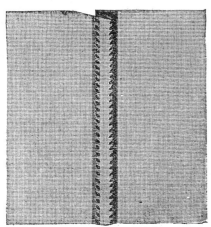

Fig. 5.—A Seam, Sewn and **Felled.**

be large enough to hold a moderate amount of work and all its appurtenances, without being of such a size as to be inconvenient to carry about; and there should be in it divisions or partitions for keeping cotton, needles, buttons, &c., apart and in order.

Now as regards outfit, the first requisite is a good supply of **Needles** of different sorts and sizes; these should be of the best quality; if they bend, the steel has not been properly tempered. The largest needle factories in the world are situate in the neighbourhood of Redditch, in Worcestershire, and it is said that each needle passes through 126 hands before it is ready for sale.

Morrell, Milward, Kirby, Johnson, and Walker, are leading makers. The needles most in demand for plain sewing are denominated "sharps," and these are of three descriptions—drilled eyed, calyx eyed, and gold eyed; some workers prefer the gold eyed, but the calyx eyed are pleasant to use, they carry the cotton easily, and are easy to thread; Nos. 6, 7, and 8 are most useful sizes. "Betweens" are shorter than "sharps," and "blunts" are shorter still, and also thicker, to suit the heavy work of stay makers, tailors, and shoemakers. Crewel needles are rather nice to employ in sewing, the eye is rather long and will slip readily through the material. "Darners," as the name implies, are intended for darning purposes; they have long eyes, some will take thick worsted, others are only fit for cotton and silk. Rug needles are short and thick, with large long eyes and blunt points, and are used for Berlin wool canvas work. Chenille needles are similar but are possessed of points. An ample needle book, containing a leaf of flannel for each class of needle, will be found extremely useful. The stock of needles may be kept from rusting by strewing a little stone alum in the packets; and if the worker's hands are inclined to dampness, it is advisable to keep a little of the powder in a small box handy to rub on the fingers. Rusty needles can be restored to their original brightness by drawing them through an emery cushion.

Machine Needles constitute a class to themselves, and each machine carries its own special needle.

Sewing Cotton may be either glazed or unglazed, and five or six reels of useful sized white and one or two reels of fairly strong black must be considered necessary. There are several brands that may be depended upon—Coats, Clark, Taylor, Chadwick, Ardern, and others. The reels are numbered according to the size of the cotton, and vary with the respective makers; coarse cotton is employed for coarse work and fine cotton for sewing fine material.

Marking Cotton is to be had in Turkey red and navy blue, ingrain colours, and though the custom of marking with ink has lately very much superseded cross-stitch marking, we must say that we greatly prefer the latter style and trust it may soon be revived among the upper and middle class; it is well worth the trouble. In a future issue we hope to give illustrations of pretty letters and initials for cross-stitch marking on pocket handkerchiefs and underlinen.

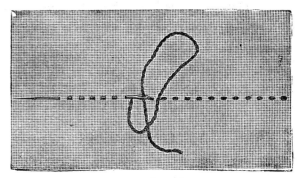

Fig. 6.—Running.

Trafalgar or **Moravian Cotton** is quite soft and free from twist; the Moravian nuns did exquisite work with this cotton, but now it is only employed for darning on net.

Embroidery Cotton.—Brooks' is a loose soft make, sold in skeins, and much used for English white embroidery.

Dewhurst and Sons' Coloured Embroidery Cottons embrace upwards of a hundred different shades, which are nearly all thoroughly ingrain and will bear hard washing.

Darning Cotton is employed for darning cotton stockings, and Strutt's best knitting cotton, in fine sizes, is useful for the same purpose. Messrs. W. D. and J. Strutt also manufacture coloured crochet cottons in forty shades, while they are the makers of macramé twine, &c.

Thread, made of linen fibre, is much stronger than cotton, and is appropriate for sewing linen, holland, and other strong fabrics; when not in use it should be kept wrapped up in a thread case, as also should flourishing thread, lace thread, and any coloured threads or cottons that are sold in skeins.

See that your **Thimble** is well made and a nice fit. A silver thimble is to be preferred, and will with care last a long time; steel ones are very strong; brass thimbles are apt to discolour the finger, but if lined with celluloid this objection vanishes. Those made of ebony and ivory are suitable for doing embroidery and lace work; gold thimbles are far too expensive for ordinary use.

There are various kinds of **Scissors,** and you can scarcely do without a large strong pair for cutting out; a medium pair with thin blades for general use; a small pair with two sharp points for fine work and embroidery; and also a pair of buttonhole scissors.

Among the other **Requisites** for plain needlework we must specify a box of mixed pins; a bodkin for running in tapes; a stiletto for piercing eyelet holes; pieces of tape of various widths; linen buttons and pearl buttons in assorted sizes; white and black hooks and eyes; a skein of bobbin with which to make piping; a small sharp penknife for unpicking; a lead pencil to define the width of hems and tucks; a yard measure marked with inches; an emery cushion; and a piece of wax for strengthening cotton.

6

GENERAL RULES.

WHEN purchasing linen and calico see that the threads are close and even and of the same thickness both in warp and woof, that there are no specks and knots, and that the selvedge is smooth and firm.

All linen and calico should be washed, stretched, and pressed by mangle or iron before it is cut; this will clear away whatever stiffening there is in the fabric, and make it easier to pass the needle through.

Linen, lawn, and holland should be cut by a thread; chintz and cretonne by a crease.

Calico, muslin, and flannel will tear, but the process is apt to pull the fabric, and therefore though it may take longer, it is wiser to cut by the thread.

Cutting out whole sets of things together tends to economy, as the various small parts will run in one with another; hence it is better to cut out six or twelve garments of a sort at once than to cut only one at a time.

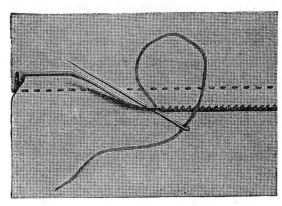

Fig. 7.—Running and Felling (Wrong Side of Material).

Garments are, as a rule, made lengthways of the fabric, that is, with the selvedges running from head to foot, and it makes a great deal of difference both in the appearance of the article and in the subsequent wear whether this rule is observed or not, irrespective of the fact that this is the *right* way, and the other way is *wrong*; the warp threads pass longitudinally up the fabric and are strong and tight and will not stretch; the woof threads on the contrary run across the material from selvedge to selvedge, and are considerably more loosely woven than the warp threads, and if pulled between the thumb and finger will give slightly.

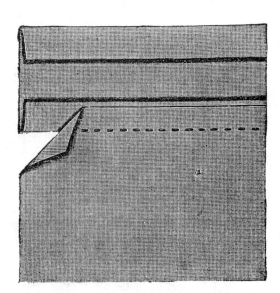

Fig. 8.—Putting on a False Hem.

Waistbands, wristbands, shoulder-straps, and collars, are always cut lengthways with the selvedge of the material, as it is not required that they should stretch or give.

Piping is always cut on the cross, or *bias*, as it is sometimes called; bindings for strengthening the openings of drawers and other similar purposes should be cut on the cross, as here "stretch" is desirable.

In cutting crossways, first fold the end of the piece of material like a half handkerchief, so as to lay the raw edge evenly against the selvedge, and then

cut off the half square; use this half square from which to cut narrow strip for piping, and if it does not suffice, you can cut more strips off the bias end of the material.

To cut off a yard crossways—Proceed in the first instance as instructed above, and when the half square has been cut off, measure a yard along each of the selvedge sides, nick the margin, fold and crease the material slantingly across from nick to nick, and cut by the crease.

Coarse fabrics require stronger sewing than fine ones, and the stitches need not be so small, but must be set closely together. When the material is very stout it should be sewn with thread in preference to cotton, unless the cotton be strengthened by waxing.

Never pull the sewing cotton too tightly, or the work will be puckered; a puckered hem is very unsightly.

The needle and cotton should be adapted to each other, and likewise to the quality of the material, taking care that the eye of the needle will carry the cotton conveniently without either pulling or breaking it.

Never attempt to sew with a bent needle; it cannot be trusted to do nice work.

Never bite or break the sewing cotton, but cut it with a pair of scissors.

The cotton should always be used the way it unwinds from the reel, as the friction of the needle's eye rubbing against the fibre will sometimes cause it to fray or break; for this reason, experienced workers will thread the needle before cutting the cotton from the reel.

The needle, while being threaded, is held in the left hand, and the cotton in the right; subsequently you take the work between the thumb and first finger of the left hand and hold the needle in the right. The thimble should be worn on the second finger of the right hand.

Do not press the needle through by the aid of the thimble alone, but help it through with the assistance of the thumb, and broken needles will be of rare occurrence.

See that the edges of the fabric are perfectly even before commencing sewing operations; then be careful to commence neatly, join the needlefuls of cotton invisibly, and finish neatly.

Do not spare trouble in the matter of "basting" or "tacking," as it is called; to do this carefully will save time in the long run, and the more you measure and prepare your work, the more satisfactory it will turn out to be.

Hold the material between the forefinger and the thumb of the left hand; and if required to be held still more firmly, carry it round the tip of the forefinger and press the second finger closely against it.

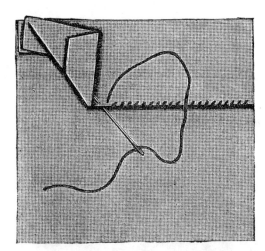

Fig. 9.—A False Hem (Hemming Process).

To work well you need not stoop, nor need you sit cramped up. A natural, easy position should be maintained, and the work should be held in such a manner that you hardly need to bend your head at all.

Never pin your work to your knee, to do so is ungraceful. If you wish to fasten it to something use a square or oblong cushion weighted with lead, and stand this on the table and pin the material upon it, and sew with the work stretched over the first and second fingers of the left hand. In this position a hem, a run, or a fell can be very quickly done.

Children should be taught from the first to fix and prepare their own work. They are generally fond of sewing with coloured cotton, which should be encouraged, as it shows the stitches more visibly than white. A piece of soft material should be given them to practise upon. When they have mastered the stitches their industry may at once be turned to useful account—not the hemming of dusters and pocket-handkerchiefs, of which they soon tire, but the making of some small garment that will be serviceable to themselves or to others. It is well to teach a child to think of others, and the little girl who makes a pinafore "all by herself" for a poor child, learns a more valuable lesson than the actual needlework. But in teaching her to work for the poor never let her think that "anything" will do; on the contrary, the sewing has need to be extra strong by reason of the hard wear it will most certainly receive.

[28]

MEASURE FOR CALICO, FLANNEL, CLOTH, SILK, AND OTHER FABRICS.

2¼ inches	...	...	...	make	1 nail.
4 nails or 9 inches	...	...	...	,,	¼ of a yard.
2 quarters or 18 inches	...	...	,,	½ a yard.
3 quarters or 27 inches	...	...	,,	1 Flemish ell.
4 quarters or 36 inches	...	...	,,	1 yard.
5 quarters or 45 inches	...	...	,,	1 English ell.
6 quarters or 54 inches	...	...	,,	1 French ell.

PLAIN SEWING.

THE term "plain sewing" is generally applied to calico work, but it really embraces any description of needlework which is of a purely useful character, and consequently it includes the making of underlinen, household linen, infants' clothing, and dressmaking, and also the mending of the same.

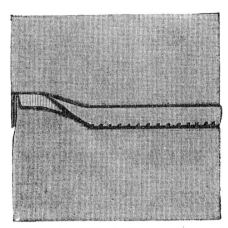

Fig. 10.—A Mantua-Maker's Seam, or Hemmed Seam.

The following are the principal stitches in use: Hemming, sewing or seaming, felling, tacking, stitching, hem stitching, running, whipping, tucking, herringboning, overcasting, buttonholing, gathering, gauging, pleating, quilting, patching, darning, fringing, and marking.

Fig. 1.—HEMMING.

HEMMING is one of the most important and certainly one of the most indispensable stitches appertaining to plain needlework. No garment is complete without a hem; pocket-handkerchiefs are hemmed, sheets are hemmed, tablecloths and nearly all articles of household linen are hemmed—that is to say, the raw edge of the material is turned down and folded over and held in place by a neat row of stitches, and this fold, or hem, as it is called, serves the double purpose of strengthening the edge of the material, and making at the same time a kind of ornamental border. A great deal of hemming is nowadays accomplished by means of the sewing machine, but into this we need not enter, as those who possess a machine will understand the *modus operandi*; enough to say that the effect resembles the stitched hem (Fig. 2), and by reason of the extreme neatness and regularity of the stitches the machine work far excels anything that can be done by hand.

A hem may be any width, from a narrow ⅛ of an inch hem, such as is put at the edge of a muslin frill, to the inch-wide hem at the bottom of a nightdress, and on to the 3-inch or 4-inch hem at the bottom of a petticoat or a dress. See that the material is cut perfectly straight; if possible, let it be cut even by a thread; hold the wrong side of the material towards you, and turn down the raw edge to a depth of from ⅛ of an inch to ¼ of an inch, more or less, according to the width the hem is intended to be when finished, and press the fold firmly as you go along; then make a second turning the actual width the hem is required, and flatten this down between the thumb and finger. It is a good plan to have a card nicked to the width of the hem and measure from time to time as you proceed. If the hem be at all wide it had better be tacked to keep it in place; the tacking stitches should run through the first fold of the hem, and if a long stitch and a short one be placed alternately it will be found more efficacious than all long stitches. Hem from right to left. Begin work by placing the hem on the first finger of the left hand, close by the root of the nail, and retain it in position by pressure of the left-hand thumb on one side and the second finger on the other side; take the needle, which already has been threaded, point it away from the chest, pass it through the first fold of the hem, and draw the cotton through until within half an inch from the end, when tuck the end under the hem with the point of the needle, so as to keep it fast without the assistance of a knot, which is always clumsy. Now you will be prepared to make the first stitch—thus: Insert the point of the needle in the material, just below the edge of the fold, direct the needle in a slanting position leftwards, and taking up two or three threads of the material, bring it out just above the edge of the fold, as see Fig. 1, and draw through. You will observe the stitch secures the hem upon the material; every succeeding stitch is taken in the same manner, and at a distance of two or three threads apart one from the other. When it is required to take a fresh needleful of cotton you will cut the old cotton within half an inch of the end, recommence as instructed above, and tuck *both* ends neatly under the hem. Finish the hem by making two stitches one over the other, and slip the needle up under the hem before cutting off the cotton. In hemming, avoid pulling the cotton too tightly, or the material will be puckered; if hemming round a curve, such as the bottom of a rounded apron, or an armhole or neck, employ care in fixing, for if the curve be *concave* the hem most likely will need stretching to cause it to lie perfectly flat; and, on the other hand, if the curve be *convex*, it will require easing. When you are hemming a square always fix and hem two opposite sides first, and then the other two opposite sides, so that the corners may correspond. Hems in woollen fabrics which will not lend themselves readily to the turning-down process, must be tacked as they are laid down, bit by bit.

Fig. 2.—A STITCHED HEM.

A NEAT and pretty inch-wide hem is represented in Fig. 2. This is worked in back stitching, and is the kind of hem most suitable for sheets and napery. It has the same appearance as the hem made by a sewing machine. Let the edge of the material be cut perfectly straight by a thread, and proceed to turn down first a ⅜-inch fold and then an inch-wide fold; count four or five threads from the bottom of the hem, and draw out a thread or two threads to afford space to stitch upon; the threads that remain will determine the size the stitches are to be. Begin on the right-hand side and work to the left. Secure the end of the cotton invisibly within the hem, and bring up the needle to the front of the work on the line of drawn thread; now the stitching is to go through all three layers of material, insert the needle two threads to the right of the place where the cotton is emerging, and bring it up two threads to the left, and draw through; again insert the needle two threads to the right (which is the place where a stitch is already passed through), and again bring it up two threads further to the left; it now is in the position shown in the engraving, and the procedure is repeated till the hem is accomplished. The folded side on which you are forming your stitches is the right side of the work.

Fig. 3.—HEM-STITCHING.

HEM-STITCHING is employed upon pocket-handkerchiefs, and at the present time it is very fashionably used on sheets, pillow slips, sideboard cloths, afternoon teacloths, and tray cloths of all descriptions. Commence by drawing out four threads of the material at a distance of two inches from the margin. Fold the hem very exactly, and let the edge of the hem lie perfectly level with the upper edge of the drawn threads, as you see it in Fig. 3; then having the needle threaded, bring it out three threads above the fold of the hem; insert

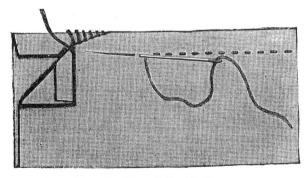

Fig. 11.—French Double Seam.

the needle between the open threads immediately under the place the cotton is emerging, and passing it leftwards take up three open threads on the needle and draw the cotton through, insert the needle again in the same place, and now turning it in a slightly upward direction through the hem, bring it out above the place where the cotton appears; that is to say, three threads above the fold of the hem and three threads to the left of the preceding stitch, as represented in the engraving, and draw the cotton through and proceed in like manner to the end of the line of drawn threads. You will observe that it requires two motions to make a stitch; the first motion is taken from right to left in the open drawn threads, and the second motion confines the group of three drawn threads in a cluster, secures the hem, and brings the cotton in position for working the next successive stitch.

Fig. 4.—SEAMING, OR SEWING.

SEAMING, or sewing, is the method by which we join two pieces of material together. If the two pieces have each good selvedges these require to be placed evenly side by side, and to be pinned together at short distances, or tacked, to keep them level; you then hold the work upright between the forefinger and thumb of the left hand and sew the selvedges over and over, pointing the needle always towards you, as shown in Fig. 4; the stitches should be just deep enough to hold the selvedges firmly together, they should lie in a slanting direction, working from right to left, and not be more than three threads one from the other. No knots are permitted in seaming; let the end (or ends) of cotton project from between the selvedges, and sew it (or them) over with the first few stitches. When the seam is finished, the finger should be placed under it while the thumb-nail flattens it down; or it may be laid on the table and flattened with a short bone paper knife, or with a tooth-

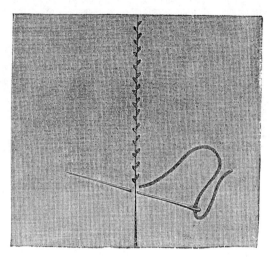

Fig. 12.—Fine Drawing.

brush handle. Sometimes, as for instance when sewing the side seams of chemises and nightdresses, the material is cut on the slant, and the raw edges have to be joined together; you will turn the raw edge of one piece down once, and turn the edge of the other piece down double the width because the half width of this is turned back again for the fell. The folds are placed inside, and the seaming is executed as represented in the engraving, Fig. 4. Thus, the *seam* is sewn on the *right* side of the work, and the fell ensures neatness on the wrong side or inside. After the *seam* is accomplished it must be pressed perfectly flat; and you will turn the work inside out, to get at the

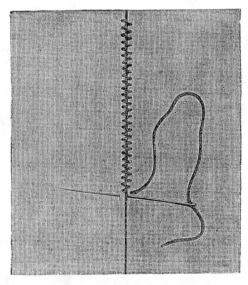

Fig. 13.—Old German Seam.

fold, which now has to be felled down, just the same as if hemming. A long fell is rather awkward to manage, because you must contrive to grasp the whole length of the material in the space between your thumb and forefinger before you can conveniently hold it upon the finger for hemming down. Beware of puckering. If there should be any inaccuracy in the evenness of the fold it **may** be smoothed away with the point of the needle.

Fig. 5.—A SEAM SEWN AND FELLED.

THE engraving, Fig. 5, exemplifies the right side of a completed seam of sewing and felling. The method of arranging and working the seam is described above. The line of stitches on the left-hand side of the seam are illustrative of the sewn stitches and those on the right-hand side are the felled stitches.

Fig. 6.—RUNNING.

HERE we have a representation of a line of stitches running straight across a piece of material, as see Fig. 6. Nothing could be more simple. Yet this is one of the most useful stitches in plain needlework, being by far the readiest method of joining together two pieces of any kind of material; besides being employed in tucking and in gathering, as will be explained further on. Running is produced by passing a needle and cotton in and out of the material at regular intervals; the size of the stitches will depend upon the quality of the material; a very usual way of running is to take up three threads and leave three threads. Several stitches may be taken on the needle at a time if the softness of the fabric will permit, and a back stitch should be put occasionally to keep the work firm. Seams in underlinen are frequently run and felled in preference to being seamed and felled; they are done quicker, and the work sits flatter. Prepare the seam by turning down the raw edge of one piece of calico in a ¼-inch fold; lay the other raw edge upon this a few threads from the top, and

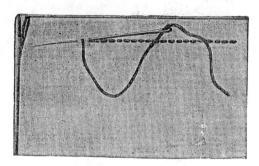

Fig. 14.—Stitching a Wristband.

run the two pieces together, taking the stitches through both fabrics about three threads lower than the fold. The right side of the work is inwards, and the running stitches do not show at all on the right side When the running is accomplished the "fold" must be pressed flat and felled down in the manner depicted, Fig. 7; the fell stitches are taken through to the right side of the fabric and must be done neatly.

To run together the seams of dresses and petticoats you will lay two selvedges evenly together, with the right side of the material inside, and run along, taking the stitches through both pieces at about ¼ inch below the selvedges. If the edges happen to be raw leave a greater margin. Suppose one breadth be gored and the other straight, the gored breadth should be held next to the worker.

Fig. 7.—RUNNING AND FELLING.

OUR engraving, Fig. 7, shows a run and felled seam in process of working; you can see the manner in which the fold is turned down, and the method of running the seam as explained in the preceding paragraph. The needle is set through the material in the act of felling. The seams in garments should correspond, or pair, one with the other; that is to say, if the first seam be

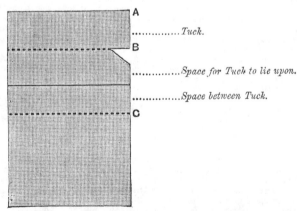

Fig. 16.—Diagram for Measuring Tucks.

commenced at the top of the article the corresponding seam should be commenced at the bottom; this rule also holds good with the seams of sleeves, and the observance will make all the difference between a well-arranged garment and a faulty one.

Figs. 8 and 9.—A FALSE HEM.

THE attachment of a strip of material upon the edge of a garment in imitation of a real hem is called a "false hem." It is not necessary in every case that the material of the false hem should be the same fabric as the garment, though generally it is so if using calico or muslin; but for such things as the bottom of a stuff petticoat or dress skirt, the false hem is needed to be so wide that it may very well be formed of twill, holland, or lining, to economise the more expensive material. Cut a breadth of lining, or as many breadths as joined together will suffice to go along the bottom of the skirt, and the width you desire the false hem to be; place this against the fabric, the right side of the strip against the right side of the fabric, the two edges even one with the other, and run them both together about ⅜ of an inch from the edge; then turn up the strip and carefully flatten the folds, as see Fig. 8; turn the false hem in position upon the wrong side of the garment, the raw edge being previously folded under, and hem it in its place after the manner of a real hem, as see Fig. 9. A false hem of this description is usefully employed to lengthen children's frocks; the hem of the frock should be undone and ironed flat, and thereby the additional length is secured; you then put on a calico hem in the manner instructed above, which hem should be somewhat wider than the piece that has been let down. A false hem for strengthening the top openings of drawers should be about one inch in width, cut on the bias, so as to stretch or give to the curve of the drawers.

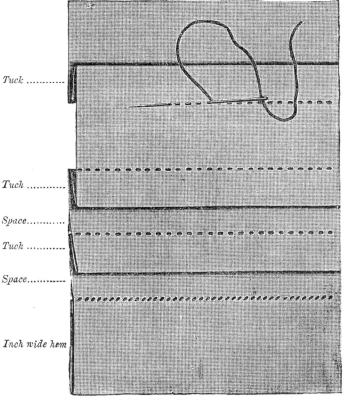

Tuck ....
Tuck ....
Space...........
Tuck ....
Space...........
Inch wide hem

Fig. 15.—Tucking.

Fig. 10.—A MANTUA-MAKER'S SEAM, or HEMMED SEAM.

THIS is often used in dressmaking for sleeves that have no lining, for seams of skirts, for making pockets, &c.; it is neat on both sides, and is effective in keeping in raw edges of material; thus it is a seam much employed in the making of fancy bags and other trifles, which must look nice, though it is expedient to attain that object with as little labour as possible. Lay the two raw edges of the material together, straight and even, the right sides inside, fold both over, fold both over again, and hem the fold in the usual manner, taking the stitches firmly through. The seam will be perfectly strong; the hem will stand in a ridge, as see Fig. 10, instead of laying flat as it would if it had been run and felled.

Fig. 11.—FRENCH DOUBLE SEAM.

THIS seam is especially useful for thin stuffs, and most of all for such as are cut on the cross and are liable to fray, as it prevents fraying, and looks neat on both sides; it is not so thick as the mantua-maker's hem, and is effected by running instead of hemming. Lay the two raw edges of the material one upon the other, the wrong side inside, and run them together ¼ inch or further from the edge. Then turn the material over at the seam, with the right sides now coming inside and the two raw edges enclosed between, and run the material together again, taking the stitches a trifle below the edges to make sure that no frayed threads are visible when the seam is accomplished. Fig. 11 shows the two runnings, and also a portion of the edges folded within.

Fig. 12.—FINE DRAWING.

SEAMS of this description are usual in old linen work, but at present the stitch is almost exclusively employed in tailoring, and if a woman is an adept at it and can thus cleverly repair rents in her husband's or boys' coats, it may be a means of saving many a shilling. The stitch is simplicity itself, but skill is required to draw the edges of the cloth quite closely together without at all overlapping each other, and of course without fraying the cloth. If rightly done the join is almost imperceptible. See that the cloth is cut perfectly even, and hold, stretched lengthways on the forefinger of the left hand, the two edges that are to be joined; point the needle from you through the edge of

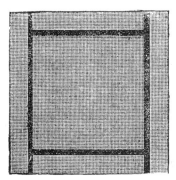

Fig. 17.—A Square Gusset (wrong side) showing the Turnings.

one piece, placing it in the position shown in Fig. 12, then point it in a similar position through the other piece, and draw the thread firmly and closely, bringing the edges of the cloth to meet, and continue thus, taking a stitch on each side, alternately, till the seam or join is finished. It then should be pressed on the wrong side with a hot iron. When sheets get old, and it seems desirable to bring the selvedge in the middle and place the worn parts outside, the selvedges should be joined by fine drawing, as it is so much smoother than top sewing.

Fig. 13.—OLD GERMAN SEAM.

THIS bears a great resemblance to fine drawing, but whereas that is chiefly adopted by tailors, the German seam, Fig. 13, is useful for joining together any two selvedged pieces of linen or other fabric. The stitches are taken first on one side and then on the other side, within the selvedge, and a distance of only two threads apart, sewing towards you; the cotton must be drawn until

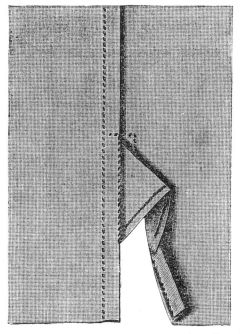

Fig. 18.—A Square Gusset as it appears when Completed.

the edges meet, but not overlap. A perfectly flat seam is produced. Seams of this kind are occasionally met with in old linen embroidery; and at one time when sheeting was made narrower than it now is, it was quite common to see the old German seam uniting two breadths together.

Fig. 14.—STITCHING A WRISTBAND.

It is more absolutely necessary to have the fabric cut perfectly straight and even for *stitching* than for any class of work, and to ensure evenness it should be cut true to a thread. Wristbands and collars will never sit well unless the linen is straight selvedgeways, so be particular on this point. Wristbands and collars are made of linen, whether the entire shirt be linen or not; in fact, they are generally required to be of three thicknesses—*i.e.*, two pieces of linen and a lining of calico. Cut the band the size and shape required, some are quite straight, others have rounded corners: put the two pieces of linen together, the piece of calico at the back, and run all neatly together on the two short sides, and one long side, at a distance of about a quarter of an inch from the margin. Then turn over one of the linen sides to hide the running and the raw edges, and you will find you have linen front and back, and the lining in the middle. Press the edge quite even on the three sides. The right side of the band will be that side upon which the fold of the edges is least conspicuous, and on this side the stitching is to be executed. Now decide at what distance from the margin the stitching is to be, and extract one or two threads to mark the line for the stitching; do this on the two short sides as well as on the long side, unless the corners are rounded, when a faint pencil line will serve the purpose. Tack the opposite long side to keep the linen in proper position, and begin by slipping the needle and cotton between the material, bringing it up close to the right-hand end of the drawn thread, and *on* the line of drawn thread, insert the needle through the band two threads behind the place the cotton is brought out, and bring it up two threads in front thereof, then insert the needle two threads back (which is precisely in the place where the last stitch ended), and bring it up two threads forward, and continue in the same way, working in one continuous unbroken line of stitches. The wrong side of the stitching must look almost as neat as the right side, though the stitches are longer, and this can be ensured by carefulness in putting in the needle always the same way—*i.e.*, always *below* the

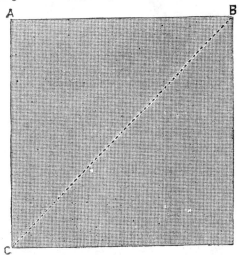

Fig. 19.—Square of Material to make a Pair of Triangular Gussets.

stitch, bringing it out *above* by guiding it at the back with the first finger of the left hand, or else contrarywise, by putting the needle in above the stitch and bringing it out below. You will soon get used to placing the needle regularly, and will discover the advantage of doing so. Fig. 14 shows a portion of a wristband in progress. When you require to begin a fresh needleful you must pass the needle and cotton to the wrong side and darn in and out neatly, and slip the new needleful between the materials, bringing it out two threads in front of the preceding stitch, and go on as before. Stitching must of necessity be worked on double material to afford substance behind the drawn thread; of course only one stitch can be made at a time, consequently it is slow work, but those who can do it nicely are generally fond of it.

Fig. 15.—TUCKING.

Tucks are folds of material used mostly for the purpose of ornamentation round the bottom of petticoats, drawers, children's frocks, skirts, and pinafores, also on infants' robes, and they certainly are very pretty, and add greatly to the appearance of the garment upon which they are employed. Our illustration (Fig. 15) shows an inch-wide hem and three tucks. These tucks are all the same width, and are formed and kept in place by a line of running stitches, as see the stitches on the needle in the course of making the third tuck. Sometimes tucks are graduated in size, putting the largest above the hem, and narrowing each tuck successively, until the top tuck is very, very narrow indeed. Sometimes they are arranged in groups, an inch-wide hem and three ¼-inch tucks, an inch-wide tuck, and again three ¼-inch tucks, and so on. When you have decided upon the form your tucks shall take, you had better make a cardboard diagram after the style of Fig. 16, so that each may be accurate by measurement; the nick in the cardboard will show you where to fold the material and where to work the running, and you will measure continually as you go on. Observe that a tuck always occupies three times its width, the upper or surface side of the tuck, the under side, and the width

of material that it lies upon, and you also have to calculate for a little clear space of material *between* the tucks, as they show to better advantage when placed at a moderate distance from each other. When arranging wide tucks you may estimate for the space to be half the width of the tuck itself—for instance, if you are making inch-wide tucks, calculate half an inch for the

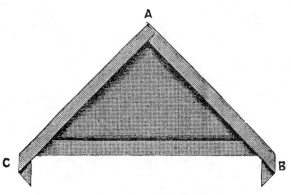

Fig. 20.—First Proceeding.

distance between the tucks; and if the tucks are intended to be half an inch wide you may estimate a quarter of an inch as the correct interval of space. Very narrow tucks require a greater proportion of space or they appear overcrowded; it will not be too much to leave one-eighth of an inch space, or even three-sixteenths of an inch space, as an interval between tiny tucks measuring one-eighth of an inch wide. Much will depend upon the good taste of the worker.

Fig. 16.—DIAGRAM FOR MEASURING TUCKS.

It is absolutely necessary to be provided with some kind of guide or gauge to ensure evenness and accuracy in tuck-running, and therefore in Fig. 16 we illustrate a cardboard diagram for determining the width of tucks and the width of spaces between the same. Any piece of cardboard, even the half of

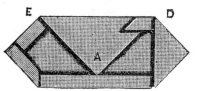

Fig. 22.—Third Proceeding.

a postcard, cut lengthways, will answer the purpose. Let the top of the card, A, stand for the folding of the material; cut a notch, B, on one side of the card so far below the top as you desire the width of the tuck to be. This notch denotes the place where the running of the tuck will be effected. Draw a pencil line across the card to mark off precisely the same width as the tuck, and thus afford surface sufficient for the tuck to lie upon when it is turned downwards on the fabric, and then consider the interval you desire to allow between the tucks, or between the first tuck and the hem, as the case may be, and denote it by a few dots across the card, simulating the line of stitches that have been already set in for the previous tuck or hem. The remainder of the

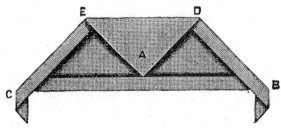

Fig. 21.—Second Proceeding.

card is left blank. Now, supposing you have completed the hem and are about to commence the first tuck, you will place the card on the right side of the material, the dotted line, C, against the stitches of the hem, and fold the material back at A, creasing it as you go along. You may crease the whole of the tuck at once, or only a part, as you prefer, and if it be a wide tuck it will be safer to tack it in place, or pin it, rather than rely upon the crease alone; either way, you will commence running at B, and be careful to measure the depth constantly while the running is in progress; or, what is infinitely easier, mark the depth faintly with a black-lead pencil, and run upon the line; take a back stitch now and then in the course of the running. When the first tuck is finished and turned down, you will proceed with the next in the same manner, and so on until all are accomplished.

Figs. 17 to 24.—GUSSETS.

A GUSSET is a small piece of material, either square or triangular in shape, let into the end of a seam to afford play to the opening of the seam, and to prevent it tearing or splitting by reason of the strain that otherwise might be brought to bear upon it. Gussets always go in pairs, and a nice-fitting, well-arranged pair of gussets are an ornament to the garment upon which they are placed. A man's shirt presents a favourable exhibition of gusseting, as it usually requires four pairs—viz., a pair of large square gussets at the top under-part of the sleeves, a pair of tiny ones at the opening of the wrist, a pair of neck gussets, and a pair of side gussets. We do not intend to enter fully into the art of shirt-making, but will here give the necessary instruction for cutting and setting in gussets. The seam in which a gusset is to be placed may be either a sewn seam uniting two selvedges, or it may be a run-and-felled seam; if the former it is all right, but in the latter case the fell must cease a few stitches before the termination of the seam, because, as it is essential to make a smooth corner to receive the corner of the gusset, it will be necessary to snip the fell across just at the end of the sewing (on the wrong side of the work), and gradually to slope off the bit of calico that stands in the way of turning down a straight narrow hem on this side of the opening; you will understand at once the mode of accomplishing this purpose when you hold the work in your hand. The completed gusset, with a portion of the seam, and the hemming up the opening of the same, is clearly represented in Fig. 18; a gusset contrived in this manner is exceedingly neat. You begin operations by cutting a square of material, measuring from two inches to three inches across or larger if desired; be very particular to cut a perfectly *true* square, straight *by the thread* on all four sides. Turn down two opposite sides, then turn down the remaining two sides of the square, as shown in Fig. 17. Place a corner of

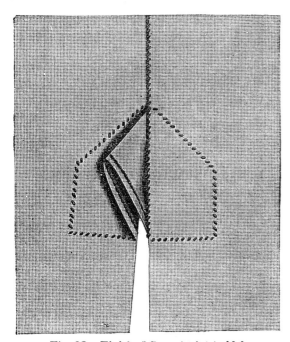

Fig. 23.—Finished Gusset (right side).

the gusset in the corner of the seam, and top sew it on two sides to the sides of the opening, going not quite to the end of the side of the gusset, but very nearly as far, then fold the gusset over on the bias, in the form of a triangle, arrange it upon the wrong side of the material, and hem it neatly thereto; the hem of the gusset may appear as a continuation of the fell, so far as it extends, and the hem of the material will then carry on the line of stitches in unbroken regularity, as see Fig. 18. A similar hem is apparent on the opposite side of the opening. A row of fine back stitching upon the edge of the bias will complete the gusset.

A triangular gusset is somewhat differently treated. Fig. 19 represents a three-inch square of material, which, if cut diagonally across by the dotted line from B to C, will produce a pair of triangular gussets. Take one of these triangles, hold it with the wrong side of the material facing you, and fold the two opposite corners together to induce a crease to denote the centre; open it again, and fold over the raw edge on all three sides of the triangle, the bias side first, then the two other sides, and it will appear as Fig. 20. Fold the corner. A bias-ways down upon the centre crease until it reaches the raw edge of the bottom turning, as see Fig. 21, where the bias is denoted by D and E. Now turn up the corners B and C, mitre fashion, to meet D and E, and *cut off* these little corners, leaving only so much as will afford a fold of material upon the sides of the gusset, which now assumes a pointed oblong shape; Fig. 22 represents the progress that has been made, the right-hand side of the oblong being still mitred up, and requiring to be cut to correspond with the left-hand side, from which the mitre has already been removed. Now hold the right side of the garment towards you, with the seam in a convenient position to receive the gusset. Place point A of the gusset exactly in the apex of the seam, and hold the edge of the selvedge (we are supposing this to be a selvedged seam) and the edge of the gusset firmly between the

thumb and forefinger of the left hand; begin to sew at the bias where marked D, and sew up to the point A, make a few strong stitches here in the apex of the seam, and continue sewing until you reach E on the opposite side of the bias; do not break the cotton, but turn the gusset over to the wrong side of the garment, pin it most carefully in place, the centre crease of the gusset upon the seam and the sides stretched out to a true angle, having the threads of the mitred corners of the gusset *true* with the threads warp and weft of the material; it may be necessary to stretch the long bias fold of the gusset in order to accomplish this, but it MUST be managed, for if the gusset does not lie smooth and flat, and thread by thread level with the threads of the fabric upon which it lies, it will not look well. When, however, it is arranged to your satisfaction, you will hem the gusset neatly round; still do not break off the cotton. Turn the work again to the right side, and embroider the gusset

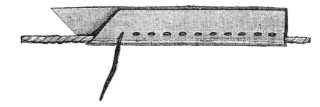

Fig. 25.—Piping. Showing Method of running Cotton Cord in a Bias Strip of Material.

with a neat row of back stitching along the bias edge. Fig. 23 shows the right side of the gusset as it appears when completed, and Fig. 24 shows the wrong side with the gusset hemmed and stretched out flat.

Figs. 25 to 27.—PIPING.

PIPING was at one time very much in request for binding and finishing off the armholes and necks of slip bodices, to strengthen the armholes of dresses, to draw in the tops of frills and flounces, and for other decorative purposes, but at present it is only moderately employed. However it is useful to know how to make it if wanted. Required, a skein of cotton cord, or bobbin, and several strips of material about an inch in width, cut on the cross. The strips must be joined neatly together to produce a length sufficient for the piping you want. Some people carefully tack the cord within the strip in the manner shown in Fig. 25, and afterwards attach the piping upon the edge of

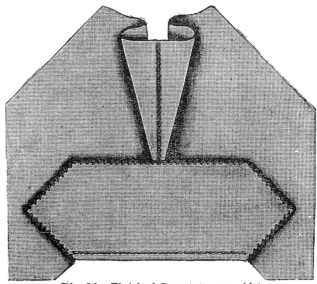

Fig. 24.—Finished Gusset (wrong side).

the material; others manage cleverly to enclose the cord within the strip and run the strip in its proper position, as see Fig. 26, all in one operation. The stitches do not pass through the cord at all, only through the fabric. Fig. 27 represents the right side of a piece of material with the roll of piping along the top; the corner is turned down to render the piping clearly in view. If the piping is to go round armholes it will stand in the position Fig. 26; you will pin the right side of the sleeve against the piping, with all the raw edges perfectly even and back-stitch the whole firmly together over the original stitches of the running; when this is done the raw edges must be smoothly shaved and overcast, to keep them from ravelling. Piping for the neck must be differently treated, it will appear like Fig. 27 upon the right side, and must be hemmed down on the wrong side; the cord, therefore, instead of being put exactly in the middle of the strip must be kept towards one side, to make one raw edge wider than the other, and the raw edge that is the widest must be held towards you as you run the piping on ; it then will come outside when the piping is turned down for hemming, and the edge will fold under the other edges, and keep all neat ; being on the bias it will stretch or contract more or less to the shape required.

Fig. 28.—GATHERING.

GATHERING is the term used in plain needlework to define the art of drawing up a long piece of material into the compass of a shorter piece ; thus, the upper part of a shirt, chemise, or nightdress, is gathered into a neckband or yoke ; sleeves are gathered into wristbands ; the legs of drawers are gathered into kneebands, and the tops into a waistband ; skirts are sometimes gathered into waistbands, although for this purpose pleating is generally preferred, as it lies flatter ; flounces are frequently gathered, so also are frills. The gathering stitch bears a great resemblance to the running stitch illustrated in Fig. 6. Now it is quite possible to make a good gathering with

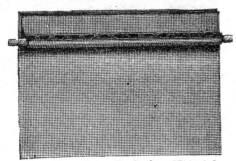

Fig. 26.—Piping Tacked on Material.

stitches of perfectly even length ; but the best authorities advise the taking up of three threads and missing four, or the taking up of four threads and missing six, and certainly if this regularity be kept up, the process of "stroking" is very much simplified as the gathering thread is brought more towards the front of the material, making consequently a greater "hollow" to "stroke" into ; our engraving, Fig. 28, will show what is meant. The right side of the fabric is held towards you. The cotton used for gathering should be a size or two coarser than that employed for sewing ; some people gather with double cotton, thinking that if one thread breaks, the other will support the gathers, but the plan cannot be recommended, as the double thread is so likely to twist and knot. A good margin should be left above the gathering thread. Several stitches may be taken on the needle before drawing the cotton through, and instead of holding the fabric flat and firm with your thumb, you should employ the thumb to push each stitch on the needle as you go, so helping the formation of little rucks, as will be understood by considering the position of the needle as it stands in Fig. 28 ; draw through when the needle gets tolerably full. Before beginning to gather, you must carefully

Fig. 27.—Piping as it looks on Right Side.

observe that the part to be gathered is cut evenly, and also you must measure it into halves and quarters, perhaps even into eights, marking the distances with a coloured cotton about an inch below the line, whereon the gathering will be done, or by inserting pins ; do not spare any pains in the matter, but do it with precision, and mark also in the same way the half, quarters, and eights of the band upon which the gathers are to be set ; time spent in careful preparation is never wasted, because the work will look so much better in the end. When the arrangement is complete the gathering is executed, working from right to left at a quarter of an inch distance or more below the edge, in the manner already described. If you find any difficulty in keeping the gathering stitches straight you may fold down the material and turn it up again, and so make a creased line which will answer for a guide. A needleful of cotton should be taken for each half, or each quarter, as seems most convenient. Never make a join in the middle of a quarter. When the length of gathering is accomplished, draw the threads up close, pull the material above and below the gathering to partly straighten the gathers in their place, put a pin at the quarter if one is not there already, and secure the gathering thread by firmly twisting it round the top and end of the pin ; do each quarter in the same way, and the work will be ready for stroking.

Fig. 29.—STROKING GATHERS.

KEEP the right side of the fabric towards you, take a strong needle, and holding the work between the forefinger and thumb of the left hand, the thumb being pressed *below* the gathering thread, begin striking on the left-hand side, raising each gather gently with the point of the needle and stroking into the little ruck between the gathers with the needle in the position shown in Fig. 29 till all the gathers lie evenly and smoothly in a row ; you may have to tighten the gathering thread as the stroking proceeds, and you should pay a little attention to the edge of the material above the thread and see that that also lies smooth and even. The operation of stroking gathers can very well be carried on without the aid of a table and a cushion, although we have included these in the engraving ; the usual custom is to hold the work conveniently in the left hand, and to push each gather, as you stroke it, under the left-hand thumb.

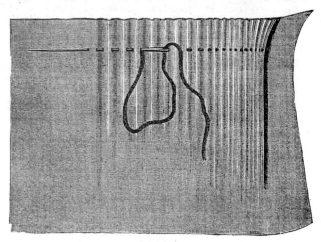

Fig. 28.—Gathering.

Fig. 30.—SEWING IN GATHERS.

RELEASE the gathering threads from their respective pins, open the gathers, and pin the half, quarters, and eighths to the corresponding divisions of the band, and placing the folded edge of the band exactly over the gathering thread, again confine the gathering thread on a pin ; now distribute the gathers evenly below the band, putting in any number of pins that are requisite to keep them regular ; small pins are best for the purpose. Hold the work much in the same way as you would hold hemming, and hem each gather in succession, one

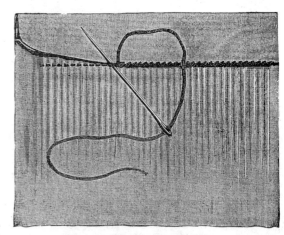

Fig. 30.—Sewing in Gathers

by one, to the band, taking up about two threads of the gather and about two threads of the band, as will clearly be understood by consulting Fig. 30. When the whole length is hemmed you will take out the pins, turn the garment wrong side out, arrange a folded margin of the band *upon* the gathering thread, pinning it as precisely as you before pinned the right side, and hem along, taking the stitches *over* the gathering thread, and being specially careful that no stitch is visible on the right side ; do not pull the cotton too tightly, and avoid puckering by keeping the work well stretched over the two first fingers of the left hand.

Fig. 31.—GAUGING.

GAUGING is pretty work for the fronts of pinafores, aprons, and children's dresses. Its beauty, however, depends upon the lines being perfectly straight and accurate. Our example, Fig. 31, shows "smooth" gauging. The stitch is precisely the same stitch as that used in gathering; in fact, there are here

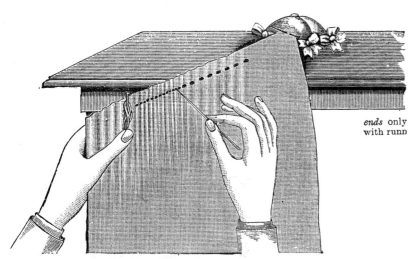

Fig. 29.—Stroking Gathers.

five lines of gathering ranged one below the other, and equi-distant one from the other. The stitches are exactly the same size in every row, stitch under stitch, taking up as nearly as possible the same parallel threads of the fabric. A guide to ensure the evenness of the lines must be contrived with cardboard. When the five lines are gathered the several cottons must be drawn up tightly so as to press the rucks closely together; then if the gauging is rightly done, a pull of the material above and below the gauging will straighten the rucks in their place and cause them to sit regular without any stroking. Now loosen the gauging, and arrange it on a foundation in the way most suited for the purpose for which it is required. Other varieties of gauging are produced by grouping the lines in wider or narrower spaces; for instance, two lines may be grouped a quarter of an inch one from the other, followed by a half-inch space, and then two more lines corresponding to the first two, and again a space, and the two lines repeated. A clever needlewoman will be at no loss for ideas. What is called "rough gauging" is worked on the same plan as Fig. 31 so far as regards the first, third, and fifth lines; but the second line of

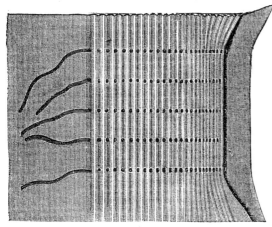

Fig. 31.—Gauging.

stitches must take up the fabric that was missed in the first line, and the fourth line resembles the second; the result is a mass of irregular fluting, which must be kept close together to look well. It is employed chiefly for the fronts of children's frocks.

Figs. 32 to 35.—BUTTONHOLES.

BUTTONHOLES are used in conjunction with buttons, to fasten or close the openings in garments; they are used on waistbands, on wristbands, and on the fronts of shirts and nightdresses, and are, besides, largely employed in dress-making and in tailoring. Great skill is required to make a *good* buttonhole, and skill can only be acquired by practice; no stitch in plain needlework, excepting, perhaps, gathering and setting in gathers, demands such precision and attention to detail. An expert needlewoman will love these stitches more than any easier stitch, because they afford evidence of her cleverness and ability. If several buttonholes are to be made in a row, they must all be cut

the same size exactly, using for the purpose a pair of buttonhole scissors; any inaccuracy in the cutting will spoil the appearance of the work; they may either all be rounded or all barred, as best suits the taste of the worker. Rounded buttonholes, as Fig. 34, are usually employed upon calico work; but sometimes they are made with one end round (the end that comes against the button) and the other end barred; buttonholes in dresses are frequently of this latter description, so also are tailors' buttonholes, and such buttonholes as are used upon cloth garments. A buttonhole with two barred ends, as Fig. 35, is very strong and neat.

Buttonholes are of necessity worked upon double material, either on a band, a hem, or a fold; if a buttonhole is needed on any part of a garment where the fabric is single, you must begin by felling a sufficiently large piece of material on at the back to form a support. The diameter of the button must regulate the size the buttonhole-slit is required to be; place a button exactly on the spot where the buttonhole is to be formed, and by a scratch with the point of the needle, or with a pencil, mark the margin right and left, *not* all the way round, as you desire to denote the *ends* only of the buttonhole slit. If the buttonhole is to be strengthened with running stitches they must be run before the slit is cut. Fig. 33 shows

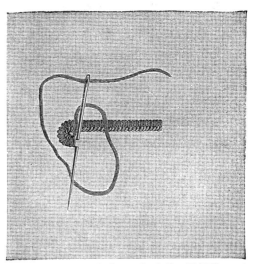

Fig. 32.—Buttonhole worked the Old Way.

an outside line of running stitches, others would be worked in nearer to the slit; or a good plan is to simply lay a thread or two upon the surface of the material when the slit is cut and button-stitch over it; the thread can be drawn up when the buttonhole is finished and will serve to keep the slit from widening; the ends should be run in on the wrong side of the fabric.

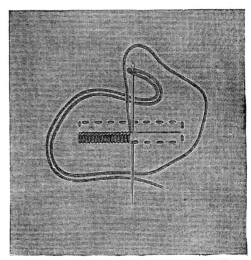

Fig. 33.—Buttonhole worked the New Way.

You may cut the slit with an ordinary pair of scissors if you have not a proper buttonhole pair at hand; it is very useful to know how to manage such an operation in case of need, but you must be especially careful to make a perfectly accurate cut straight *by a thread*. A badly cut buttonhole can never look well, for if it be not cut straight neither can the stitches be placed in a straight line. Double the material evenly at the exact centre of the buttonhole, make a small snip, and open out the material again; now insert the point of the scissors in the snip and cut to the mark—*i.e.*, to the length of the buttonhole, right and left.

14

A buttonhole should be worked with stronger cotton than that employed in the sewing of the garment, and as long a length should be threaded into the needle as will suffice to make the entire buttonhole; for instance, it will require probably half a yard to work a buttonhole half an inch in length. The stitches must be all uniform in depth, and the "twists" or "knots" should be drawn up tightly in a perfectly even line upon the margin of the slit, so that they form an edge as firm and as strong as a piece of fine wire.

Fig. 32 is an example of buttonhole stitch worked upon linen in the old way. Hold the buttonhole slit lengthways along the forefinger of the left hand, and confine it in that position by pressure of the thumb and the third and fourth fingers, the thumb being just below the place where the needle is to be inserted. Begin on the left-hand side of the lower edge of the slit, and work from left to right. Insert the needle within the slit, pointing downwards, and bring the point up through the fabric about four or five threads (an eighth of

pass it from left to right under the point of the needle, then draw the needle through, releasing the cotton from pressure as you pull the knot to the top of the slit with a gentle inclination towards the left-hand side. This method produces a very decided twist, or knot, which, however, can at pleasure be more highly raised by the following little addition, which is very quickly managed; when you have drawn up the cotton till only a very small loop remains, pass the needle from back to front (that is, with the needle pointing towards you) *through* the loop, and complete the drawing-up process. Form every stitch in the same manner, missing always one thread of the fabric between the stitches.

Fig. 34 illustrates a buttonhole with round ends, worked according to the instructions given explanatory of Fig. 32.

Fig. 35 shows a buttonhole completed with two barred ends. These ends partially close over the button and effectually prevent the buttonhole from

Fig. 34.—Buttonhole with Round Ends.

Fig. 36.—Sewing on Cash's Initial Letter (First Process).

an inch or so) below the slit, and draw the cotton through till within a short distance of the end. Hold the end to the right at the back of the material in such a position that the buttonhole stitches will be formed over it and cover it. Again insert the needle within the slit, pointing downwards, and bring the point up through the fabric on the same level horizontally as before, and at a distance of one thread from the cotton; let the needle stand thus, and use the thumb and finger of the right hand to bring the cotton behind the top of the needle from left to right, and pass it under the point of the needle from right to left—in the manner depicted in Fig. 32—then draw the needle through, and pull up the cotton until it forms a little twist on the edge of the slit; every successive stitch is formed in the same manner, always missing one thread of the fabric between the stitches. When you reach the corner you must turn the material gradually to get it in a convenient position; here the stitches must diverge like the rays of a star, and you must draw the knots up

bursting. The sides are worked first. The ends must be first of all "stranded," by making five or six stitches—*i.e.*, threads of cotton, reach across from side to side, or span over, from the foot of one line of buttonhole stitches to the foot of the opposite line of stitches; these strands are all to lie on the surface, which is effected by taking up a few threads of material on one side of the stitching, then crossing the end of the buttonhole, and taking up a few threads of the material on the opposite side, and so on alternately. When you have the strands laid you will button-stitch over them, making the "bars" or "bridges" appear as shown in the engraving. Some people work the button-stitch simply upon the strands; others consider it best to penetrate through the thickness of material.

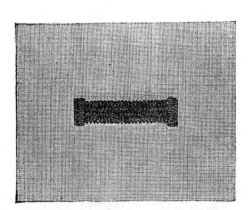

Fig. 35.—Buttonhole with Barred Ends.

Fig. 37.—Initial Letter sewn on.

tighter than usual, while you miss two threads between the stitches till the corner is rounded; then work along the other side of the buttonhole, and round the other end in a similar way; finish by passing the needle and cotton through the top of the first stitch to the back of the work, run behind the stitches for a short distance, and cut off the cotton.

Fig. 33 represents a portion of a buttonhole worked the new way. Begin as instructed above, commencing at the left-hand corner of the lower edge of the slit, and work from left to right; hold the cotton well to the left, pressing it against the material under the third finger of the left hand, insert the needle behind the slit, pointing downwards, and bring the point up to the front on the same level horizontally as you started, that is, at a depth of four or five threads below the slit, and missing one thread from the cotton, and while the needle stands thus and your finger still presses upon the cotton, employ the thumb and first finger of the right hand to bring the double cotton from the eye, and

Figs. 36 and 37.—SEWING ON INITIALS.

THESE woven initials are Messrs. J. and J. Cash's patent. They can be bought in all letters and in monograms, and names can be woven to order. The expense is trifling, and those who cannot do cross-stitch marking and yet dislike ink marking had better procure a few for attachment upon underclothing, they being especially handy for marking socks, stockings, flannel garments, &c., and all drapers stock them. The method of sewing them on is perfectly easy. Cut the letter from the tape upon which it is woven, place it upon the linen in the position shown in Fig. 36—*i.e.*, upside down as it were, with the front of the letter against the inside of the hem at the bottom of the garment; work a row of tiny stitches across the tape in the manner represented in the engraving. This done, turn the initial over, and folding in the opposite edge of the tape, hem it down flat upon the garment, and the initial will appear as in Fig. 37.

WELDON'S
PRACTICAL PLAIN NEEDLEWORK.

(SECOND SERIES.)

How to Whip, Patch, Mark, Bind, Pleat, Sew on Hooks, Eyes, Buttons, and Tapes, &c.

FORTY-FOUR ILLUSTRATIONS.

PLAIN NEEDLEWORK.

"So long as garments shall be made or worne;
So long as hemp, or flax, or sheep shall bear
Their linnen wollen fleeces yeare by yeare;
So long as silk wormes, with exhausted spoile
Of their own entrailes, for man's gaine shall toyle:
Yea, till the world be quite dissolved and paste,
So long, at least, the Needle's use shall last."

"NEEDLEWORK is an art so attractive in itself; it is capable of such infinite variety, and is such a beguiler of lonely as of social hours, and offers such scope to the indulgence of fancy and the display of taste; it is withal—in its lighter branches—accompanied with so little bodily exertion, not deranging the most *recherché* gown, nor incommoding the most elaborate and exquisite toilette, that we cannot wonder that it has been practised with ardour even by those the farthest removed from any necessity for its exercise.' So wrote the Countess of Wilton in her Book of Needlework, and needlework is indeed an art so indissolubly connected with the convenience and comfort of mankind at large, that it is impossible to suppose any state of society in which it has not existed.

Although the click of the sewing machine has, to a certain extent, superseded the little noiseless shining badge of industry, and the products of the loom have rendered much of its service unnecessary, still, every wise mother will instruct her daughters in the art of plain sewing, for those who have been so trained will make all the better progress and advancement in the higher branches of needlework, such as is called artistic needlework, which includes embroideries of every kind, drawn thread work, &c.

In our first issue on Plain Needlework, which forms No. 98 of "Weldon's Practical Needlework Series," we fully illustrated and explained the correct methods of executing a number of stitches. We now enter more fully into the subject, and place a second series in the hands of our readers, hoping that its wide circulation may do much to promote the extension of this useful occupation among young people, who should be encouraged to take up plain sewing far more frequently than is usual at the present time, and busy themselves either in making their own underclothing, or in working for the benefit of their less fortunate sisters and brothers, for clothing neatly made and given

to those who need it will far outweigh in value any money gift, both to the giver and the receiver, and the womanly thought and tenderness that have been stitched into the seams may ease many a sore and burdened heart.

Fig. 38.—SEWING ON BUTTONS.

THE ways of sewing on buttons are many and various, as will be seen by the accompanying engraving (Fig. 38), which shows in full actual size the most approved methods. Of these seven are linen and three are pearl buttons.

Buttons are sold by the card at so much per dozen; the best quality should be procured, as they are stronger and wear better than cheap makes. Linen buttons vary in size from those as large as a shilling to tiny ones less than a threepenny-bit. The newest style are made with metal backs, and have two small holes pierced in the centre, a rim of metal being bound round each hole, and these are attached to the garment by simply sewing through from hole to hole. Linen buttons are generally preferred for articles that have to undergo mangling, as they will bear the weight of pressure better than pearl buttons. Pearl buttons are used on shirts and other articles of underclothing that are ironed by hand. Buttons must always (for the sake of strength and resistance of the strain to which they are at times subjected) be sewn upon *double* material, and this is their position when they are attached upon a waistband, a fold, or a hem; but if it should be required to put a button upon single material it will be necessary first to fell a little square of the same material on the wrong side of the fabric to afford the necessary substance, and then sew the button in the usual manner. Now as regards the method of sewing on buttons. It is not correct to begin with a knot; you should commence by making two or three small stitches in the material just where it is decided to place the button. These will secure the end of the cotton and will be covered by the button. The cotton must issue from these stitches on the wrong side of the garment. No. 1 (Fig. 38) represents a button sewn to the garment by a ring, or circlet, of small back stitches. This is a good method, it is strong, and equalises the tension upon the button. The ring may be faintly marked with a black-lead pencil to ensure a true circle, or can be indented by the pres-

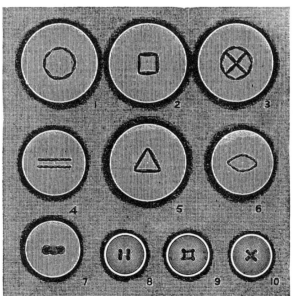

Fig. 38.—Approved Methods of Sewing on Buttons.

sure of the round top of the pencil upon the button. It must not occupy more space than shown in the engraving, in fact, slightly less would be desirable; the back-stitching is of course accomplished by passing the needle through and through, from the wrong side of the garment to the upper surface of the button, and back again, following the marked guide. **No. 2** shows a button held in place by a small square of back stitches; the square must be formed in the exact centre of the button, and the lines must be perfectly straight—that is, it must be a *true square* of stitches, or it will not look well. In **No. 3** we see a button attached by a circle of back-stitching worked in the same manner as No. 1, and further embellished with a star radiating from the centre of the button to the stitches of the circle; this star is composed of four long stitches, but can be perfected by adding four others intermediately between, taking care to form the star as neatly and as clearly on the wrong side as on the right. Very frequently a button is sewn on by an eight-pointed star without any outer

Fig. 39.—Whipping. Old Method.

circle of stitches. **No. 4** is explanatory of a button secured by two parallel lines of stitching running from right to left of the button, in the direction the buttonhole slit will lie when the fastening is effected; the stitches do not traverse the entire width of the button, but stop at a short distance within the margin: this method of sewing has much to recommend it, and is in fact one of the best methods, as the buttonhole lies easily in position without being at all stretched or widened. **No. 5** shows a triangular sewing of back stitches, which is very simple to accomplish. **No. 6** illustrates the sewing on of a button by back-stitching in the form of an oval; the oval must be pencil-marked, or in some way defined upon the button, to ensure a correct shape, then the stitches will be worked over the mark, or making such deviation therefrom as will improve the appearance of the oval, taking them of course through and through in the manner instructed above, with the oval arranged to lie in the direction most adapted to meet the buttonhole slit, which probably will fall horizontally from right to left, though sometimes, if on the front opening of a garment, it may

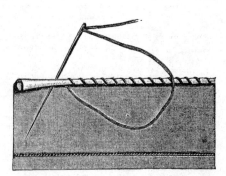

Fig. 40.—Whipping. New Method.

lie in the opposite direction, perpendicularly, upright: this oval method is very good and neat, and deserves to be employed more frequently than it is, as it takes space where space can most easily be afforded, and does not stretch or widen the buttonhole. **No. 7** represents a metal-lined button pierced with two holes, and the sewing-on process is effected by taking the stitches through from hole to hole. **No. 8** shows a pearl button of the kind used on shirts, this is pierced with four holes, and the stitches are taken through and through, and are visible perpendicularly on the surface of the button and horizontally on the wrong side of the garment. **No. 9** demonstrates a pearl button secured by sewing square-ways from hole to hole; the stitches should present the same appearance on the reverse side. **No 10** represents a pearl button whereon the stitches are taken cross-ways from hole to hole, this is neat and looks well; about two threads of cotton each way or three threads each way are quite sufficient to ensure strength. Now as regards the proper

method of **fastening off the cotton** when the button is secured in its place by either of the ways enumerated above; it is quite feasible to make a few stitches on the inside of the fabric and cut off the thread; but the right plan of proceeding is to raise the button a little edgeways and bring up the needle and cotton between the material and the button, and then wind the cotton a few times round the sewn stitches to form what is called a "shank" or "stem," which will protect the stitches from friction and therefore render the sewing more durable, and likewise will serve to raise the button slightly from the material and so ease the operation of buttoning; the cotton must not bind the stitches too tightly, and when a

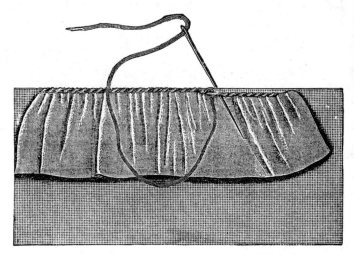

Fig. 41.—Sewing on Whipping. Old Method.

few windings, say five or six, are accomplished, pass the needle again to the wrong side, make a back stitch or two, and cut the cotton. It is most desirable that buttons should be sewn on strongly.

Figs. 39 and 40.—WHIPPING.

WHIPPING is a satisfactory method of gathering muslin and such other fine material as will lend itself readily to the treatment. It is almost exclusively

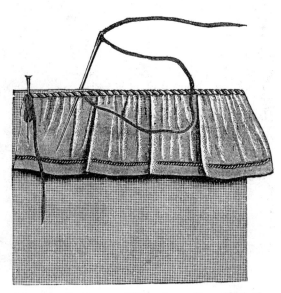

Fig. 42.—Sewing on Whipping. New Method.

applied to frillings. The muslin must be torn across, or cut carefully by the thread, from selvedge to selvedge, as the frill hangs much better this way. The lower edge should be hemmed with as narrow a hem as fingers can form. The edge that has to be whipped must be trimmed perfectly smooth, and carefully apportioned into halves and quarters, each portion being marked with a crease, or by the insertion of pins. The band, upon which the whipping will be sewn, must also be halved and quartered in the same manner, so that when the whipping is accomplished the centre of it may be pinned to the centre of the band, and the quarters to the quarters, and thus the fulness will be distributed with regularity, not full in one part and scanty in another. The rule is to allow the frill to be quite double the length of the band to which it is to be attached, and more frequently than not a little extra is allowed to afford additional fulness. The cotton with which you whip must be strong and even, and it is wise to use one needleful to the first half and another needleful to the second half of the whipping, or if a very long piece has to be whipped you may take fresh needlefuls at the quarters; it is very awkward if the cotton should break when adjusting the fulness, and therefore great care should be exercised to draw the whips in place without hard pulling. Hold the wrong side of the muslin towards you, the edge that is to be whipped being uppermost, resting on the forefinger of the left hand; secure the end of the cotton at the right-hand corner; the edge of the muslin is now to be rolled over very closely and tightly towards you by means of

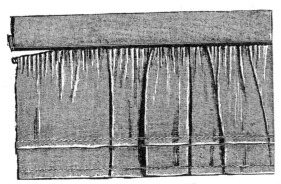

Fig. 43.—Frilling. Whipped and Sewn on Material.

an upward and downward gentle movement of the left-hand thumb. You may have to damp the thumb to ensure a nice even roll, and you certainly can roll only a short piece at a time—skill in the proceeding can, however, be best acquired by dint of practice, and in due time practice will lead to perfection. By the old method of whipping you will insert the needle below—*i.e.*, *within* the roll, and bring it out at the top, as see Fig. 39, which is the easiest way of procedure; or pursue the newer method, as see Fig. 40, of pointing the needle towards the chest from the top of the roll, bringing it out within the roll: either way, place the stitches at an even, regular distance apart, never through the roll, but through *one thickness* of fabric only, that the cotton may draw readily; and its capability should be tested at every inch or two, but do

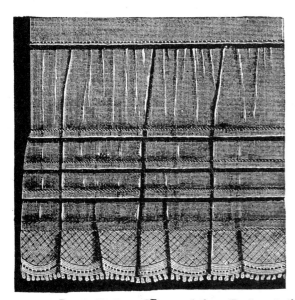

Fig. 44.—Wide Frill with Lace, Hem, and three Tucks; Gathered, and Back-Stitched on Material.

not draw too much or the frill will get twisted. If you strike whipping with a large pin, in the same way as gathering, it adds much to its neat appearance in setting on, and makes it more easy to sew.

Figs. 41 and 42.—SEWING ON WHIPPING.

WHEN sewing the whipped frill to the band, hold both together in your hand, with the right side of the band towards you, and the right side of the frill facing thereupon, therefore the roll of whipped stitches lies still towards you as it did during the execution of the whipping; pin the quarters of the frill to the quarters of the band; draw the whipping thread to the

required length, and retain it in that length by twisting the end round a pin; adjust the whipping evenly, attaching it to the band with additional pins if needful, and sew along, taking a stitch in the hollow of each whip. Notice especially that your sewing stitches must lie precisely in the same direction as the stitches of the whipping, therefore if you have accomplished this by the old method, Fig. 39, you must sew from left to right, in the manner shown in Fig 41; while if you have whipped by the new method, Fig. 40, the sewing will be effected in the usual way from right to left, as exemplified in Fig. 42.

Fig. 43.—FRILLING: WHIPPED AND SEWN ON MATERIAL.

OUR engraving, Fig. 43, shows a frill whipped and sewn upon a band of material. The frill is of cambric, cut to a thread or torn the weft way of the

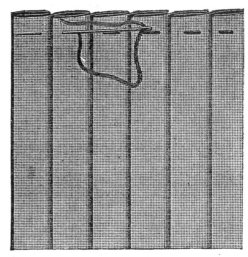

Fig. 45.—Pleating.

material, that is, from selvedge to selvedge. The width of frills is entirely a matter of taste, and, of course, varies with the purpose for which they are to be used. A frill that is to be goffered rarely exceeds two inches in width. The one represented in our engraving is designed for nightdress trimming, and takes a two-inch strip of material. A hem (one-eighth of an inch) is lightly hemmed along the bottom, and a tuck (also one-eighth of an inch in depth) stands at a distance of about a quarter of an inch above the hem. Measure your cambric by the band upon which it is to be placed, remembering it should be quite double the length of the band to allow for proper fulness. If one strip of cambric does not suffice, others must be cut and joined very neatly to

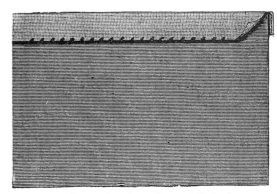

Fig. 46.—Binding. Simple Method.

the first, either by seaming the selvedge ends together or by a neat run and fell; or, supposing the frill is to be round as for a wristband, the ends must be joined together before commencing operations. Begin with the hem, then do the tuck; instructions for tucking are given on pages 9 and 10 in the first series of " Weldon's Practical Plain Needlework." Then divide the frill into half, quarters, and eighths, marking each with a thread of coloured cotton or by inserting a pin Hold the wrong side of the frill towards you, and proceed with the whipping in the manner explained above. The band must be marked in divisions of half, quarters, and eighths, to correspond with the divisions of the frill, and these eighths must be pinned together, holding the right side of the band towards you with the right side of the frill inside to face it. Arrange the fulness evenly, securing it here and there with extra pins as seems necessary to keep it in place. Twist the drawing cotton round the head and point of the adjacent pin to prevent it slipping, and with the frill next you, and having the work firmly pressed between the thumb and forefinger of the left hand, attach the frill to the band by the action of sewing or seaming, taking a stitch to a whip, and being especially careful to regulate the whips accurately that the stitches may be even in size and of equal distance apart from each other. Press the stitches flat when the seaming is accomplished. Fig. 43 represents the right side of the frill and band.

Fig. 44.—WIDE FRILL, WITH LACE, HEM, AND THREE TUCKS.

GATHERED AND BACK-STITCHED ON MATERIAL.

A HANDSOME wide frill is represented in Fig. 44. It is formed of strips of cambric three inches in depth. The hem is one-eighth of an inch wide; the

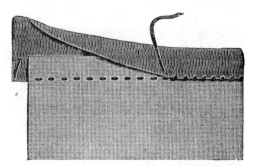

Fig. 47.—Binding, Showing a Run and Fell.

three tucks correspond with the hem, and are arranged at regular intervals of a quarter of an inch apart from each other. An edging of fine Valenciennes lace is sewn lightly on the margin of the hem, which lace must not be stretched in the least, but put easily, as probably when washed it will shrink more than the cambric to which it is attached. The top of the frill is gathered, it then is laid behind a fold of material, pinning quarters to quarters and eighths to eighths, as in the preceding paragraphs, and the two are caught together with a line of back-stitching. This method of putting on a frill necessitates a false hem on the wrong side of the garment, to effect which you will hold the wrong side of the garment next you, and lay the edge of the false hem level with the edge of the frill, with the false hem itself held downwards over the

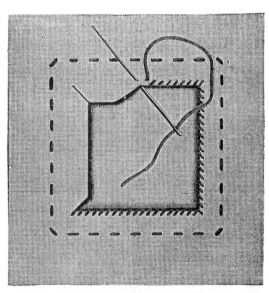

Fig. 48.—A Patch Tacked and Commenced.

frill, concealing the upper portion of the frill from view; then run the edge of the false hem in place, taking the stitches as nearly as possible upon the line of the backstitching, but not on any account letting them show through upon the right side of the work. When this running is accomplished you will turn the false hem up and proceed as if formulating an ordinary hem.

Fig. 45.—PLEATING.

PLEATING is extensively employed in dressmaking, and affords a ready means of arranging the fulness of frills, flounces, and skirts, without making an uncomfortable thickness or bulkiness, as might be the case if the fabric, being of flannel or cloth, were fulled by gathering. When you pleat material

you cause it to lie in flat, smooth folds. The engraving, Fig. 45, shows a row of pleats adapted for many purposes; observe that the material when pleated is of threefold thickness, all the pleats are the same size, and all lie in the same direction. The skirt of an infant's petticoat or frock is frequently pleated in this manner, but remember that one half of the pleats should face to the left and the other half to the right. It is optional whether or not to tack the pleats as represented in the illustration. Experienced sewers will no doubt consider it sufficient to place a pin to hold each pleat, and the only objection is that the pins are liable to fall out unless the work be carefully handled. If the fulness of the skirt will not allow of the pleats being threefold in thickness, a little space must be left between each, and if, on the contrary, the fulness is excessive, they may overlap. Flannel petticoats are generally pleated and set into a band, which band may be either shaped or straight, as preferred. Lay the edge of the band at a safe distance below the edge of the pleats and hem it neatly thereto, on both right and wrong sides.

In Double Pleating the pleats lie both ways—i.e., back to back—one pleat to the right and the next pleat to the left. This looks very well, but patience must be exercised to arrange all the pleats in uniform size.

Box Pleating, which consists of two, three, or more pleats laid one over the other, absorbs a quantity of material, and therefore is specially suitable to "band in" extra full skirts where generally a large box pleat is required on each side of the back; also it is used with good effect as a heading to deep flounces; while perhaps its greatest value is to make quillings and ruchings, in which form it is much employed for millinery purposes and for the ornamentation of fancy articles. A quilled or ruched box pleating is seldom more than from two inches to three inches deep. First make the right-hand top fold half an inch wide, then the right-hand bottom fold three-quarters of an inch wide, make left-hand folds to correspond; these folds should all meet at the back and consequently the back pleats will jut out on each side a quarter of an inch

Fig. 49.—A Patch Hemmed on Both Sides.

beyond the front pleats, hold them in position, or pin them, while with a needle and cotton you tack or back-stitch straight along the centre of the fabric; leave a quarter of an inch space, and make another similar pleat, and so on to the end; thus the pleats are confined in the centre of the ruching and the fulness rises on each side. A fuller ruching is made by arranging three pleats over each other. The edge of the material is frequently "pinked," or may be left raw, according to taste.

Figs. 46 and 47.—BINDING.

THE word "binding" has a double signification; it is used to denote the action of strengthening the edge of any material, or the edge of any garment, by encasing it in a folded covering to prevent the fraying of the edge and to make it firm, neat, and strong; and is also applied to the covering by which the edge is encased, whether that covering be tape, narrow ribbon, galloon, or braid, which are all well suited to the purpose, and are generally used as occasion requires. There are also many varieties of miscellaneous bindings manufactured specially for carpets, for cocoa-nut matting, and various upholstery purposes, and likewise stay bindings and boot bindings. The bottom of a dress is nearly always strengthened or bound with worsted braid, which is doubled and laid in position, one half on the right side and the other half on the wrong side of the edge, and attached thereto by hemming, taking the stitches through in the manner shown in the illustration, Fig. 46; this is the simplest form of binding. People who employ a sewing machine will no doubt stitch the braid instead of hemming it, while some, after folding the braid double, would stitch it behind the edge of the dress, letting it show a little below, but not covering the front at all. Others may prefer to make a roll of the braid instead of allowing it to sit perfectly flat. To effect this, lay the braid upon the right side of the material about an eighth of an inch from the edge, run braid and material together a trifle above the lower extremity of the braid, then turn the braid over on the wrong side of the fabric and fell it with neat invisible stitches. Fig. 47 illustrates this process of running, and also shows a small piece of felling. Men's coats and boys' jackets are in this manner bound with silk braid. Galloon, a kind of thin ribbon made of a mixture of cotton and silk, was formerly much employed as a binding for flannel, but is now seldom used, it being considered better taste to hem flannel garments with herringboning, or to ornament them with buttonhole-stitched scallops in the manner which will be explained and illustrated when we treat of flannel work.

but it is absolutely necessary to be done if we would keep our things neat and tidy, and preserve them in use for any considerable time. The difficulty comes in the fixing, for the most simple stitches are employed. A patch may be any size, and almost any shape; square or oblong patches are the most convenient to manage. Cut your patch the same way warp and woof as the fabric it is to lie upon, and quite an inch longer each way than the thin part it is to replace, and be careful that all four sides are precisely even to a thread, turn down the raw edges, place the patch upon the front of the decayed or worn part also even to a thread, and be sure to arrange the pattern, if there be any, so that the patch and the original material shall exactly correspond. Fix the patch by tacking

Fig. 50.—A Patch Seamed and Felled. Right Side.

Binders, such as are placed to strengthen the armholes of shirts and night-dresses, are invariably made of calico or linen, the same that is used for the garment; they must be cut selvedgeways, fixed carefully without a pucker or a wrinkle, and hemmed neatly inside the garment.

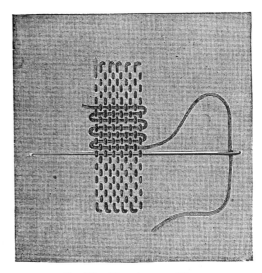

Fig. 52.—Darning on Linen.

it to retain it in place, and commence operations by hemming the four sides of the patch to the original material, keeping the corners true to a right angle; press the work flat and smooth, and turn it over to the wrong side; here cut away the worn portion, leaving only so much of the original fabric as will form a hem, tuck the edges in straight and even, nicking them a little at each of the four corners to enable them to sit well, and proceed to hem or fell the fabric upon the patch in the manner represented in Fig. 48: this representation is designed to show the position of the tacking stitches. The process of hemming the patch upon the right side of the fabric is not yet accomplished

Figs. 48 to 51.—PATCHING.

"THE greatest help to making is mending." Every rent in dresses, skirts, underclothing, or household linen should receive attention as soon as it occurs. The old adage, "A stitch in time saves nine," is deserving of remembrance, for there is nothing that brings its own reward so soon as intelligent care in

Fig. 51.—A Patch Run and Felled. Right Side.

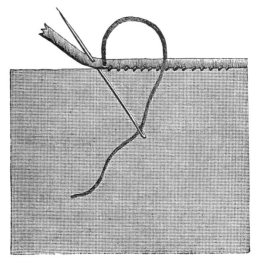

Fig. 53.—Sewing on Cord.

dealing with one's own belongings. If the mischief be only a small tear, or only a few threads frayed away and missing, a darn may be sufficient to repair the damage; but if the injury is of greater extent, resulting in a badly worn part and a hole, it will be wise to procure a suitable piece of material to use as a patch, to replace the worn-out portion. The patch should be of material as much resembling the original fabric as possible (with calico, linen, or print, this can be easily managed), and if it can be provided from a fairly good portion of another similar garment so much the better, but in any case the patch should *not* be of strong new stuff, because the strain of the new would assuredly prove too great for the old fabric and would by-and-bye necessitate another patch larger than the first.

Now patching is not a pleasant occupation; it is rather tiresome and tedious,

—in fact, it is matter of individual choice whether you first hem the right side and afterwards fell the wrong side, or *vice versâ*, and also it is to a great extent a matter of choice and convenience whether the patch is laid upon the right side or on the wrong side of the fabric that needs repair; the former, however, is the old established method; the principal consideration is to get the patch cleverly fixed and put on, and the result consequently successful. Fig. 49 illustrates the appearance the work should assume when the patch is finished.

Fig. 50 exemplifies another method of patching by means of a seam and a fell—this plan is more especially adapted for repairing sheets and other large articles. Take the sheet where it is to be patched, and crease it upon the right side about two inches beyond the part that is worn, let the crease be carried along all four sides, guiding it, of course, by a thread that it may be perfectly accurate, then take the patch, which previously has been cut to the required size also by a thread, turn the raw edge half an inch in on the wrong side and seam the right side of the patch to the right side of the sheet, taking care to firmly secure the corners; then press the seam; turn the sheet over, cut away the worn part, turn the edges in, nicking the corners so that all will be quite straight, flat, and even, and fell the turned-down edges upon the patch.

A very neat patch is shown in Fig. 51; this is effected by the process of running and felling, and though rather more difficult of accomplishment than either of the methods described above, it is well worth trying and is really simple enough when once you get accustomed to turning the corners. It is better suited to large patches than small ones. Prepare the fabric by creasing the outline of the place the patch is to cover, as described in the foregoing instruction, also turn in the edge of the patch in like manner, but this is only done to obtain a duplicate crease to work by, and the edge may at once be restored to its former condition. Now place the right side of the patch against the right side of the fabric, not over the place the patch will occupy when finished, but quite to the right-hand side thereof, with the crease of the patch precisely over the crease of the fabric. Run the two creased sides together from corner to corner; turn the work over, and you will find it fall into its allotted position. Now you come to experience the difficulty of getting a few running stitches in to turn the corner nicely without pulling or puckering; you may have to enlarge the hole, and put your fingers through to get at the corner, but it *can*

Fig. 55.—A Loop, used in conjunction with a Hook.

be done by the exercise of patience, and you will go straight along the second side to the next corner, and so on to the completion of the patch, which will be finished by felling the inside in the usual way.

Cloth is too thick and heavy to turn the edges for patching, therefore the edges of the patch must be neatly buttonhole-stitched (taking the stitches about the sixteenth of an inch apart), or darned upon the article, and the edges of the hole treated similarly upon the patch.

Fig. 52.—DARNING ON LINEN.

DARNING is a method by which new threads are supplied to take the place of threads that have become thin and worn out. There are several kinds of darning, but we shall at present confine our attention to plain darning on linen, which is the simplest, as well as the most practical and useful. It should be remembered that needles used for darning are made very long and thin; the work may be accomplished with ordinary sewing cotton, soft Moravian cotton, or flourishing thread; the finer the material the finer must be the needle and cotton. If ravelling can be got at the darn can be made almost imperceptible. All darns should be effected on the wrong side of the fabric; you may take up two threads and leave two, or take up one thread and

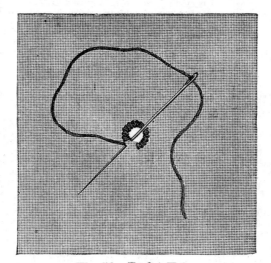

Fig. 54.—Eyelet Hole.

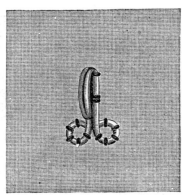

Fig. 57.—A Hook attached to Material.

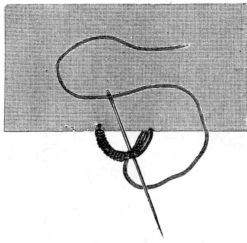

Fig. 56.—A Button-Stitch Loop, made at the end of a Band.

leave three; run the needle its whole length in and out before drawing it through. Make the first running up and down perpendicularly the selvedge way of the material, *i.e.*, the warp way; run a little beyond the thin part for greater strength; the cotton must not be drawn tightly, and it is advisable to leave loops at each end in turning to allow for any shrinkage in the wash.

Proceed in straight rows forwards and backwards, and alternate the stitches by taking up in one row the thread left in the preceding row; if there is a hole carry the cotton over it and continue the darning on the opposite side; when the darn is large enough the position must be reversed for crossing, which is effected by taking up the mending cotton only, pick up one thread of cotton and miss one, as shown in our engraving, Fig. 52. The stitches must be placed rather close together both ways, so that the darn, when completed, may be firm and strong. Cuts and tears are apt to be diagonal or three-cornered; the tips of these should first of all be drawn together with very fine cotton, by what is termed "fine drawing" (see Fig. 12 in No. 98 "Weldon's Practical Needlework Series") and afterwards darned, commencing in the centre and working to the sides.

Fig. 53.—SEWING ON CORD.

A CORD is sometimes sewn on infants' frock bodices, and on ladies' slip bodices and camisoles to give strength to the neck. The sewing should be executed with fairly strong cotton or fine thread. Hold the cord close against the edge of the garment, and take small hemming stitches, inserting the needle in the manner represented in the engraving (Fig. 53). Do not stretch the cord, but rather ease it as you sew, for it will be sure to shrink more or less the

Fig. 58.—An Eye attached to Material.

first time of washing, and the neck will be puckered if it should happen to shrink very much.

Fig. 54.—EYELET HOLE.

EYELET holes are sometimes placed at the neck or waist of a garment to afford an outlet for a tape, cord, or ribbon, but their chief use comes in for dressmaking purposes, so handy are they to receive a hook, and so much neater than eyes and stronger than loops. They must needs be worked upon double material, and this they have when made upon bands, or when employed as receptacles wherein to secure the hooks of a dress bodice. You will require a stiletto to pierce the holes and a few needlefuls of machine silk or tailors' twist for working. The hole is simply encircled with close, firm overcast stitches. Begin thus: Slip the needle between the folds of the material, and bring it up on the right side a little distant from the hole, and draw through, push the end of the silk within the folds of the material, hold the material tightly, and tightly overcast the edge of the hole all round, working from left to right. The mode of procedure and the exact position of the needle and silk in the act of forming a stitch will be understood by consulting Fig. 54, which represents a nearly finished eyelet hole. When it is quite completed, pass the needle to the wrong side and make a back stitch, and slip the needle as far as you can within the material and cut off the silk. If nicely worked the edge of the eyelet hole will feel as firm as if wired. Eyelet holes are sometimes buttonhole-stitched, the needle is placed precisely in the position described above, and the silk is passed under the point of the needle before drawing the needle through. The links of the stitches should lie flat round the outer margin of the circle, not close against the hole.

Fig. 55.—A LOOP, USED IN CONJUNCTION WITH A HOOK.

LOOPS of the kind shown in Fig. 55 are often employed in dressmaking, and when used in conjunction with hooks form convenient fastenings for dress bodices, jackets, sleeve wrists, and other purposes. The foundation of the loop consists of several strands of cotton, which, being confined together by buttonhole stitching, are formed into a sort of bar, into which the hook can pass and be secure until the time comes to release it. It is essential that the loops be worked upon double material. Mark the place where the loop is to be, thread your needle with cotton or silk, and slip it through the folds and bring it out on the right side of the material a little to the left of the mark; insert the needle from the front to the back of the material a little to the right of the mark, and bring it out again in the place from whence it started, draw the cotton up and you will see the first foundation strand lying upon the surface of the fabric; make five

Fig. 60.—Eye Sewn upon a Band and neatened with Buttonhole Stitches.

hand corner of the loop to be; the distance is determinable by the size of the button—the larger the button the greater the space; draw the cotton through till you get a loop sufficiently large to pass freely over the button, then insert the needle from the right side to the wrong side of the band in the place where you just now commenced, and draw through, which forms a second strand to the loop, and proceed in this manner, first on one side and then on the other, till there are strands sufficient to make a good strong loop; leave off on the left-hand side, and bind the stands together with buttonhole-stitching, forming a kind of cord, as will be understood by consulting Fig. 56, which shows the work in progress. When you reach the end of the loop you will fasten off by making one or two back stitches on the wrong side of the band.

Figs. 57 and 58.—SEWING ON HOOKS AND EYES.

FIGS. 57 and 58 show the ordinary method of attaching hooks and eyes to material. If you examine a dress that fastens by means of these appliances you will see that the hooks are sewn upon the under or wrong side of the margin of the bodice, and that the eyes are upon the surface or right side, in a position corresponding to the hooks. Owing, however, to the dictates of fashion, eyes are, at the present time, very little used for dressmaking purposes; eyelet holes and loops have superseded them, but they still are usefully employed upon waistbands. Observe that the hook is sewn with its back to the material by stitches that pass over and through each of the round rings, as well as by other stitches that cross the shank. The eye is sewn by the rings only.

Fig. 59.—Hook Sewn in reverse position.

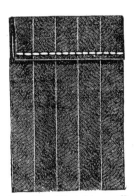

Fig. 63.—Finishing off end of Waistband Webbing.

Fig. 64.—Finishing off end of Waistband Webbing.

Fig. 62.—Patent Eye.

or six more strands in the same manner; these must all be the same length (about a quarter of an inch), and lie parallel one with the other; when this is done, you proceed to bind the strands together—you have your needle and cotton on the left-hand side—hold the cotton down under the left-hand thumb, pass the needle (with its point towards the chest) *under* the strands and *over* the cotton held by the thumb, and draw through just as if forming an ordinary buttonhole stitch, only in this case the needle passes simply under the strands and not into the material at all; proceed till the strand is covered with buttonhole stitches, and you get to the right-hand side, where pass the needle through to the back of the material, slip the needle a little way through the folds of the material, and fasten off. The beauty of the loop consists in the regularity and firmness of the buttonhole stitches; the links of the stitches fall against the lower side or bottom of the loop, and the hook, therefore, will rest on the top smooth edge.

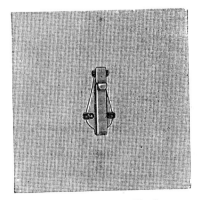

Fig. 61.—Patent Hook.

Figs. 59 and 60.—SEWING ON HOOKS AND EYES. ANOTHER METHOD.

IT is sometimes considered advisable to place a hook in reverse position, that is to say, with its back uppermost and its tongue against the material, and so far as loose-fitting garments are concerned the practice is regarded with favour, because as the tongue presses against the material, the hook is more likely to remain fastened than if attached in the ordinary manner. Of course under this condition the upper part of the hook has to be movable, and therefore it is secured to the material by means of the rings only, and a few additional stitches pass across the bottom of the shank from one ring to the other, as shown in Fig. 59. In Fig. 60 we see an eye sewn to the end of a band, the round rings are hidden under a fold that is made for the purpose, and the attachment is effected by means of stitches passing from the right side to the wrong side of the band, and *vice versâ*, and consequently passing also through the round rings;

Fig. 56.—A BUTTON-STITCH LOOP MADE AT THE END OF A BAND.

THIS loop is placed upon the end of a band with the object of forming a catch for a button. It is worked upon the same principle as the loop portrayed in the foregoing example, but the method varies slightly. The end of the band is supposed to be previously hemmed or stitched. Secure the needle and cotton on the edge of the fold of the hem in readiness for commencing at the left-hand corner of the loop, insert the needle from the right side to the wrong side of the band in the place where you desire the right-

the eye is made neat by working buttonhole stitches with silk over the wire.

Figs. 61 and 62.—PATENT HOOKS AND EYES.

THE peculiarity of these little appliances will be at once remarked and commented upon. They are not so extensively used as they might be, considering that they are manufactured on purpose to supply a supposed need. We all know that ordinary hooks, if placed upon the front of cloaks, blouses, and other loose apparel, have a most uncomfortable trick of unfastening of their own accord, and if the tongues of the hooks catch into any neighbouring lace or trimming, the annoyance is very great. The patent hook entirely obviates this sort of thing, it fastens and unfastens with a kind of spring, and cannot be unloosed from its eye unless loosed purposely. Both hooks and eyes are secured to material by stitches passing through little rings, as will be seen in Figs. 61 and 62.

Figs. 63 and 64.—FINISHING OFF ENDS OF WAISTBAND WEBBING.

THE ends of waistband webbing or belting, as it is sometimes called, must be made neat and presentable by turning in the raw edge and securing it in a

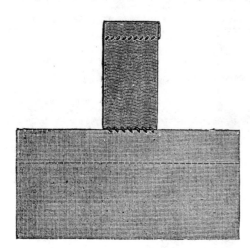

Fig. 65.—Sewing on a Tape String. Right Side.

tidy manner. Simple hemming seldom answers, because the webbing is thick, and the strain is liable to be greater than the stitches can bear. A hem, back-stitched with thread, as shown in Fig. 63, is very satisfactory, excepting that the double fold of material is apt to be bulky; but remember that if this method be adopted it is not possible to do the stitching as if working upon the end of a piece of tape; instead, the needle must pierce through and through, up and down, to get a perfectly firm grip of the webbing, and attention must be paid to commencing and fastening off in a strong, secure way. In Fig. 64 we show another method that possesses considerable merit, but looks better on the wrong side (the side seen in the engraving) than on the right. The band is folded once only, the raw edge is concealed beneath a line

Fig. 66.—Another Method of Sewing on a Tape. Right Side.

of cross stitches, and thus the fold is held securely in position. On the other side of the work the stitches are ranged in two straight lines. It might be possible, by working in a zigzag sort of fashion, to produce the cross stitches with exactitude upon both sides of the webbing.

Figs. 65 to 71.—SEWING ON TAPE.

TAPE is constructed of either cotton or linen, and is woven in a loom after the manner of ribbon. It may be had in many and various widths. Cotton tape is rather thin, but answers well for numerous purposes; linen tape is the strongest, and the kind known as "India tape" is very soft. Tape is

employed to make strings for various articles of wearing apparel, and in this capacity is used upon the bands of aprons and drawers, upon children's pina-fores and infants' frocks, and many other things; it also comes in handy to make loops on towels and kitchen cloths as a provision for hanging them upon a hook. Tape should be sewn perfectly flat, without a wrinkle or a crease; the stitches must be firm and regular, and if the material should happen to be double, as is the case when attaching a tape upon a hem or a band, every stitch must show through clearly, or else no stitches whatever show through at all. The tape is generally placed as deep as its own width, and so forms a square on the material.

Now first as regards **Strings**—Turn to Fig. 65, and you will see the most

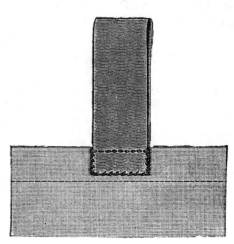

Fig. 67.—Sewing on a Tape Loop. Right Side.

usual method of setting a tape string upon a garment. Commence by cutting the tape to the length the string is required to be, and at one end turn down a narrow single fold, not more than one sixth or one quarter of an inch in depth, take the article upon which the tape is to be sewn (we will imagine it to be the hemmed side of a pinafore), hold the wrong side of the hem towards you, and place the single fold of the tape against the wrong side of the hem, and proceed to hem the tape upon the hem of the pinafore; begin at the right-hand side; hem three sides of the tape. Whether the stitches are taken through to the right side of the pinafore is a matter of taste; it is no doubt stronger if they go through, but neater if they do not. When the three sides are fairly secured, fold the tape down level with the edge of the article,

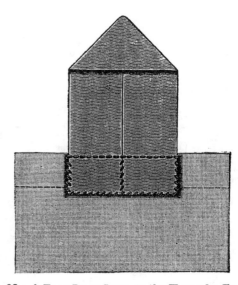

Fig. 68.—A Tape Loop Sewn on the Hem of a Towel.

and seam the fold of the tape to the edge of the article, and fasten off neatly; these seamed stitches are visible in the engraving, the hem being at the back is not apparent. Make the end of the tape neat by turning down and hemming a little narrow hem to prevent the tape from ravelling. Strings always go in pairs, and when the first string is put on, the other must be sewn to correspond.

Fig. 66 represents another and more tasteful arrangement for attaching a tape string. Make a single narrow fold at one end of the tape and place it against the wrong side of the hem of the article that requires a string, letting the fold come just a trifle below the stitches of the hem, and fell the two selvedge sides of the tape upon the hem; turn the article to the right side, and work a little row of back-stitching close to the edge of the article to connect the tape firmly thereto, and work another little row of back stitches over the stitches of the hem, just as you see them in the engraving; these stitches pass through the fold of the tape. Ornament the end of the string with a line of buttonhole-stitch overcasting, which, if deeply set in, will effectually prevent the tape from fraying.

Next, with regard to sewing on **Loops** of tape.

Fig. 67 shows the possibility of securing a loop of tape upon the side of a cloth in a neat and satisfactory manner. Cut a four-inch length of tape, make a

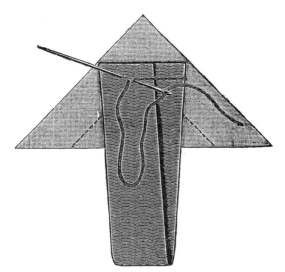

Fig. 69.—A Loop of Tape Sewn on the Corner of a Towel.
First Detail.

narrow fold at one end, and place that against the folded side of the hem, and fell it on its three sides. Do not break off the cotton, but bring the other end of the tape upon the right side of the fabric, thus folding the tape double, and so forming a loop; hem this end in like manner, precisely even with and opposite to the first hem, then work a line of back-stitching through all, taking the stitches level with the edge of the article, and the loop will appear as illustrated.

Fig. 68 represents a loop sewn on the hem of a towel; the top of the loop is folded to form a three-cornered point. Place the two ends separately, but

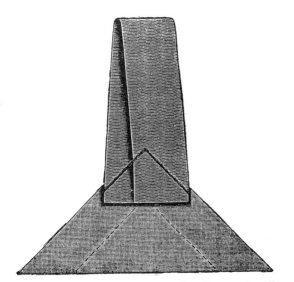

Fig. 70.—A Loop of Tape Sewn on the Corner of a Towel.
Second Detail.

lying side by side as in the engraving, turn in and fell them down on each extreme selvedge side and along the bottom, and stitch the edge of the hem of the towel to the loop on the right side; then slip the needle to the middle of the ends, and join the two together just so far as they rest upon the towel.

Fig. 69.—Here we see the first process to be performed when a loop of tape has to be secured upon the corner of a towel or cloth. The tape should be cut about five inches in length, it then is to be doubled obliquely, and laid in angular position across the corner of the towel, on the side upon which the towel is hemmed, with the loop lying down upon the towel, and the ends

facing the corner. Take a needle and cotton, and beginning on the right-hand side, back-stitch the tape firmly upon the towel in a straight parallel line at a little distance from the raw edge. The loop is then to go through the second process (Fig. 70) by being turned upwards, and again stitched to the towel, and this time the towel must be held towards you, and the stitches must follow the angular outline of the corner.

Fig. 71 illustrates another method of fixing a loop on a corner. It has a pretty appearance, but is scarcely so durable or so firm as the method detailed in the preceding example. The loop is in the first place to be stitched in angular position across the corner in the same way as represented in Fig. 69; it then is turned upwards and ornamented with cross stitches; two cross stitches are worked one above the other on each side of the loop, and four or five similar stitches occupy an intermediate position, and rise to the point at the corner of the towel. They, of course, go through one fold only of the hem, but may be duplicated on the right side of the hem if considered desirable; these cross stitches are very clearly represented, and may easily be copied from the engraving.

Figs. 72 to 75.—MARKING.

CROSS STITCH.   EYELET STITCH.   LEVIATHAN STITCH.

ONCE upon a time, not many years ago, it was the general custom to mark all one's personal linen and all the household cloths and napery with cross-stitch marking, and very pretty indeed it looked. In those days every girl was taught to work a sampler, in which the greatest pride was taken, as, if satisfactorily accomplished, it would be framed and hung up in either sitting-room or bedroom, as a visible sign and token of the proficiency of the worker. Many

Fig. 71.—A Loop of Tape affixed by Cross Stitch.

of these old-time samplers are in existence at the present moment; some, more elaborate and wonderful than their compeers, prove attractive exhibits at annual art exhibitions; and indeed the generality are an actual tangible proof of the neatness and patience of a former generation; they comprise a handsome wide border, within which are depicted the letters of the alphabet, and numeral figures, worked in various styles, followed by an appropriate verse or text, with also a number of little trees and flowers, birds and animals, crosses and crowns, and all manner of variety of little devices intermixed with ornamental lines, and concluding with the name and age of the worker, and the year of its achievement. We seldom now, excepting perhaps in Board Schools, employ our children's time in working samplers, yet **marking** is exceedingly useful, and ought never to be neglected. Those who can do it, like it; and certainly, unless ornamental embroidery is employed, nothing looks so well, or wears so long, as red ingrain cotton marking on pocket handkerchiefs, bed linen, hosiery, or underlinen; the cost of cotton is merely a penny, the marking can be done at odd moments, and it is permanent and neat, it cannot readily be unpicked, and it does not spoil the fabric as marking ink is apt to do.

The varieties of stitches used for marking on linen are cross stitch, eyelet stitch, and leviathan stitch; of these cross stitch is the most universally adopted—it is so called because the stitch forms a cross on the right side. Marking cotton is ingrain—i.e., fast coloured. It can be had either in red or blue, on reels or in skeins; the red looks well upon white material. To work cross stitch, bring the needle and cotton to the front of the material, in the small space or hole between the threads, this will be the bottom left-hand corner of the stitch; count two threads to the right, insert the needle at the top right-hand corner, and take up two threads, pointing the needle in a straight direction towards you, and bringing it up at the bottom right-hand corner, level with the cotton, but two threads therefrom, as shown in Fig. 72; draw the needle through and you will find the *half* of a cross stitch; now insert the needle at the top left-hand corner, two threads above the starting point, slant it to the right, and bring it out at the bottom right-hand corner where the cotton is, as see Fig. 73, *or* at the nearest point ready for beginning the next stitch, and draw through, and you will find a perfect cross stitch; every cross stitch is formed in the same way: you may place them one over the other, or one below the other, as the case may be; you should form the first half of every stitch from left to right, and allow the cross to lie from right to left, *every cross to slant in the same direction.* Keep the wrong side as neat as you can. Fasten off by running the cotton under a few stitches on the wrong side, and cut the end off close. Thread the needle with the end left at the commencement, and fasten it off in the same way, unless you have previously confined it by working stitches to cover it; knots are not admissible.

Eyelet stitch, Fig. 74, consists of eight amalgamated stitches, each worked from the centre of the stitch to the outside, taking up two threads with each

subject. Each article of body and house linen should be distinctly marked, and in such a manner as to be easily seen when the article is folded. It is more general for body linen to have the initials of Christian and surnames only of its respective owners, but some persons prefer the surname in full.

Chemises and nightdresses are marked just beneath the opening in front, but should the former have no slit, the name should be placed on the band at neck, or a few inches below it, or even on right-hand side of hem. Bodices are marked on the hem after the last buttonhole; petticoats and drawers on the right-hand side of the band, although if this is a drawn one the marking comes in front. If corsets are marked, it should be on one of the gussets on right-hand side.

On collars the name is placed on the band at back, and on cuffs the same plan is followed; or if there is no band it should be next to the last buttonhole, inside of course. Gentlemen's shirts are marked on the little flap, just beneath the front, while for socks and stockings the correct place is about an

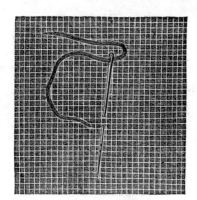

Fig. 72.—Cross Stitch. First Proceeding

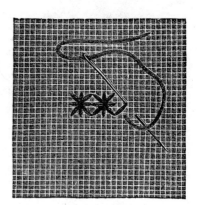

Fig. 74.—Eyelet Stitch.

stitch; it is a pretty stitch. The junction of the cotton draws a tiny "eye" in the centre, but it takes time to work, and therefore is not in frequent use.

Leviathan stitch, Fig. 75, is employed when letters or figures are required to be worked on a large scale; each stitch embraces four threads, and is four times crossed; any letter therefore worked in leviathan stitch will be just double the size of the same letter worked in cross stitch. The engraving represents two stitches complete, and a third stitch commenced; when you draw the needle through you will find the stitch stands in the form of a single cross; the next movement is to insert the needle in at the top midway between the two corners of the stitch, and bring it out to the left adjacent to the central crossing of the previous stitch, and draw through; then insert the

inch from the seam on right, and an inch and a half from the weit or hem. Some ladies' stockings have the instep ornamented with an embroidered monogram, and occasionally a very elongated narrow monogram replaces the clocks.

Red marking cotton is ordinarily used for socks and stockings, or Cash's woven names or initials are very handy for marking woollen goods. On handkerchiefs it is allowable for young ladies to have their Christian name embroidered in full, but it is *only* for young ladies that this is correct. If entitled to a coronet it is placed above the initials, and is used on the body linen as well as other articles.

Sheets, pillow-cases, towels, table-cloths, serviettes, together with all kitchen cloths, are generally marked an inch or two from the hem in the left-hand

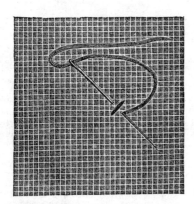

Fig. 73.—Cross Stitch. Second Proceeding.

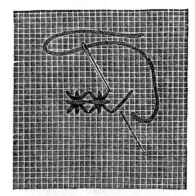

Fig 75 - Leviathan Stitch.

needle on the right-hand side midway between the top and bottom corner, and bring it out two threads below—*i.e.,* at the bottom corner—and draw through, which completes the stitch.

Fig. 76.—AN ALPHABET OF PLAIN LETTERS AND FIGURES FOR MARKING HOUSEHOLD LINEN.

THE correct marking of all linen is an important affair to a good housekeeper, and to have it properly done in all its details denotes an orderly mind; but it is a duty which is somewhat neglected, or only imperfectly carried out, and in many instances this is mainly owing to a want of knowledge of the

corner, and about an equal distance from the selvedge at side, in red marking cotton. If, however, the monogram is embroidered on sheets, it is placed in the middle of the width, the foot of the letters reaching nearly to the hem, so that when the sheet is turned over it faces you. Both for these and for pillowcases the letters are long, about three inches, but some much longer. Some pillow-cases have the monogram or initials in the centre of the width, just above the hem; on others, again, they are placed in the centre, surrounded by a wreath, but these latter are generally intended only for show, and are removed at night. White embroidery cotton is used for this elaborate marking. On counterpanes, the monogram or crest ornaments the centre, but should in no case be used together. It is a good plan to adopt a certain style of monogram and use the same design for everything in the house—linen, note paper, plate, buttons, &c.—varying, of course, the size as well as the manner of marking on the linen.

If towels are embroidered it is about four inches from the hem (the foot of the letters to the hem) and on the middle fold; occasionally the monogram or crest is seen in the centre, but this style is not so usual and is even more awkward for folding, for it must be borne in mind that the marking must always be on the outer fold, and on house linen the number of each article is necessary and the date.

The alphabet, Fig. 76, shows the working of a complete alphabet of capital letters, small letters, and figures, as usually employed upon household linen and under garments. The names may be worked in full, or initials selected, at the option of the worker. Where there are two or three letters or more to be marked, the cotton should be neatly fastened off at the end of each letter, and not carried on from one to the other. Four threads are generally left between the letters.

In marking household linen, it usually occupies four lines and sometimes three, thus—

E. M. Smith
G. C.
12
1894

at all difficult of execution; in fact, when learnt, they are quite as easy to work as the plain letters of the previous example, as they are merely cross stitch. Initials may be selected, or the name be marked in full, according to the taste and desire of the worker.

The capital letters in our sampler measure five-eighths of an inch high, and are worked in simple cross stitch, taken over three squares of the canvas each way; that is, they cover nine squares in all.

The small letters and figures, which are half an inch high, are worked in the same manner, and over the same number of threads.

Those who have the time should certainly give preference to cotton marking, which unfortunately has much been neglected since the introduction of marking ink. Children especially should be taught to mark with cotton, and every child should be encouraged to work a sampler, as in the good old days, when a square of canvas was not only ornamented with the alphabet and figures, but with flowers, animals, and fancy designs, terminating with the name and age of the worker, also the date.

A very old sampler, worked about the middle of the eighteenth century, terminated with the following curious lines—

Fig. 76.—Plain Letters and Figures for Marking Household Linen.

The first line, the name; second line, glass cloth; third line, the number of the article; and fourth line, the date. Or some prefer to merely mark them thus—

E. M. Smith
12
1894

Chain stitch is also used for marking purposes, as well as satin stitch, French knots, very narrow braid, back stitch, &c., but all these are for large and elaborate monograms or single letters, and which must be fully treated in a separate book.

Fig. 77.—FANCY LETTERS AND FIGURES FOR MARKING HANDKERCHIEFS AND WEARING APPAREL.

THE capitals and small letters shown in Fig. 77 are especially pretty for marking pocket handkerchiefs and articles of wearing apparel. They are not

" Elizabeth Hyde is my name,
And with my needle I worked the same;
That all the world may plainly see,
How kind my parents have been to me."

GENERAL RULES.

ALL linen, calicoes, &c., should be washed previous to cutting out.

Linens, lawns, cambric, holland, and such materials should be cut by the thread.

Longcloth, muslins, flannels, and such fabrics will tear; but all small articles, such, for instance, as a gusset, a patch, &c., should be cut.

Cutting out several of the same articles at once often saves waste, therefore it is better to cut half a dozen chemises or half a dozen drawers at a time.

Frills and flounces are usually cut widthways of the material.

Material for piping purposes, also broad hems or facings, are cut on the true bias.

In cutting any fabric crosswise, or on the bias, first fold the end of the material cornerwise like a half handkerchief, which brings the raw edge evenly against the selvedge side, then cut off the half square, from which cut the strips for piping.

14

To cut off a yard of material crosswise, first cut off a half square as just directed, then measure a yard along each of the selvedge edges, crease it slanting across, and cut it off here.

Velvet, satin, silk, and such goods can be bought cut the crossway as well as the straight.

When purchasing longcloth, cambric, flannel, &c., buy the proper width for the article required, so that it may be cut out to best advantage.

Much waste arises from the material being a trifle too narrow or too wide. If too narrow it means joins, which besides taking more material calls for more labour in sewing, while if a few inches too wide, this strip has to be torn off and possibly will be of no use.

See that the edges of your work are perfectly even before turning down, as this will ensure an even hem, and a nicely made garment.

Cotton is preferable worked the way it unwinds from the reel, and for this reason, ladies often thread the needle before cutting off the cotton.

Thread should be used for all kinds of linen work.

Cottons are used for calicoes, muslins, cambrics, and such goods.

Cottons and threads, especially coloured ones, should be kept (when not in

In marking linen for use in the household of a married couple the initials of both husband and wife should be combined.

For instance, supposing the Christian names of Mr. and Mrs. Morris to be Harold and Gladys, the linen should be marked H. G. Morris, followed by the number and date, as below—

H. G. Morris.
12.
1894.

The wife's personal linen would be marked G. Morris, and the husband's H. Morris.

It is as well to put a list of the linen in the linen chest or cupboard, and in the case of loss of any article, or the addition of any new article, note must be made of same.

Monograms on linen are best embroidered in French or Irish embroidery cotton, and it is also desirable that the linen be washed before being embroidered.

Nightdress cases should have the lady's name handsomely embroidered thereon.

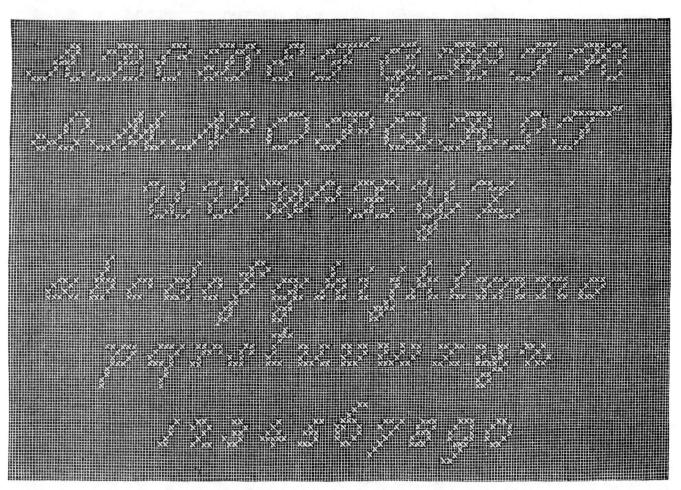

Fig. 77.—Fancy Letters and Figures for Marking Handkerchiefs and Wearing Apparel.

use) rolled up in brown paper, which prevents the air fading or decaying them.

Sewing silks are best encased in soft wash leather.

Embroidery muslin, which ranges from 4¾d. the yard upwards, and measures 44 inches wide, is very suitable for making frills, while the better qualities at 6¾d. upwards will be found well adapted to camisoles, summer chemises, &c., as it is beautifully soft, wears well, and is so cool and nice.

Indian longcloth is also nice for summer underwear; while for trimming purposes, torchon lace and insertion are wonderfully durable.

Feather-stitched braid both in white and colours can be had for joining edgings and insertion, or for making neat the neck and sleeves of underwear.

Coarse torchon laces, both in linen and wool, are used for trimming flannel petticoats.

Undervests are best knitted with fine wool or silk, or else woven ones purchased, as these fit the form so much closer and better than do those made from flannel.

Coloured cambrics, silks, and batistes are used for underwear, trimmed with Valenciennes lace.

White china silk washes splendidly, and makes extremely nice underwear.

Pillow shams, which are placed over the pillows during the daytime and folded up at night, are often most elaborately embroidered, while some show a drawn-thread bordering and bold monogram in centre.

Mountmellick work is admirably adapted to the ornamentation of pillow shams, quilts, toilet mats, and covers.

Slips to place on top of the sheet when it turns down are also of fine linen with drawn-thread border and monogram in centre.

For summer use white or coloured cambric or dimity bedspreads are nice. They are bordered with a gathered frill of the material, which can be edged with lace or be trimmed with insertion.

Mottoes round bedspreads are often used, such as—

"To all, to each, a fair good night,
And pleasing dreams and slumbers light."

Bedspreads of coloured silk, satin or sateen, covered with guipure lace, are effective and nice for summer use.

Serviettes are now ornamented with a single letter or monogram worked in the centre in satin stitch.

Muslin bedspreads, with the spots worked over with coloured silk and the muslin mounted on sateen, are extremely effective, and with care they wash and wear well.

WELDON'S
PRACTICAL PLAIN NEEDLEWORK.

(THIRD SERIES.)

How to Feather-Stitch, Patch, Quilt, Honeycomb, Braid, &c.

FIFTY-SIX ILLUSTRATIONS.

PLAIN NEEDLEWORK.

Figs. 78 to 80.—FEATHER STITCH.

THESE pretty stitches are employed in plain needlework to ornament the fronts, necks, and sleeves of chemises and nightdresses, the bands of knickerbocker drawers, and other articles of underlinen. Sometimes they form a substitute for fine back stitching, and at other times are used in addition thereto. As a rule, for cotton goods they are worked with Strutts' white crochet cotton of rather coarse make, or with flax thread, or, if colour is required, employ Evans' Maltese thread which will wash beautifully. If feather stitching is to be embroidered as a heading to tucks on a flannel petticoat, you may use "flannel silk," which is unshrinkable and keeps its colour, or Andalusian wool is suitable and looks well. Feather stitching in silk is also used to ornament flannel blouses, infants' and children's flannel underwear, &c. The great point is to set in the stitches with regularity, and to keep the feathers all one uniform size, never letting the line get wider or narrower as the work proceeds. It is impossible to count threads upon calico or linen, therefore the size of the stitches and the distances one from the other must be gauged by the eye. This requires practice; but the work is so easy and so quickly accomplished when once it is understood, that the time spent in learning will eventually be repaid. Feather stitch is usually worked along the centre of a narrow band; if the band is wide, a row of feather stitch is placed on each side. In ornamenting the front of a garment the feather stitch should always be commenced at the neck and worked downwards. A crewel needle should be employed in preference to a sewing needle.

Fig. 78 represents **Single Feather Stitch.** Here we have a series of single stitches, or feathers, branching out from each side of a central vein or mid-rib. A novice in working had better trace one perpendicular line on the material as a guide for this mid-rib, which forms the centre of the feather stitching. Have the needle threaded with cotton, and bring up the needle and cotton on this line; then hold the cotton under the left-hand thumb, insert the needle a little distance to the right-hand side, a little higher than the place the cotton springs from, and, pointing it in a slanting direction, bring it up on the traced line a trifle below the place it was previously brought out, pass the point of the needle over the cotton held by the thumb, and draw through. Thus you have a stitch made on the right-hand side. Now again retain the cotton by pressure of the left-hand thumb, turn the needle completely round, and insert it on the left-hand side a little distant from the mid-rib, slant it towards the centre, and bring it up on the traced line a trifle below the preceding stitch; pass the point over the cotton held by the thumb, and draw through, and you

Fig. 78.—Single Fig. 79.—Double Fig. 80.—Treble Feather Stitch. Feather Stitch. Feather Stitch.

will have a stitch upon the left-hand side. Now again hold the cotton down and make a slanting stitch on the right-hand side, and next hold the cotton down and make a slanting stitch on the left-hand side, and proceed in this manner, making the stitches radiate alternately right and left for the length desired. The cotton must not be drawn too tightly, or it is apt to pucker the material; it is better to leave it moderately loose in case of any shrinking when the article is washed.

In Fig. 79 we see **Double Feather Stitch**, so called because two stitches are worked, one below the other, forming double branching lines on each side the mid-rib. The needle is always placed slantways in the material as instructed in the previous example. This double feather stitch is universally approved, and is a great advance upon the single feather stitch.

Fig. 80 shows **Treble Feather Stitch**, another variety of fancy stitching, rather more elaborate than either of the preceding, but a general favourite when mastered. Observe that the mid-rib is not perfectly rigid, it bends alternately to the right and to the left with each grouping of the stitches.

Figs. 81 and 82. — CORAL STITCH.

CORAL stitch is another useful stitch for ornamenting under-garments. It bears a great resemblance to feather stitch, though not worked in precisely the same manner. Perhaps it is of the two more quickly accomplished; the result, at all events, is very pleasing. Coral stitch is of two kinds—single and double—and the same preliminary remarks that apply to feather stitch will apply to it also.

Fig. 81 exemplifies **Single Coral Stitch.** A learner had better trace on the material two perpendicular lines at a distance of not more than a quarter of an inch apart, as a guide to ensure evenness. Having the needle threaded with cotton bring it up on the line to the left. Remember that every stitch is to be taken with the needle pointing straight towards you, hold the cotton under the left-hand thumb, insert the needle on the line to the right, and take up a few threads quite straight by the line; the point of the needle must pass over the cotton held by the thumb, and then the stitch may be drawn up. Again hold the cotton under the thumb, and now make a stitch straight on the line to the left, bringing up the needle over the cotton held by the thumb; and continue thus, working a stitch alternately on each side right and left.

Fig. 82 shows that particularly effective stitch known as **Double Coral Stitch**, which some years ago was so extensively used upon babies' muslin frocks and pinafores. It is worked very similarly to single coral stitch, the only difference being that it is slightly wider, as an additional stitch is made midway between the side stitches.

Fig. 83.—HERRINGBONE STITCH.

HERRINGBONE stitch is occasionally used as an ornamental stitch upon garments made of linen and calico, but it is still more extensively employed in flannel work, for the purpose of keeping a hem or a seam down flat without making a double fold in the material. It will protect a raw edge, and therefore obviates the necessity of a hem or a fell. In this capacity the stitch will again be referred to when we treat of the making and mending of flannel articles. At the present time we will simply explain the method of working herringboning. It is executed in a straight line, horizontally, beginning on the *left*-hand side and proceeding to the right, and when it is worked it resembles a series of small crosses, which require to be formed with perfect regularity, or the effect will not be good. A learner may be guided by two lines drawn upon the material about a quarter of an inch apart from each other, or wider or narrower, as the width of the herringbone is desired to be; but very soon, when accustomed to the stitch, it will be quite easy to manage

Fig. 81.—Single Coral Stitch.

Fig. 82.—Double Coral Stitch.

without any guide whatever, the eye will be a sufficient criterion of its accuracy. Thread the needle and bring it up to the right side of the material, on the top line, at the extreme left-hand side of the work; insert the needle in the bottom line in a perfectly straight direction from right to left, taking up a few threads of the material. Do not allow the cotton to pass under the point of the needle, but keep it well behind, that is, on the side where the eye of the needle is. Draw the needle through, take a stitch in the same manner on the top line, then another on the bottom line, and so on; and the cotton of the last stitch forms a *cross* over the stitch preceding. Notice especially to take up precisely the same amount of material on the needle for each stitch, and let the same space be left between the stitches. Draw the cotton just tight enough to lie smoothly, but not so tight as to pucker the material.

Fig. 84.—FANCY HERRINGBONE STITCH.
TO RUN RIBBON IN.

HERE is a novel design for working herringbone stitch upon a pinafore, or other garment, in such a manner as to produce a casing for a coloured ribbon to be run in; the appearance of the ribbon lying on the white fabric and covered with the network of herringbone stitch, is very quaint and pretty. Study the illustration, Fig. 84, and you will observe the work is executed in two distinct rows of stitches. Coarse crochet cotton is employed for the purpose. The first row is worked in exactly the same manner as the narrow line of herringbone stitch shown in Fig. 83, but it is much wider; in fact, the original is half an inch wide, and the engraving represents the full actual size. The stitches are taken at proportionate distance one from the other, remembering that space must be left to accommodate the second row of stitches between the stitches of the first row. You may work the first row for the length required, and then return and commence the second row; or you may, with two needles, accomplish a portion of the two rows simultaneously, as depicted in the engraving. Be careful to place the stitches of the second row exactly *opposite* the stitches of the first row, that the cotton may fall in true diamond fashion, with the meshes of the network crossing in the very centre of the insertion. A coloured ribbon, or a piece of narrow ribbon velvet, is drawn under by the help of a bodkin

---

Fig. 85.—LACET BUTTONHOLE STITCH.

OUR engraving, Fig. 85, shows an insertion worked in lacet buttonhole stitch, which is very useful for trimming purposes, as it can be arranged in bands, or be laid between tucks, and though in the original it measures one and a half inches in width, it is capable of being either wider or narrower, as required. A band of coloured material, ribbon, or sateen, or Turkey red twill—whichever seems most suitable—is first of all let in between the fabric of the article, and upon this the lacet buttonhole insertion is executed with coarse silk, coarse crochet cotton, or flax thread. Begin every row on the left-hand side, and work from left to right. Commence with the top row—Bring the needle and cotton up through the band, just below the fold of the fabric, hold the cotton under the left-hand thumb as in ordinary buttonholing, insert the needle a trifle to the right, at a little distance above the fold, pierce also through the

band, and bring the needle out in a perfectly straight downward direction through the band only, pass the point of the needle over the cotton held by the thumb, and draw through; every successive stitch is made in the same way. When working the second and following rows, you put the needle above the loop of the previous row, insert it through the band, and bring it out a little distance lower through the band, passing the point of the needle over the cotton, and draw through. The illustration represents the needle in the act of forming a stitch. You must not draw the cotton tightly, but allow it to fall in graceful loops to simulate lace. The loops of the last row of the buttonhole stitch are attached to the lower fold of the fabric by simple catch stitches. If you are working a round band of insertion you can in each round connect the last stitch to the first in an almost imperceptible join.

Figs. 86 and 87.—LACE WHIPPED.

WHEN Torchon or other lace is used for trimming underlinen it is first whipped and then seamed on. The whipping is executed simply by picking up the small open loops that lie on the top margin of the lace. Use rather fine cotton; hold the needle in the position shown in Fig. 86. Insert the

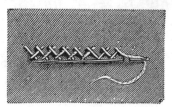

Fig. 83.—Herringbone Stitch.

needle from front to back to pick up each loop in succession; a whole needleful may be held at one time, and when the needle is conveniently full the cotton is drawn through. The lace should first of all be quartered and halved as explained in the instruction for whipping on muslin (see Figs. 39 and 40, page 4, of No. 103 of this series, which is the 2nd Series of "Plain Needlework"), that the fulness may be distributed evenly upon the article that is being trimmed.

Fig. 87 shows the same lace seamed on a band of linen. Hold the right side of the band towards you, place the right side of the lace upon it, the whipped edge of the lace against the edge of the band, and unite the two by the process of seaming, taking the stitches very neatly and regularly. If possible, sew one little loop with each stitch. People sometimes seam on lace in the reverse position—*i.e.*, with the band towards the worker; it comes to the same thing in the end, and may be just as easy for those who have accustomed themselves to it, but it is more difficult to regulate the fulness, because the end of the whipping thread will come at the right hand instead of at the left, and the little loops are not so readily perceptible for the needle to pass through each.

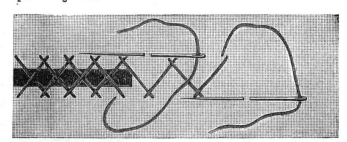

Fig. 84.—Fancy Herringbone Stitch to run Ribbon in.

Fig. 88.—A BAND OF INSERTION.

HERE we show the method by which a band of insertion is let into a garment. The material of which the garment is made is generally cut to admit the insertion. You will commence operations by folding each cut edge of the material to the depth of about three-eighths of an inch, letting the fold lie on the uppermost or right side. Turn the edge of the insertion down on the wrong side, and now place the folded edge of the insertion over the folded edge of the material, and tack both together, taking care that the insertion is placed perfectly straight and level. Work a row of feather stitch or coral stitch upon each side of the open work, as represented in Fig. 89, taking the stitches quite through to the back of the material, for the purpose of retaining both fabrics together. When this is accomplished, the tacking thread should be removed. It is a good plan to fell a strip of linen upon the wrong side of the material behind the embroidery, as it affords support to the insertion, and causes it to wear better.

Fig. 89.—A BAND OF INSERTION AND AN EDGING.

OUR engraving represents the placing of a band of insertion and an edging. The upper edge of the insertion is arranged as instructed above. The lower edge is not feather stitched until the lace has been gathered and sewn on, which is done by laying the wrong side edge of the insertion upon the gathered edge of lace and securing these together by running, putting in a back stitch frequently to prevent any undue stretching of the fabrics. Run a neat strip of material at the back of the gathering stitches, which strip may be only just so wide as to reach to the lower portion of the open work, or sufficiently wide to serve as a backing to the insertion and be felled behind the top row of feather stitching. Complete the trimming by working the second row of feather stitch along the bottom of the insertion.

Fig. 90.—A FLANNEL HEM.

WHEN it is desirable to make a hem at the bottom of a flannel garment, the fabric is not turned down twice as if hemming cotton goods, for with a thick substance like flannel the double fold would be thick and clumsy; therefore

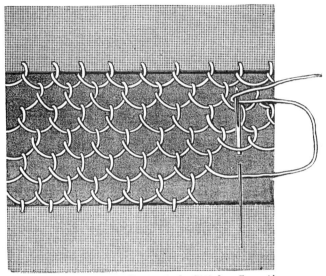

Fig. 85.—Lacet Buttonhole Stitch. Insertion.

one fold, the depth of the hem, is all that is required, and this fold should be tacked carefully in place previous to herringboning it in the manner shown in the engraving, Fig. 90. The ordinary herringbone stitch is used, the working of which is explained in Fig. 83 of the present issue. The top row of stitches should be placed about one-eighth of an inch above the raw edge and they pierce through the double flannel, while the lower row of stitches are set just below the raw edge and consequently pass through only one thickness of the flannel, but as they press against the raw edge they effectually prevent unravelling and retain the hem in a firm and even position.

Figs. 91 to 94.—FLANNEL SEAMS.

FIG. 91 represents the ordinary method of running two breadths of flannel together to form a seam. If it be new flannel you must first of all tear away the list which forms the selvedge, which is generally of a darker colour than the flannel and varies from a quarter of an inch to an inch in width. Place the two pieces of flannel together, one over the other, the right side (that is to say the side having the most fluff or nap) inside, and the edge of the piece that is next to you a trifle lower than the edge of the back piece; and with a needle and cotton run both together in simple running stitch, as see engraving, being very careful to keep the flannel even and to avoid puckering. When the running of the seam is accomplished, you will open out the breadths of flannel, and bring the raw edges flat upon the fabric, allowing the widest edge to overlap and fall completely over the narrow edge. Proceed then to herringbone the seam, as shown in Fig. 92; take both rows of stitches through to the right side of the flannel, where they will assume the appearance of two lines of neat running. Flannel seams vary in width according to the quality of the flannel; as a rule a thick flannel requires the fell to be considerably wider than a fine flannel. The seams of babies' flannel garments should be exceedingly smooth and neat.

In Fig. 93 we see another way of running and herringboning a flannel seam. Here the two edges are placed evenly together, and joined about a quarter of an inch or three-eighths of an inch from the edge, by a line of running stitches worked as Fig. 91 is done; then the flannel is opened out, and the edges are spread flat, one to the right and the other to the left of the join. The herringboning is carried along the exact centre of the seam, the stitches being in fact taken across the join, one stitch above the join and one stitch below, alternately. This makes a smooth strong seam and one which will wear to

the last thread of the fabric, for as the running is practically backed by the herringboning, it is not at all likely to give way.

A third method of running and herringboning a flannel seam is shown in Fig. 94. It is commenced by placing the edges of the flannel quite evenly together and running a line of stitches within a short distance of the margin; then open out the flannel and spread the edges flat, one to the right and the other to the left of the seam, and herringbone each edge on its own respective side, as see engraving. This treatment effectually prevents any unravelling of threads, and results in a very smooth, neat seam, which however is scarcely so strong as those worked by either of the foregoing methods, as the running thread receives no protection whatever, and therefore is liable to break if subjected to any unusual strain either in wear or in washing.

Figs. 95 to 97.—A FLANNEL PATCH.

GREAT skill is required to properly patch a flannel garment; still, as it is often necessary to be done, and as it is a credit to have one's clothes neatly and properly mended, it is well worth learning how to accomplish a patch with accuracy and dexterity. A patch is generally square in shape, though it may be oblong, round, or even triangular if occasion demands. The flannel used for the patch should be as nearly as possible of the same quality as the flannel of which the article is made. The edges of the flannel patch are never folded under, but the work is effected entirely in herringbone stitch, which protects the raw edge on both sides of the garment; that is to say, the edge of the worn flannel immediately surrounding the hole is herringboned upon the patch, this being the right side of the garment, and reversely the edge of

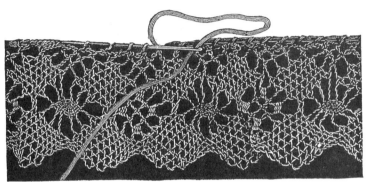

Fig. 86.—Lace Whipped.

the flannel that forms the patch is to be herringboned down upon the wrong side of the garment. First discover the selvedge way of the garment, and endeavour also to discover the selvedge way of the piece of flannel you are about to use for the patch, and mark each by inserting a pin in a corresponding direction. Remember that the patch should be sufficiently large to cover all the thin part surrounding the hole. Place the right side of the garment downwards upon the table in front of you, selvedgeways perpendicularly right and left; lay the right side of the patch downwards over the hole and worn part of the garment, the threads of the patch being parallel and perfectly even with the warp and woof threads of the garment. Tack the patch down upon the garment within half an inch or so of the edge, being particularly careful as regards accuracy. There must be no looseness or irregularity, but

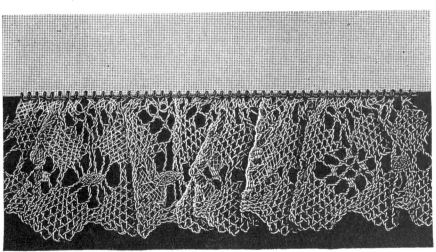

Fig. 87.—Lace Whipped and Sewn on.

the patch must lie perfectly smooth and even against the garment. It now is in readiness for attachment by herringbone; at least you may now, if you like, herringbone this side (the wrong side), or you may turn to the right side of the garment and cut away the worn part, tack round the hole if needful, or put pins at the corners to hold the flannel steady. The herringbone is commenced at the lower left-hand corner, by bringing the needle and cotton up in the actual corner by the raw edge; work from left to right; take one stitch a little distant from the raw edge through both thicknesses of material, then a stitch below the raw edge through only single material, and so on alternately, gauging the size of the stitches by the eye, and bringing the last stitch of the side close against the next corner. Fig. 95 shows the herringboning up this side the patch, and Fig. 96 represents in detail the correct method of mitring the stitches to turn the corner, preparatory to working along the next following side. All the corners must be mitred to correspond. When this herring-

Fig. 88.—A Band of Insertion.

boning is finished you may turn again to the wrong side of the garment and herringbone the outer margin of the patch. Fig 97 shows the right side of a finished patch. Observe the perfect regularity of the square of herringbone stitching, and also the skilfulness displayed in the mitring of the corners. The square of herringboning that you worked round the outer margin of the patch is defined by the appearance of two rows of small neat stitches resembling two rows of running.

Fig. 98.—A SCALLOPED HEM IN FLANNEL.

HERE is a neat scalloped hem to go round the bottom of a flannel petticoat. This is particularly easy to work, quickly done, and at the same time very effective looking. The engraving (Fig. 98) shows the hem and scallops in actual working size. First of all, a real hem is to be turned down and back-stitched or machine-stitched on the inside of the petticoat, or a spare strip of flannel, if stitched on, will answer the purpose, as it does not in the least signify about having a fold at the bottom; the object is to produce a double thickness of flannel to work the embroidery upon. The embroidery may be executed with Andalusian wool, flax thread, or white silk. Trace the outline of the scalloping upon the flannel, and mark a dot in the centre of each scallop to denote the place where the spot is afterwards to be worked. The buttonhole stitch scalloping is worked in the usual way, the stitches are set closely together, and are all of equal height. The spots are produced in satin stitch, setting the needle in from right to left, making a very small stitch at the top and at the bottom of the spot, with longer stitches towards the widest part across the spot. The work should be pressed flat with a warm iron before the scallops are cut out.

Fig. 99.—NARROW BUTTONHOLE SCALLOPING.

THIS engraving shows a simple narrow edge worked in buttonhole scalloping. It is suitable for use on a baby's flannel garment, and may be produced with either silk or wool. The stitches assume a straight line along the top of the edge; the needle is set in the same direction for every stitch, always with its point towards you, and the stitches are graduated in length to the formation of the scallop, being short at the corners and gradually lengthening in the centre of each scallop.

Fig. 100.—QUILTING.

QUILTING used to be very much employed in the making of quilts and counterpanes, and many of these were quite works of art, so elaborately were they quilted, not only in diamonds, squares, and oblongs, but in really handsome geometrical designs and flowery scroll patterns. At the present time, however, quilting is chiefly reserved for such articles as are wadded for warmth, as winter petticoats, cloaks and mantles, and the long cloaks, hoods, and bibs of infants, as well as for making up tea cosies and lining work-baskets. Three thicknesses of material are required for quilting—i.e., satin, for the surface of the work; flannel, domette, or wadding for padding, and muslin (or some inexpensive fabric) for lining. If a good thick quilting is desired it is usual to substitute wool wadding in the place of the flannel; this makes the satin sit up puffily. Our engraving, Fig. 100, represents a piece of quilting worked in diamonds. Lay the flannel or wadding between the satin and the lining (if wadding, let the unglazed side come against the satin), and pin or tack these smoothly together, thus you get the three thicknesses of material one over the other. The work is properly executed in back stitch, and if a machine is available it may be machine-stitched, as this is one of the purposes for which machine stitching is preferable to handwork, on account of its greater regularity; sewing machines have their own quilting gauges, but in hand-working the distances must be carefully measured either by folds creased in the satin to serve as marks or by means of strips of paper cut to the right width. Work the first line of back stitching obliquely from right to left across the surface of the satin, taking care that the stitches pierce through to the lining; do more lines on each side of this line, at an even distance of say an inch or more apart one from the other; then cross these lines of stitching with other oblique lines in the opposite direction, and so forming diamonds. Quilting is frequently executed in the ordinary running stitch, which is a much quicker method, though not nearly so neat as back stitching.

Upholstery quilting is worked on a different plan, and requires the best and thickest wadding, a good strong lining, and some beads or buttons. Bring up the needle and cotton from the back to the front in the place designed for the corner angle of a diamond, thread a bead on the cotton, and pass the needle and cotton again to the back, sew a stitch or two for firmness, and tie the cotton tightly in a secure knot; do the same at every corner angle of a diamond, and you will see the diamonds are well defined by reason of their puffiness, as the stitches draw them in at every corner. A very pretty effect is imparted by the use of the beads or buttons.

Fig. 89 —A Band of Insertion and an Edging.

Fig. 101.—BLANKET STITCHES.

IT is the custom to put an overcasting of buttonhole stitch round the edge of blankets to ensure against the unravelling of the blanket and also to add to its good appearance, and as the stitching is generally worked with bright red wool, it makes a pretty finish, and looks both neat and cheerful. The raw edge of the blanket may be folded under or not, as preferred; the selvedge sides need not be folded. The sides that are folded should be tacked flatly before commencing to overcast. Example 1 shows the simplest form of buttonhole stitching. The needle is passed through from the right side to the wrong side of the blanket above the top of the fold, making stitches to the length of fully half an inch. These stitches appear the same on the wrong side as on the right side of the blanket. They are set at a little distance one from the other, and the "ridge" along the bottom of the stitches (which is formed by passing the needle through the loop of wool in the manner shown in the engraving) serves to strengthen the edge of the blanket to the blanket. Example 2 is more elaborate in style and displays ingenuity. The needle is always placed in a vertical direction, and the stitches slant vertically, one to the right and one to the left, meeting in a point on the edge where the ridge is, and then one to the left and one to the right meeting in a point at the top of the line of stitching, and so on alternately. Example 3 is exceedingly pretty if worked with regularity. The stitches are arranged three in a group. First insert the needle to make a stitch, slanting from left to right; then put in a very tall upright stitch, and then insert the needle to make a stitch slanting from right to left and meeting the two other stitches in the way clearly depicted in the

Fig. 103.—TURRET BUTTONHOLING.

FOR THE BOTTOM OF A FLANNEL PETTICOAT.

TURRET buttonholing, as exemplified in Fig. 103, is very effective for the bottom of a flannel petticoat, and also looks handsome for dress trimming; the wide lace which shows between the turrets gives the work a really elegant appearance. Torchon lace is the best to use upon flannel, as it will wash with the garment, but for a dress a wide black silk lace is good style. Turret buttonholing requires to be executed with the greatest accuracy; the stitches must be set in perfectly straight, regular, and even, and the corners must be mitred to pair with each other, or it will not look well. It is a good plan to make a kind of stencil plate of cardboard and use this as a guide wherewith to trace upon the material the outline of the buttonhole stitching. The lower edge of the

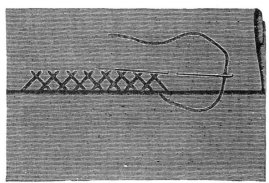

Fig. 90.—A Flannel Hem.

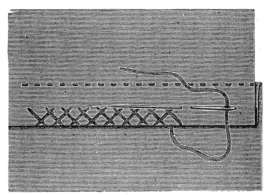

Fig. 92.—Herringboning a Flannel Seam.

engraving; thus all three stitches spring as it were from the same base, and the wool lies level against the edge of the blanket to the base of the next group of stitches. Example 4 bears great resemblance to example 2, but here there is the addition of a vertical stitch between the stitches that meet in points. Example 5 is neat and effective. Begin with two perpendicular buttonhole stitches half an inch in height, then make a stitch nearly an inch in height, and do two more stitches to correspond with the first two; thus you have five stitches, the tallest in the centre. They each must be upright, and a little distant one from the other; leave a slight space, and do another similar group of five stitches, and so on.

Fig. 102.—BRAIDING.

BRAIDING is a good deal used as a trimming for dresses, jackets, and mantles; it is quickly done, and looks handsome if a bold pattern is selected.

cardboard will, of course, be straight to begin with, and will be a guide for the bottom of the tabs; these tabs are 2 inches wide, the open space measures 1¼ inches. Draw a series of perpendicular lines at these distances, alternately, letting them stand 2½ inches high above the edge of the cardboard, and now draw a short line across the top of all these narrowest alternate spacings as far as the width of your cardboard will permit; three or four tabs will suffice, as it can be repeated; cut out all the narrow spaces, and thus you get the shape of the tabs. Now trace all the tabs upon your material, which should be double, and round the inside of each tab, and also above the top of the spacings, introduce a guiding line to regulate the width of the buttonhole stitches. In our model the stitches occupy three-eighths of an inch; also draw short slanting lines from point to point at the angles of the corners to define the direction the stitches are to take in mitring the corners. The buttonhole stitch is worked in the ordinary manner, making the stitches level with the outline, that is, three-eighths of an inch deep everywhere, excepting at the corners, where each

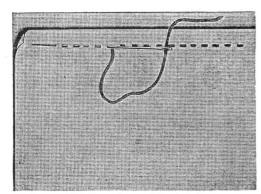

Fig. 91.—Running a Flannel Seam.

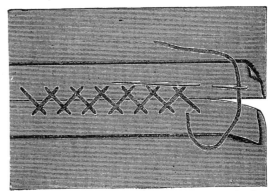

Fig. 93.—Another way of Running and Herringboning a Flannel Seam.

Now about this there need not be much difficulty, as an excellent assortment of patterns for braiding has lately been issued in Briggs' Transfer Designs, and includes borders, both narrow and wide, bodice fronts, costume sets, panels, &c. The smooth flat narrow braid is the best for the work, as it looks so much neater than that which is thick; it is sold in knots. Silk braid should be employed upon silk material, woollen braid on wool, and cotton braid on washing dresses. To sew on silk braid you should use silk drawn out of the braid, as it will match better than any sewing silk you can procure, therefore cut two or three pieces the length of a needleful, and keep them for the purpose of unravelling. To work—Having transferred the pattern to the material—Lay the braid accurately upon the traced line, and run the braid neatly and firmly upon the material, taking a back stitch every now and then; be very careful to turn the angles acutely, and to twist the curves all in the same direction.

successive stitch gets shorter and shorter in accordance with the slanting line till the extreme point of the corner is reached, when they gradually lengthen in the proportion as they before shortened, the teeth of the stitches meeting like a mid-rib, as is most clearly shown in the engraving. When all the buttonhole stitching is accomplished the material is cut away by the edge of the loops of the stitches and you find tabs of solid material alternating with cut-out spaces. Take the lace and gather it moderately full upon the back of the flannel hem, letting it hang a little below the tabs, and arranging it to fall as represented in the engraving.

Figs. 104 to 107.—HONEYCOMB.

HONEYCOMB is an ornamental stitch much in vogue for children's frocks and pinafores, ladies' blouses, afternoon teagowns, &c. It is a variety of smocking, which interesting art has already been explained and illustrated in Nos. 19, 29, and 44 of "Weldon's Practical Needlework Series." Now, as the whole beauty of smocking depends upon the evenness and regularity of the gathering, means must be adopted to keep the lines of gathering threads perfectly straight, and also to regulate the distance of the stitches one from another. This it will be almost impossible to do without a guide or chart of some sort. One method of proceeding is to take a piece of perforated cardboard, about eighteen inches long and six or seven inches wide, and in this,

the same line, then in through the second dot and out half way between this and the third dot, and so on, till the gathering thread goes the whole way along, covering the row of dots. Again thread the needle, and now run along the second row of dots in the same manner, stitch under stitch, as see Fig. 107. When as many rows are gathered as you require, draw up the threads, and keep the gathers in place by twisting the ends of the cotton round pins stuck in the material. If rightly done there will be no need of stroking the gathers down, they will lie in folds perfectly flat and even.

Quite lately, for convenience in smocking, Mr. Briggs has issued sheets of

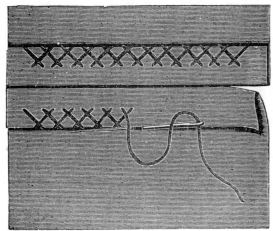

Fig. 94.—A third way of Running and Herringboning a Flannel Seam.

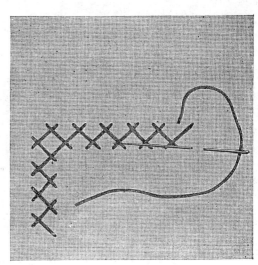

Fig. 96.—Showing in Detail the Correct Method of Mitring the Corner of a Flannel Patch.

with a sharp penknife, cut a series of small holes as shown by illustration, thus: Commence three holes from one end, cut out the little square formed by the next four holes, leave six holes intact, cut out another little square of four holes, and so on along to the other end of the cardboard, six holes left between each square cut out. Now, higher up on the cardboard, from the holes you have first cut, count four holes or five holes, according to the width you desire to leave between your lines of gathering threads, and cut another row of holes exactly over and above the row already cut, and repeat this process for the width of the cardboard. This chart will appear like Fig. 105. Place it upon the material you intend smocking, taking care that it lies perfectly straight and even, and with a pencil (using black lead on light material and yellow

transfer papers imprinted with small dots at regular intervals; these sheets only require ironing on the material in the same manner as Briggs' well-known transfer designs for crewel work, and the dots immediately become apparent, and the gathering is done from one dot to the other in the manner described above.

Another and still handier guide than the perforated card, one more generally suited to beginners, and not to be despised by those proficient in the work, is made of a sheet of ordinary stout cardboard, from which cut a strip lengthways four or six inches in width; along each edge mark spaces with pen

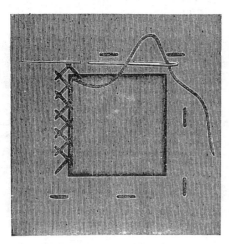

Fig. 95.—A Flannel Patch Commenced.

Fig. 97.—A Flannel Patch Finished. Right Side of Material.

lead on dark) make dots on the material through every hole of the cardboard, as Fig. 107 shows. If the card is not sufficiently large to mark the entire surface of material you intend smocking, you can lift it up and replace it in any desired position, taking care that it still lies evenly, which can be ensured by placing the top row of holes over the row last marked; be very careful not to let the cardboard slip whilst marking. The marking and the gathering had both preferably be done on the wrong side of the material, that is with the wrong side of the material uppermost, to keep the right side spotless and scrupulously clean. Thread a needle with cotton having a good knot at the end, and begin gathering by inserting the needle in the top dot on the right-hand side, bring the point up half way between this dot and the second dot in

and ink, thus, | | |, half an inch apart along one edge, and three-eighths of an inch apart along the other edge. Now put the half-inch edge of cardboard uppermost on the wrong side of the material and tick each mark, lift the cardboard as much lower down on the material as you anticipate the smocking will occupy, and tick other marks exactly below those already done. To be accurate, you will, of course, measure from the margin of the material; now draw lines from one tick to the other, the cardboard itself will serve as a ruler, and you will use a black lead for light material, and a yellow lead for dark, that the lines may be readily seen. These lines are to denote the *width* of the *stitches ;* you use the three-eighth inch edge for gathering lines, ticking as many as required for the depth of the pattern on the right-hand side and left-hand side of the material, and drawing along from one side to the other; this will appear like a series of oblong squares, and is supposed to be for working the honeycomb pattern to afford due depth to the cells. Other patterns may require some difference in the spacings; for instance, for the diamond pattern the lines may be drawn three-eighths of an inch apart both ways, forming perfect squares. An expert worker may dispense with the drawing of lines, and just simply crease the material from tick to tick. Begin gathering on the top line, inserting the needle in on the right-hand side, where the lines cross, bring up the point on the top line half way between the first and second perpendicular lines, then in at the crossing of the next lines, and out half way between the second and third perpendicular

Fig. 98.—A Scalloped Hem in Flannel.

lines, and continue, till you have gathered all along to the end of the top line ; leave the end of cotton, re-thread the needle, and proceed along each line in a similar manner (see Fig. 106), and when all are done draw up the gathering threads and secure each by passing round a pin.

Before beginning any pattern ascertain how many rows and how many gathers will be required to bring the pattern in accurately, and mark the material to allow for just so many of each and no more. All gathering threads are pulled out when the work is completed. When working on striped material, a very pretty effect may be produced by reserving the white portion for the depth and bringing the coloured stripes up to form the front ridges of the gathers.

To **Honeycomb** as Fig. 104 shows: Hold the right side of the fabric

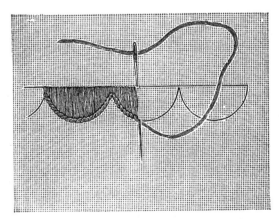

Fig. 99.--Narrow Buttonhole Scalloping.

towards you, and having your needle ready threaded with coloured silk, bring it up from the back to the front at the left-hand top corner in the first pleat and exactly over the first gathering thread ; sew the second pleat to this by passing a stitch from right to left through each, work another stitch through both pleats, then insert the needle in the same place, but in the second pleat only and bring it out in the same pleat over the second gathering thread ; catch the third pleat to this by a stitch through each, work another stitch through both pleats, then insert the needle in the same place but in the third pleat only, and bring it out in the same pleat over the first gathering thread, and proceed in this way, working a stitch alternately in each row. Two pleats are sewn together in every stitch, and the last pleat of one stitch becomes the first pleat of the next. In going from one line to another be careful always to slip the needle lengthways up and down *within* the pleat, never across.

Work the third and fourth rows as you have already worked the first and second, and continue until eight rows of dotted stitches are accomplished. Now, following Fig. 104, begin the shaping of the scallop, and work only six dots in the ninth row and five dots in the tenth row. Do four dots in the eleventh row and three dots in the twelfth-row. Then finish with two dots in the thirteenth row and one dot in the fourteenth row, and so bring the scallop to a point. Work other scallops in the same manner. When the honeycomb is completed and you release the gathering threads, you can stretch the work over a lining to the size required, while the top can be contracted to fit the neck.

Figs. 108 and 109.—FRINGING.

FRINGING does not come strictly within the definition of " Plain Needle-work," yet it may be treated within these pages, as it is now so generally employed as a finish to afternoon teacloths, sideboard cloths, towels, and other linen articles required in a house. Fig. 108 shows the simplest mode of fringing ; you see it consists merely of the perpendicular threads of the linen, as the horizontal threads have been drawn away. At a distance of about 2 inches above the edge of the linen draw out one horizontal thread to define the depth to which the fringe may extend, and use this open space as a guide to work a line of buttonhole stitch as a margin to the cloth and to prevent the fraying of any threads above the level of the fringe proper. The thread you have extracted will do nicely to button-stitch with, as it will match the linen so exactly, others can be extracted lower down when needed. Work from left

Fig. 100.—Quilting.

to right. Bring up the needle and cotton in the line of the drawn thread, insert the needle two threads higher up the linen and bring it out in the same place whence you started, and draw through. Now hold the cotton down by pressure of the left-hand thumb, insert the needle four threads to the right of the place where you previously inserted it, and bring it out in the open line four threads to the right of the former stitch, pass the needle over the cotton that is held by the thumb, and draw through, releasing the cotton from under the thumb ; work every stitch in the same manner. When the buttonhole stitch is accomplished, the whole of the outside horizontal threads are drawn away, and the perpendicular threads will hang as represented in the engraving. Some people prefer to draw the threads before doing the line in buttonhole stitch, in which case hem stitch may be substituted for the buttonhole stitching, but the above is the most satisfactory method. The openwork insertion that is seen above the fringing is worked in trellis hem-stitch, as shown by Fig. 109.

Prepare the insertion by drawing out eight threads, or more or less, according to the width you desire the insertion to be. Work from right to left. Secure the end of the cotton with which you intend working on the right-hand side of the linen, near the upper edge of the drawn insertion, bring the needle and cotton out three threads above the open insertion, insert the needle between the open threads directly under the place the cotton is brought out, and passing it from right to left take up four open threads on the needle and draw the cotton through ; insert the needle in the same place but in a slightly upward direction, and bring it out three threads above the open insertion, straight above the cotton of the stitch just worked and four threads to the left of where the cotton was first brought out, and draw the cotton through. Proceed in the same manner to the end of the row, always grouping four threads in every cluster. When the row is finished turn the work in such a way that the stitched edge of the insertion is now at the bottom and the unworked edge at the top, and work a second row of hem stitch, sub-dividing the clusters by taking up half the threads of one cluster and half the threads of the next cluster together (see position of the needle in Fig. 109), always taking four threads together, and thereby making the threads slant first one way and then the other, like a trellis.

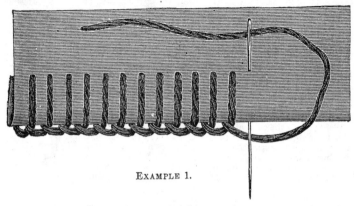

EXAMPLE 1.

A variation of this trellis insertion can be made by drawing out a greater number of threads, and grouping six threads or eight threads (it must always be an even number) in a cluster.

Fig 110.—KNOTTED FRINGE.

A KNOTTED fringe is exceedingly pretty, and is not difficult of accomplishment, though it requires a good eye to get all the knots straight and regular.

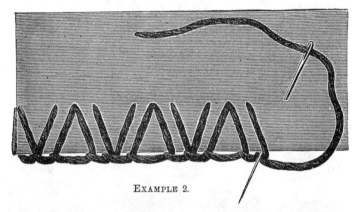

EXAMPLE 2.

The margin of the linen must be fringed to the depth of three inches. It is not necessary to edge this with stitching. The threads are separated into groups of six. The first group and the fourth group are knotted together, then the third group and the sixth group together, then the fifth group and the eighth group together, and so on, making all the knots in a straight line a short

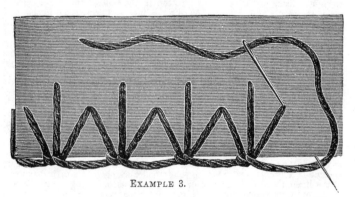

EXAMPLE 3.

distance below the solid linen; the knotted threads are then sub-divided, and half the threads from one knot are re-knotted with half the threads from the next adjacent knot, when the fringe will appear as Fig. 110. A wider fringe can be effected if you commence with a greater depth of drawn threads and tie two additional rows of knots below the two rows described above.

Figs. III to II4.—SIMPLE HEM-STITCH IN DRAWN THREAD WORK.

SIMPLE hem-stitch is the stitch most usually employed for hem-stitching pocket-handkerchiefs, sheets, and other linen articles which need a more ornamental hem than the well-known hem of plain needlework. A hem will, of course, vary in width according to the requirement of the article it is intended to adorn. A pocket-handkerchief hem should be about an inch wide, and to produce this you will require to draw out four threads of the material at a distance of 2⅛ inches from the margin on all four sides of the material to allow for hem and turning in, and by reason of two of the open lines of drawn threads crossing each other at each end of the fabric, a little square is formed at each corner, as is seen in all bought hem-stitched pocket-handkerchiefs, The turn of the hem must be folded very exactly, to lie perfectly level with the

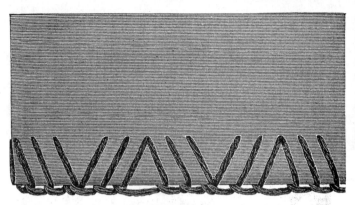

EXAMPLE 4.

upper edge of the drawn open threads, to which it is sewn in process of hem-stitching. If you are going to hem a sheet a wider hem is generally allowed, sometimes as wide as from three to four inches on best fine linen sheets, but a two-inch hem, or even one inch, will look very well for sheets in ordinary use, and as the hem in this instance will not be carried down the sides, a drawing of five or six threads at a suitable distance from the top and bottom of the sheet will suffice.

The most approved method of working simple hem stitch is shown in Fig. 111, and a little careful study of the engraving, together with the following explanations, should render it quite easy. In this example the hem is represented as being turned down in position on the upper or right side of the material, and the stitching is executed from right to left along the upper edge of the drawn open threads. Of course it is optional to turn the hem on the wrong side, if preferred; but handkerchiefs, sheets, d'oyleys, and such

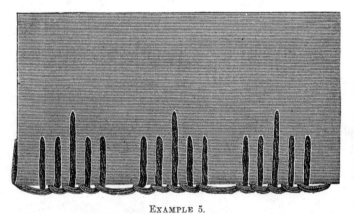

EXAMPLE 5.
Fig. 101.—Blanket Stitches.

things as are made with fabric both sides alike are generally hemmed in the way here depicted, as the fold looks pretty rather than otherwise. Get your needle threaded with whatever thread you intend working—we will always in these instructions term the working thread "cotton," to avoid confusing it with the threads of the linen material—secure the end of the cotton inside the fold of the hem at the extreme right-hand side of the piece of material, and holding the hem over the first finger of the left hand, bring the needle and cotton out two threads above the fold of the hem, insert the needle between the open threads directly under the place the cotton is brought out, and passing it from right to left take up three open threads on the needle and draw the cotton through, insert the needle in the same place as before, but in a slightly upward direction to pass through the hem in position, as in the engraving, Fig. 111, and bring it out two threads above the fold of the hem straight above the cotton of the stitch just worked and three threads to the left of where the cotton was first brought out, and draw the cotton through, * insert the needle from right to left to take up the next three threads of drawn open linen and draw the cotton through, insert the needle in the same place, but turning it in a slightly upward direction through the hem, bring it out straight above the cotton of the stitch just worked, two threads above the fold of the hem, and three threads to the left of where the cotton was before brought out, as represented in the engraving, draw the cotton through, and repeat from * to the end of the line of drawn open threads. You will observe that there are two motions in every stitch ; the first motion is taken from right to left in the drawn open threads, and the second motion confines the group of drawn threads in a cluster, secures the hem, and brings the cotton in position for working the next successive stitch. Be careful to

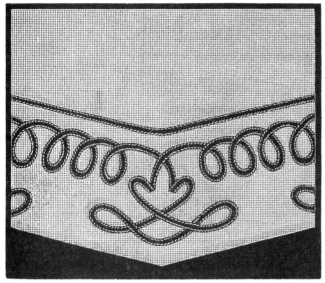

Fig 102.—Braiding.

make every stitch perfectly true and regular, and draw the cotton close, but not so tight as to pucker the material.

This hem stitch is very extensively used in drawn thread embroidery to strengthen the upper and lower edge of nearly all open-work insertions; it may be made as deep as desired, and while it forms a strengthening ornamental overcast stitch on the margin of the solid linen, it at the same time confines a certain number of open threads into clusters (two, three, four, six, or eight threads in a cluster), according to the requirement of the pattern that is to be worked, as will be explained in succeeding examples.

Fig. 112 shows another way of working simple hem stitch, and which very much resembles the hem stitch of the preceding example, and can be used for the same purposes, but it is worked in a rather different manner, and, on examination of the engraving, it will be seen that the stitches slant obliquely instead of standing perpendicularly upright, besides which the two component parts of each stitch are entwined together. Draw out four threads of linen, and turn down a hem, as instructed in Fig. 111. The hem stitching is worked from right to left. Secure the end of the cotton inside the fold of the hem at the right-hand side of the piece of material, hold the hem over the first finger of the left hand, and bring up the needle and cotton in the hem two threads above the fold, * hold the cotton under the left-hand thumb, insert the needle in the open insertion two threads to the right from where the cotton is brought out in the hem, and take four open threads on the needle (as see illustration Fig. 112), and passing the needle above the cotton held by the left-hand thumb, draw the cotton through in a sort of button-stitch loop, insert the needle in the little space you will see at the left of the cluster of threads just drawn together, and bring it out in the hem two threads above the fold and four threads to the left of the last stitch in the hem, and draw the cotton through, and repeat from *. This proceeding clusters four threads together in each stitch, and the stitch in the hem always emerges above the middle of a cluster.

Fig. 113 shows still another method of doing hem stitch, and which is worked from left to right, and the stitches slant obliquely. It is a very pretty stitch, easy of execution, and may by some workers be preferred to either of the foregoing examples. Prepare the material by drawing out four threads, and turn down a hem as previously instructed. Secure the end of the cotton inside the fold of the hem at the extreme left-hand side of the piece of material ; hold the hem over the finger of the left hand, and bring up the needle and cotton in the hem two threads above the fold, * insert the needle from right to left to take up three of the open threads, bringing the needle out exactly under the cotton that proceeds out of the hem, and draw the cotton through ; insert the needle in the same space of open threads and bring it up perpendicularly two threads above the fold of the hem, in the position represented in the engraving, which is three threads distant from the last stitch in the hem, and draw the cotton through, and continue from *, taking three threads farther to the right in each consecutive stitch.

Fig. 114 gives an open hem-stitch insertion differing somewhat from Fig. 109, but could be used for the same purpose. It is made by working a line of simple hem-stitch along both the upper and lower edge of an insertion of drawn threads ; this method of hem-stitching forms the foundation of numerous elaborate patterns, and serves a twofold purpose, as it not only strengthens each margin of solid linen, but at the same time confines the open threads in even, regular clusters. Commence operations by drawing out eight threads. Work from right to left. Secure the end of the cotton with which you intend working on the right-hand side of the linen near the upper edge of the drawn insertion, either by a knot or by a small invisible stitch on the wrong side of the fabric, bring the needle and cotton out three threads above the open insertion, insert the needle between the open threads directly under the place the cotton is brought out, and, passing it from right to left, take up three open threads on the needle, and draw the cotton through, insert the needle in the same place, but in a slightly upward direction, and bring it out three threads above the open insertion, straight above the cotton of the stitch just worked, and three threads to the left of where the cotton was first brought out (see position of the needle in Fig. 114), and draw the cotton through. This is practically the same stitch as simple hem-stitch, Fig. 111 ; but here the stitches are deeper, as they cover three threads of the solid linen instead of only two threads, and thus are better adapted for fancy purposes. Continue working in the same manner to the end of the line of drawn open threads, drawing the cotton close, but not so tight as to pucker the linen, and be very careful to confine the same number of threads in each cluster, or the bars will be irregular, and not perfectly straight. When you reach the end of the line, fasten off the cotton securely by running the end in through some of the worked stitches. Turn the work, so that the edge of the open insertion, which before was at the top, is now at the bottom, and repeat the hem stitch, taking up the same clusters of threads which you took in the first row ; the counting will not now be difficult, as the stitches of the first row will have made a little parting in the open threads between the clusters, to indicate where to place the clusters of the second row.

The art of forming groups and clusters is of very great importance in drawn thread work, and particular attention must always be paid to the working of the *first* row, for upon this, in a measure, the whole beauty of the work depends, and sometimes a very slight inaccuracy will throw out a whole pattern.

———

Fig. 103.—Turret Buttonholing.

Fig. 115.—ALPHABET AND FIGURES.

Worked in satin stitch, either with cotton, silk, or flax thread, and will be found suitable for marking small articles, such as handkerchiefs, finger napkins, d'oyleys, mats, &c. ———

Fig. 116.—ALPHABET AND FIGURES.

These old English letters and figures executed in satin stitch are for marking handkerchiefs and such small articles, and should first be pencilled upon the material, then worked over with cotton or silk.

Fig. 117.—MONOGRAM, A. W.

THIS is worked purely in satin stitch with embroidery cotton, and such a monogram will be found useful for marking handkerchiefs, scarfs, &c. It could also be worked in silk, or even flax thread, both letters in one colour, or each in a distinct shade such as pale green and pink, dark brown and blue, brown and pink, brown and maize, &c. When worked on coloured silk neck-wraps it is as well to repeat the colours in the embroidery.

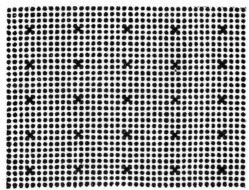

Fig. 105.—Cardboard Chart for Smocking.

Fig. 118.—CROSS-STITCH MONOGRAMS.

THESE eleven designs show useful size monograms for marking purposes, worked in two coloured ingrain cottons. The darker colour should be selected for the principal letter. Cross-stitch marking is extremely simple to execute, and a plain alphabet of capital and small letters, likewise a set of figures, are illustrated on page 13 of No. 103 of this series, where are also given full directions for marking.

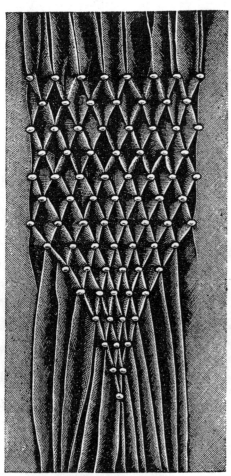

Fig. 104.—Honeycomb.

ON MENDING.

WHEN sheets begin to wear in the centre they should be patched at once; or, if this is not considered advisable, the sheet should be cut straight down the middle lengthways, when the selvedges are joined together to make a new

centre, and the raw edges are hemmed for the outside of the sheet. Treated thus, the sheets will last nearly as long again, and if the seam is neatly sewn it will not be any detriment or inconvenience. Another way is to turn the ends to the middle, in which case the join runs across the sheet, and the thin parts, which are re-hemmed, come at the top and bottom. Fig. 4 shows the quickest and simplest method of seaming a sheet, though, as you are upon selvedges, there is of course no raw edge to be turned down for felling. Some people prefer doing it in the manner shown in Fig. 13, these numbers being illustrated in No. 98, which is the 1st Series of Plain Needlework.

If blankets get thin and old they can be patched with a piece cut from another old blanket. These should never be thrown away; the very worst of them will answer for house cloths and polishing cloths. But if you happen to

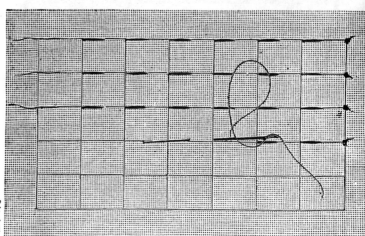

Fig. 106.—Showing Method of Drawing Lines on Material, and Gathering Commenced.

possess two or three old blankets the most beneficial way to use them is to make a soft warm quilt for the poor by tacking them together one over the other, and then quilting them within two pieces of soft print. Quilting is represented in Fig. 100. You can, with a flat yard measure, draw diagonal lines across and across the print in diamond fashion, and stitch over the lines with a machine, or run by hand, taking care that the stitches go through and through.

If you intend giving half-worn flannel petticoats to the poor, see that they are well mended, and you will much enhance the value of your present. Poor folks have little time for mending, and small ability to do it properly. Patch all thin places, and if there are any tiny holes let them be darned with wool as you would darn hosiery. See that buttons and strings are all right.

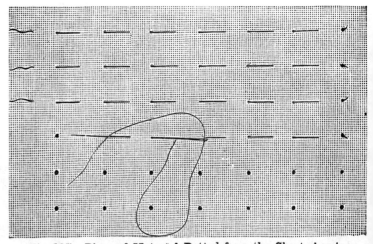

Fig. 107.—Piece of Material Dotted from the Chart showing Method of Gathering.

Table-cloths are frequently disfigured by being cut accidentally with a knife, and all such little cuts should be darned as soon as perceived, or they will fray, and be much more troublesome to repair after they are washed than if attended to immediately. Sometimes the corners of table-cloths get torn by reason of being pegged on a line to dry, in which case the corners may be neatly rounded off and hemmed.

The wear of men's shirts can be lengthened by setting on new collars and new wristbands, and indeed nothing looks worse than to see these worn all frayed and ragged when a little proper attention would put them to rights. Any places that get thin under the arms should be patched; the patches will not be seen under a waistcoat.

In patching lined clothing the patch may be slipped between the lining and the cloth.

All underlinen should be repaired before it gets too bad; in fact, all the family garments should be looked over after passing through the laundry, and the things that require mending should be consigned to the mending basket to await a convenient opportunity. Some people mend as much as they can before sending the things to be washed, and indeed it is a very good practice, and much to be commended.

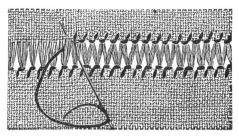

Fig. 109.—Trellis Hem-Stitch.

USEFUL HINTS.

HOSIERY should be strengthened before being worn by darning a strand of wool or cotton in the stocking web of the heels and toes; this makes the stockings wear a great deal longer, and is especially advised for children's stockings and socks. Boys' stockings should be strengthened in the knees also. Strengthening is effected by running neatly and longtitudinally over the stocking web, taking up one thread and missing three. A long slim

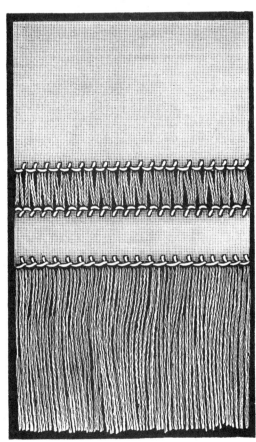

Fig. 108.—Fringing.

needle should be employed. Run the needle in and out its whole length before drawing through, then, when you turn and go upon the next line of the stocking web, you will take up the centre thread of those you missed and miss the three next, so always taking up one and missing three throughout the strengthening process, and leaving a little loop at the top and at the bottom of the darn in case the strengthening should shrink in washing. Use wool as nearly as possible the same kind and colour as the original stocking for strengthening a wool stocking; if any difference, it may be a trifle finer.

Strutts' Angola mending is much used. Brooks' embroidery cotton is good to employ for white cotton stockings.

To sew on buttons exactly where they should be is a difficult task for many, but may be easily accomplished in this way: Place the garment upon the table in front of you, and lay the side containing the button holes over the other side, just as it is to be when fastened. Now pin the pieces together at top and bottom, and keep them on the stretch while you stick a pin through each buttonhole into the fabric where the buttons are to be sewn. If you are careful to hold the garment aright you will have the pins stuck in just where the buttons are to be. Open out the garment, letting the pins slip through the buttonholes; you can then place them in firmer, and they denote the position for sewing on the buttons.

Many mothers find it difficult to keep the feet of an infant or young child covered and warm through the winter nights. This is the way in which it can be managed: Cut the back breadth of the little nightgown eight or ten inches longer than the front, make a deep hem, and fold up the extra length like the flap of a sachet. The fold should be held in place by three buttons and corresponding buttonholes; the child can never kick through this, and yet it allows perfect freedom of action, which is impossible when the nightgown is drawn in at the bottom, bag fashion, with strings.

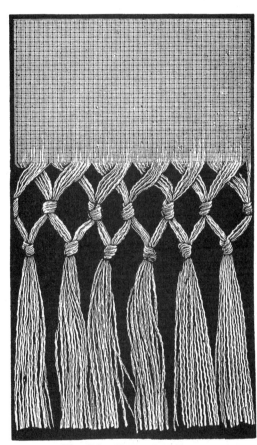

Fig. 110.—Knotted Fringe.

A nightingale is a most comfortable thing for an invalid or elderly person to wear sitting up in bed. One can be made of 2 yards of scarlet flannel. Fold the flannel exactly in half and cut a slit 6 inches deep on one side of the fold. Now bind the whole way round the flannel, including the slit, with narrow black ribbon or with black mohair braid. Measure 8 inches from the top of the slit, and fold the corners of the flannel back on each side like a sailor's collar, and catch this together at the top with a bow of ribbon to form the back of the neck, and put another similar bow at the bottom of the slit; a fancy button may be sewn upon each turned-down collar, if liked. The two lower back corners of the flannel are also turned back in triangular fashion, and connected with a bit of elastic, or they may button over, to form a place to slip the hands through; the points of the turned-back angles may be ornamented with buttons to match. Ribbon strings are put to tie the nightingale under the chin.

14

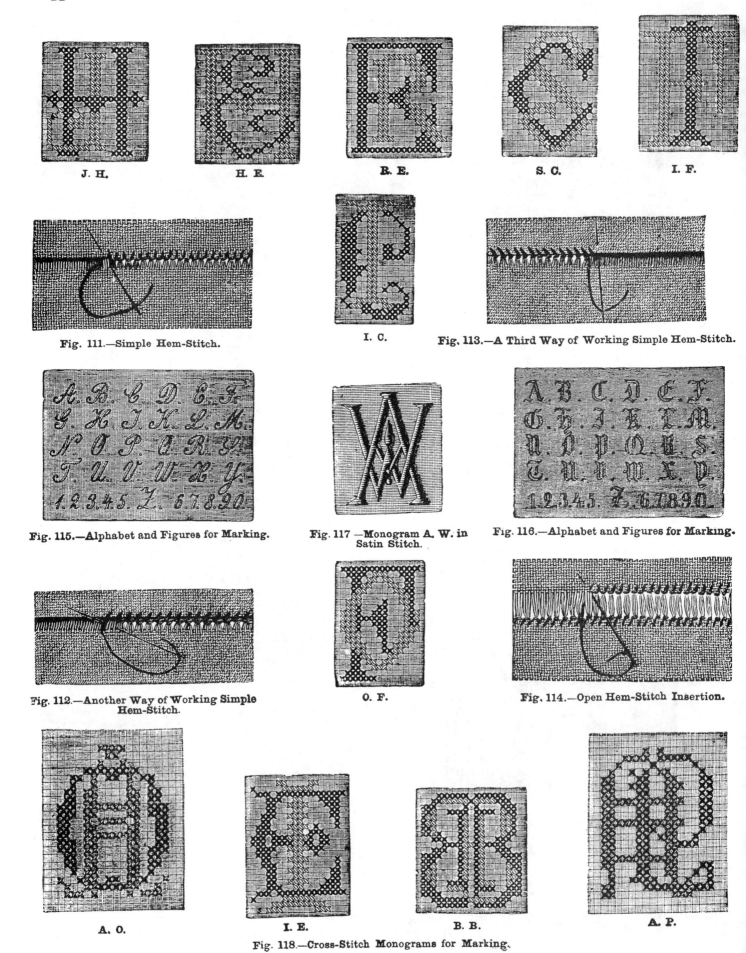

J. H.

H. E.

R. E.

S. C.

I. F.

Fig. 111.—Simple Hem-Stitch.

I. C.

Fig. 113.—A Third Way of Working Simple Hem-Stitch.

Fig. 115.—Alphabet and Figures for Marking.

Fig. 117.—Monogram A. W. in Satin Stitch.

Fig. 116.—Alphabet and Figures for Marking.

Fig. 112.—Another Way of Working Simple Hem-Stitch.

O. F.

Fig. 114.—Open Hem-Stitch Insertion.

A. O.

I. E.

B. B.

A. P.

Fig. 118.—Cross-Stitch Monograms for Marking.

[60]

WELDON'S
PRACTICAL MONOGRAMS AND INITIALS.

(FIRST SERIES.)

Original Designs for Marking Household Linen, Handkerchiefs, Book Covers, Sachets, &c.

THIRTY-THREE ILLUSTRATIONS.

EMBROIDERED MONOGRAMS & INITIALS.

"The great variety of needleworks which the ingenious women of other countries as well as of our own have invented will furnish us with constant and amusing employment, and though our labours may not equal a Mineron's or an Aylesbury's, yet, if they unbend the mind, by fixing its attention on the progress of any elegant and imitative art, they answer the purpose of domestic amusement; and, when the higher duties of our station do not call forth our exertions, we may feel the satisfaction of knowing that we are, at least, innocently employed."—MRS. GRIFFITH.

EMBROIDERY is the art of adding to the surface of woven textures a representation of any object through the medium of the needle threaded with the material with which the work is to be executed. The word embroidery is derived from the French *broderie*. We are indebted to the East for the invention of embroidery—an art that has not inaptly been termed the mother of painting.

The Greeks, however, gave the honour of the invention of this art to Minerva, and although its discovery claims the priority of many centuries, embroidery is still practised in every nation, for—

"Our country is fild
With ladies and with gentlewomen, skild
In this rare art."—TAYLOR.

Although it really seems to have attained a higher degree of perfection in France than in any other country, for here it is that one can buy the most lovely embroidered lingerie and mouchoir anywhere to be obtained.

Mr. Lane ("Manners and Customs of the Modern Egyptians") says: "Their leisure hours are mostly spent in working with the needle, and many women, even in the houses of the wealthy, replenish their private purses by embroidering handkerchiefs, and employing a *della' leh* to take them to the market, or to the hhaaree'ms for sale."

Embroidery for marking household linen, underclothing, handkerchiefs, &c., although it has certainly not fallen into abeyance, has been receiving less attention of late than its importance merits; for although marking ink is all very well in its way, and undoubtedly offers a quick method of marking linen goods, it certainly cannot lay the least pretension to daintiness or refinement, and we should hope there are yet many women who still prefer to see their belongings marked with a daintily embroidered design. Embroidered monograms and initials for marking and adorning household linen, underwear, handkerchiefs, book covers, cushions, is therefore a subject well worthy attention, and we therefore devote this issue to designs suitable for every purpose that monograms and initials are required.

The variety of stitches that can be used is infinite, comprising, as it does, satin stitch, which takes the first place as favourite, then overcast, crewel, eyelet holes, coral, back stitches, also chain, cross or Russian stitch. The choice of threads is as varied as are the styles, sizes, and designs for the letters. There are Strutts' knitting and embroidery cottons, and flax threads for house linen, fancy linen tea-cloths, sideboard slips, &c.; Moravian thread for handkerchiefs, d'oyleys, and fine work; washing silks and coloured thread galore; also Messrs. Carl Mez and Söhne's brilliant threads of all sizes suitable for linen or cotton marking, rugs, quilts, and such large pieces of work. Next come all sorts of filoselle, filofloss, gold and silver thread, passings and bullions, to say nothing of the beads, spangles, fancy cords, &c., that can so often be introduced with good effect when ornamenting such articles as cushions, portfolios, music-cases, blotters, &c.

First of all, in order to utilize the designs for monograms and letters as given here, it is necessary to fully understand how to transfer the designs to the material. Trace the design upon a sheet of tracing or tissue paper, then the linen and the traced design can either be held up against the window glass and the outlines followed with a lead pencil, or transfer paper or cloth can be used. The latter plan is especially convenient when the linen is coloured, in that the marks on the ordinary paper are not readily seen when held up to the light or when dark-coloured silk or satin is used. Both transfer paper and cloth are to be had at Berlin wool shops or stationers. If the former is chosen, the worker should choose black-lead paper in preference to blue, as the mark made by the latter tint does not readily wash out. The cloth can also be had in either white or blue, and has the advantage of sticking to the material as the pencil passes over it, thus obviating any fear of making uneven lines by the fabrics slipping out of place.

To use either the cloth or paper, the satin should be laid face upwards on the table, over it should be placed the transfer linen, with the prepared side downwards, and over this again the pattern, right side uppermost. The three layers should be either held together with drawing-pins or with weights at the edges, so that they will not slip, and the outlines are then to be followed with the point of a knitting needle, crochet hook, or even with a bodkin, provided that when used with firm though even pressure, it passes over the design without tearing the paper. After all the outlines have been followed both layers of paper should be removed from the satin, when the design should be found clearly and distinctly marked in its right place upon the material.

No. 1.—Embroidered Initial for Household Linen.

The letter thus traced, the method of working it must be decided upon. When a somewhat elaborate style of embroidery is required, it is as well to avoid puckering the material by stretching it in a frame. For handkerchiefs and similar work of small extent a round tambour or drum-head frame is very convenient. Such frames are to be had at an extremely low cost at most fancy shops, and their great advantage is that the work can be stretched in a moment without the trouble of sewing that is necessary for the ordinary embroidery stretcher.

After the work is finished it is always an improvement to lay a damp cloth over it, and to iron it at the back with a tolerably hot flat iron. When bullion and similar ornamentation have been used the work cannot be laid on the table while it is ironed, but must be held out taut, wrong side upmost, by two people while a third passes the iron over the back of it. Even when the work has been executed in satin stitch it is as well, if it is in high relief, to iron it in this way, or to lay the embroidery flat upon several folds of thick blanket This will be well understood by workers of Mountmellick embroidery.

When an initial has been worked upon any material such as holland, the back should be rubbed over with a little embroidery paste before it is cut round and appliqué to the handsomer fabric. This will prevent the edges from ravelling unduly.

No. 1.—EMBROIDERED INITIAL FOR HOUSEHOLD LINEN.

HERE is shown an effective and quickly executed letter for the purpose of marking sheets, pillow cases, table linen, &c., worked in satin stitch an French knots, the broad parts of the stem being padded or filled in first b closely set lines of running stitches as explained in description of Nos. 2 and 3.

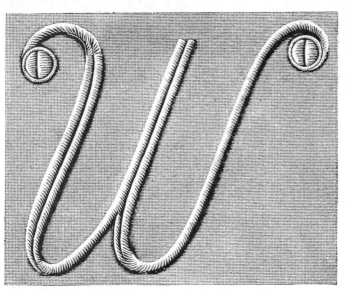

No 2.—Satin-Stitch Letter for House Linen.

Nos. 2 and 3.—SATIN-STITCH LETTERS FOR HOUSE LINEN.

PLAINLY worked letters of varying sizes are most frequently used for the marking of sheets, table-cloths, and similar large pieces of napery. For such letters there is no stitch equal to satin stitch, both for general richness of appearance and durability.

It is necessary for the letter to be in somewhat high relief to get the proper effect. With this end in view the whole of the space between the outlines must first be filled in with closely-set lines of running or darning stitches as the diagram here shows. Over these must be made a second series of stitches and even a third, if the raising made by two sets does not seem to be enough. The relief is generally required higher in the middle than at the sides of the design, to give a nice roundness, and to manage this it is necessary to add another line or two of darned stitches down the centre. Some workers raise the letters by couching several strands of embroidery cotton over the design, adding more threads wherever it is thought advisable to add to the relief.

Diagram showing Method of Working Raised Satin Stitch.

In working padding of any sort, it must be remembered that satin stitch cannot be made successfully over any space that is at the utmost half an inch broad. The strands of the thread in such a case become very readily disarranged, and it is, besides, very difficult to induce them to set evenly one below the other. When a wide space has to be filled it is better to divide it into two divisions, making a double row of stitches across the letter in its widest part. Such an arrangement is shown by Illustration No. 2, which represents the letter W in its natural working size, but which can be still further enlarged if desired. The thick down-strokes will be seen to be worked as above mentioned. This matter must be borne in mind while the padding is being placed, and a line of material without any covering should be left all down the centre of the widest part. In the same way the boss with which each end of the letter is finished off is divided thus into two and here the division is still clearly defined. When satin stitch is worked over only two threads or so of the material it is known as overcast stitch and generally needs by way of padding one line only of darning or running stitches. This is shown in the line which encircles the bosses.

When satin stitch is correctly worked it should need no outline, but the stitches should set so exactly even with each other as to appear almost as if woven in one piece. So, too, there should be a considerable amount of solidity about it when well executed, and the stitches should be so tightly and firmly placed that they cannot be disarranged with wear and tear; yet they must not

be too lightly drawn, or when the work is washed the material will pucker up. When a more ornamental letter is desired than that just described, a little fancy embroidery can be introduced, as in Illustration No. 3. Many ladies have the hem of the upper sheet decorated with a border of drawn-thread work, or edged with a frill of lace, or Cash's Patent Frilling; and when this is the case, the initial or monogram is worked above the insertion or hem, and in the middle, and also appears in the centre of pillow case, or even the pillow sham.

The letter L, No. 3, shows the addition of some decoration in the shape of leaves and small bosses or berries. The letter is worked in satin stitch, as described for No. 2, but the two round spaces or bosses at each end are, by way of variety, outlined with overcast stitch and filled in with seed or dot stitch. The latter stitch consists merely of tiny back stitches scattered here and there at haphazard upon the material. In seed stitch they are not larger than the point of a pin; in dot stitch they are more nearly the size of the head of the pin, and are often slightly raised by being worked double—that is, one exactly on the top of another.

The leaves and berries are worked in satin stitch, one larger one being worked in two parts, while the stems are made in overcast stitch. In working round patterns, such as berries in satin stitch, the padding generally consists of small running stitches taken in a circular direction, and over one another again towards the middle to raise the boss. Some workers roll up a tiny tuft of cotton wool, and catch it down with a few stitches taken across it from edge to edge of the design; but, as a rule, the work is more solid and less likely to sink with wear and washing when the padding is formed by actual stitches. When the satin stitch is to be made the boss should be begun with a short stitch taken almost along the edge of one side of the design; the next stitch should be rather longer, and from edge to edge of the traced pattern, and the next longer still. When half the circle has been covered, the remaining stitches must diminish in size again very gradually till the boss is finished.

Another method would be to work these circles or bosses as eyelet holes, either overcast or buttonholed round, the effect of which is exceedingly good. Another variation is brought about by groups of French knots instead of satin stitch, outlining each boss with a ring of crewel stitch.

No. 3.—Ornamental Satin-Stitch Letter.

No. 4.—CORDED INITIAL.

THERE is a particular make of fine white flax cord to be had at most fancy shops, and which is well adapted for the decoration of large, plain letters, such as are often required upon linen articles. This cord may be highly recommended to those workers who are unable to execute satin stitch successfully, for, by using it in masses, a good effect may be gained. White thread or strong cotton should be used for sewing down the cord.

A simple and effective way of using cord for a single letter is that shown by Illustration No. 4. Here the initial is simply outlined with a single line of cord, the space between which being ornamented with rather large French knots; or a row of cord could be carried down the centre and French knots on either side. Again, if the space between the cord be entirely filled instead

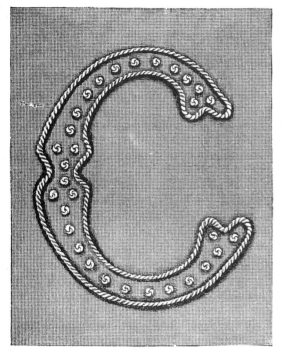

No. 4.—Corded Initial.

No. 5.—Long Initial.

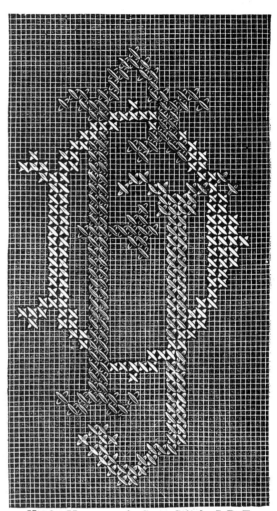

No. 6.—Monogram in Cross Stitch, J. D. F.

No. 7.—Fancy Letter.

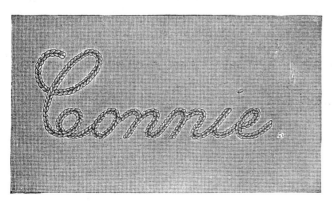

No 8.—Embroidered Name in Chain Stitch.

No. 9.—Triple Monogram, S. L. B.

of as illustrated, there would be an opportunity for the introduction of a little colour, and in that case the cord should be oversewn with some of the same tint. This would be a pretty model for interweaving with a floral design upon cloth, satin, holland, &c., for a book cover or sachet. Here the cord might well be gold, or a mixture of gold and coloured silk, while the French knots may be of brightly tinted silk, or spangles, beads, or tiny jewels could be used according to fancy. Chenille, too, would make a pretty outline for an initial of this sort.

No. 5.—LONG INITIAL.

THIS style of initial is useful for placing down the side of a book cover, a pillow slip, corner of a towel, &c., and is intended for working in satin stitch, or can be outlined with crewel stitch, &c., and centred French knots.

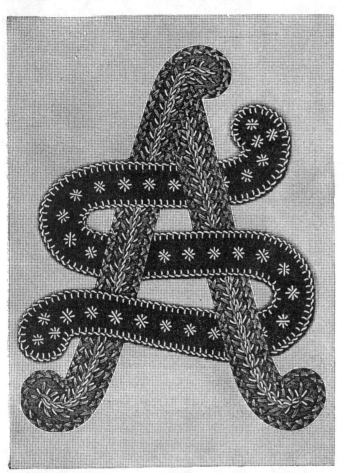

No. 10.—Monogram in Appliqué.

No. 6.—MONOGRAM IN CROSS STITCH.

THIS is composed of three letters, J. D. F., and offers an idea for the combination of any other three letters, or even two if desired. It is suitable for all purposes where cross-stitch letters are employed, such as the side of a photo frame, a work bag, book cover, &c., and our engraving gives it in natural working size. As a suggestion, the palest tint of cotton or silk should be devoted to the first letter of the name, a medium shade to the D, and dark tint to the F, which is the initial of the surname. Our specimen was executed in pale pink for the J, old gold for the D, and bronze for the F. This monogram is equally adapted to working in satin or some more fanciful stitch for book covers, sachets, &c.

No. 7.—FANCY LETTER.

A PRETTY style of letter for the ornamentation of household linen, blotter or book covers, sachets, &c., and can be worked in silk or cotton, in satin or any fancy stitch. If in satin stitch, its widest parts would be done in two rows, as No. 3 explains, or it could be embroidered in a fanciful way, as suggested by No. 1. The same shape letter is shown by No. 9, used as a monogram.

No. 8.—EMBROIDERED NAME IN CHAIN STITCH.

A PRETTY style for marking handkerchiefs, &c., it being first written on the fabric in bold roundhand, then worked over with white or coloured cotton in chain stitch. Crewel, some of the many kinds of coral stitch, and overcast stitch, to say nothing of French knots, are all available. Very fine gold thread, such as is made up of wire, and not paper, is also largely used at the present time for names of this sort when they are worked upon nightdress sachets,

handkerchief cases, and other fanciful knicknacks. If required, washing gold thread can be had, and as it is much employed in the embroidery upon tea-cloths, sideboard slips, &c., it is equally appropriate for any marking that may be placed upon them.

No. 9.—TRIPLE MONOGRAM.

HERE is shown a prettily-arranged monogram of three letters, S. L. B., suitable for working in solid satin stitch after the style of No. 3, or it could be outlined with cord, centred French knots, as No. 4. Again, it could have each letter worked in a different stitch, or even in a different colour, according to the purpose to which it is to be applied. It is suited to the marking of household linen, for blotting books, cushions, &c., and it could be cut out in cloth and appliquéd on to the article after the style shown by Nos. 10 and 11.

Nos. 10 and 11.—APPLIQUÉ MONOGRAMS.

THERE are many purposes for which an extremely large and bold monogram or initial is required, and when this is the case Illustrations Nos. 10 and 11 will be found most suitable. Appliqué is called into requisition, and the device is cut out of some totally different material to that upon which the letter is to be worked, and then sewn down to the foundation. Such letters are suitable for the centre of a coverlet or bedspread, or summer and winter carriage rugs, horse blankets, mailcart and perambulator wraps, travelling rugs, sofa blankets, and similar large articles.

No. 10 gives the initials A. S. and No. 11, A. G., executed in two distinct styles, No. 11 showing quite a simple method, while No. 10 goes into more elaboration, and, in fact, offers more scope for the ingenuity of the worker. No. 11 monogram is such as would be employed upon a holland carriage rug, where the letters would have a good effect if cut out of Turkey red or navy blue twill, while, as a rule, the colours of the livery and the upholstery of the carriage itself have to be taken into account.

No. 11.—Simple Appliqué Monogram.

The letters must first be traced upon the material chosen for them, then a very little embroidery paste should be rubbed with the finger over the back, and, when this is dry, the letters should be cut out. The object of the paste is to prevent the material from fraying unduly when it is cut. The monogram should be tacked firmly in place upon the rug in the centre just below the hem; while horse rugs or blankets are marked on the right-hand corner at back. It is a good plan to use very small stitches in the tacking or overcasting down of the edges of the letters to the rug.

There are several ways in which the edges may be worked. In the Illustration No. 11 they are outlined by tacking on a row of narrow scarlet braid, and over which is worked a series of buttonhole stitches at an eighth or quarter-inch intervals, with coarse amber flax thread. If preferred, the letters may be caught down with closely-set buttonhole stitches only, executed with flax thread of a contrasting colour, or with embroidery cotton, or even silk to match the applied material. It is a good idea, too, to use several strands of white knitting cotton, and to couch them down with coloured stitches. Yet another plan is to employ Harris' Flax Cord, which can be had in many mixtures of colour, but whatever is chosen should be wide enough to completely hide the tacking or overcast stitches which hold the letters down to the background. Sometimes, if a small amount only of ornamentation is desired, a row of French knots, at quarter-inch intervals, is worked just inside the border stitches of the letters with very good effect. Upon such strictly useful articles, however, as dogs' coats and horsecloths, this more decorative addition is omitted. Another plan is to form the letters of wide, or several rows of narrow braid. The wide

No. 12.—Ornamental Letters in Chain Stitch.

braid looks well outlined on its edge, or just beyond the edge, with French knots, worked in silk or cotton of a contrasting colour to the braid. Rows of narrow braid look well divided and outlined with French knots.

A far more ornamental style of appliqué is that shown in No. 10. Here the two letters are of different colours, the A being cut out in terra-cotta twill or cloth, and the S in navy blue, or any other combination of colour desired, both being carefully intertwined, and tacked or overcast upon a foundation as already explained. Several shades of colour are used for the embroidery; the S, for instance, has its edges worked with closely-set small buttonhole stitches executed in porcelain blue embroidery cotton, while at intervals along the centre of the letter are worked small stars or even raised dots, or French knots executed with the same cotton. The A is caught down with miniature herringbone stitch worked in bright red thread, and in working, one end of each stitch should rest upon the letter, and the other on the foundation. They should also be set tolerably close together, so that the cut margins of the material are entirely hidden, as well as thoroughly secured to the foundation. Down the centre is carried a line of fishbone stitch, or buttonhole veining, as it is sometimes called. This consists of a buttonhole stitch of nearly half an inch in length, worked first on one side, then on the other, of a central line, and in the example these stitches are about a quarter of an inch apart. This space is afterwards filled up by a set of stitches like isolated satin stitch, one of which is worked between each of the buttonhole stitches, and finally a line of crewel stitch is carried down by the side of the line which connected the fishbone stitches. These second and third sets of stitches should be worked with thread of a contrasting colour to the first, and in the original bright yellow was used.

No. 12.—ORNAMENTAL LETTERS IN CHAIN STITCH.

THIS simple stitch is very effective for working initials either in white or coloured cottons, silks, &c., according to the article they are to adorn. Our specimen was worked in butcher blue cotton, forming the leaves and shield of Turkey red cotton, and the initials can be any size desired. Cotton of a rather coarse make is required to give the raised effect. Then, after outlining the letters upon the material, go round them in chain stitch, and after this fill them in with row after row, as the illustration clearly shows. Leave each stitch somewhat loose, so that the needle may be readily passed under it on the right side; and this is more especially necessary when working upon a material to

be washed, otherwise tight stitches mean that the foundation will be drawn and cockled.

The full stops after each letter are worked in French knots. The small leaves are in Gordon knot stitch, which will be familiar to all Mountmellick embroidery workers. It is executed thus : Bring up the needle and cotton to the front of the fabric in the place where you desire to commence working, hold the cotton for an instant under the left-hand thumb, pass the needle from right to left under the cotton so held, and with a gentle movement of the thumb push the cotton upwards under the point of the needle; turn all the cotton upwards, reverse the position of the needle from left to right, and insert it horizontally to take up a thread or two of the material in the place where the knot is to be formed, that is, at the distance of one-eighth of an inch or so below where the cotton was brought out; turn the cotton downwards under the point of the needle, and draw carefully through. You will have a long stitch and a knot stitch. All succeeding knots are formed in the same way, and all equidistant one from the other. The stitch requires practice, but is done quickly enough when once you get into the way of it.

The outline of the shield is followed with spaced buttonhole stitch, arranged with one long and one short stitch; the straight edge of the stitches resting precisely on the outline. This outlining can be worked entirely in the red cotton, or in red and blue, while there are many other stitches which are equally appropriate for outlining purposes.

No. 13.—HANDSOME INITIAL FOR BLOTTER OR BOOK COVER.

SUCH a letter as that shown by Illustration No. 13 forms a sufficient decoration in itself for one side of a blotter, book cover, sachet, or work bag, centre of a cushion, corner of a fancy table cover, &c., and it is no difficult task to add more of the delicate scroll work, if in its present form the initial does not completely fill the space allotted to it.

No. 13.—Handsome Initial for Blotter or Book Cover.

If the material chosen for the embroidery is satin, moiré, brocade, or any similar material, it is advisable to stretch it in a frame rather than to run any risk of puckering by working it over the hand. Also, unless the fabric be unusually thick, it should be backed with some unbleached holland such as is used for church work. The same remark applies to velvet, but here it is, as a rule, a mistake to work a letter directly upon the material, a far better effect being gained, and the work being fresher and more highly raised, when it is executed upon some other material, and then applied to the velvet.

The initial R chosen as an example is six inches high and five wide, and being very simple in form, can easily be enlarged. Its broad, even surface entirely covered with closely-set "feather" stitches, "long and short," as they are sometimes called. If these are well worked and if the needleful of silk is discarded directly it appears in the slightest degree frayed, the effect should be that of a silk appliqué rather than hand-worked embroidery.

Some workers find that they are unable to fill in all the interstices between the stitches sufficiently with one layer of threads only. The plan then pursued is as follows; first, if filoselle be used, the whole of the letter is carefully covered with the crewel stitches made with three strands of the silk. This done, a second set of similar stitches is made with two strands only of the silk and these are placed not over, but between, those of the first working, with the object of filling up any open spaces there may chance to be between them. Finally, a third series of stitches is made with one thread and these fill up even the tiny gaps that may remain. When finished, the surface of the work should be as smooth and soft as satin with not a break to mark the beginning and end of any of the stitches. Filofloss lends itself particularly well to such a method of execution, and when the letter is shaded instead of being treated as a broad, flat surface, it is really wonderful to see the way in which the different tints blend one with the other.

Our example is worked with flame-coloured silk upon electric blue moiré,

with back or stem stitch if preferred, and look very pretty on certain shades of colour if fine gold or copper passing is employed. On many old pieces of work spaced buttonhole stitch is used for such a purpose, the short stitches bristling out along the outside of the curves.

There is a great fancy just now for making ornamental book covers and blotters of tinted linen, and these very frequently have no further ornament than that given by one huge letter, such as that now under consideration. Upon this material darning serves very well for filling in the body of the letter. Each stitch should be about a quarter of an inch in length, and about two threads of the material should be picked up between each one. No settled plan need be followed as regards the proper alternation of the stitches in each row, but they should be placed tolerably close together. A raised knot stitch has an excellent effect as an outlining, but, if preferred, there are many fine white cords and braids, known as Soutache, that may be used instead, and which will produce a still more raised effect.

There is yet another way of managing such a letter upon tinted linen. This is to cover the background with darning, and to leave the initial entirely unworked, as the darning will form it, or it could be outlined with chain stitch, after the style shown by No. 14. It could also be outlined with

No. 14.—Darned Initial.

and is bordered with a double strand of Japanese gold thread, caught down with stitches of fine flame-coloured silk. The broad surface of the letter is broken up by jewels, which are sprinkled here and there about it. Yellow topaz was the stone chosen, with a sapphire in the point where the curves of the letter meet. If the effect of these gems is not liked, large bosses of satin stitch, worked in the two colours, may be employed instead. These should be raised rather high over a padding, as already described, and look more effective when worked with a different make of silk to that employed for the letter. For instance, if filoselle or filofloss has been chosen for the initial, the bosses will look well in coarse purse twist, or, if the embroideress is sufficiently skilful, with bullion or gold thread.

The spray work with which this letter is surrounded is one of its chief beauties, softening as it does the otherwise hard outlines, and breaking up the strong contrast between the gold thread and the silk. The stitch used for this is the ordinary single coral or feather stitch, so generally chosen for the decoration of underlinen, but it is worked here with a single strand of cream filofloss. Each little stitch is placed at a somewhat greater distance from its fellow than would be the case in other kinds of work, and this is done to produce a more spiky or spray-like effect.

There are other ways of working such sprays. They may be simply followed

braid, cord, or a couching of several strands of knitting cotton caught down with coloured flax, which has very much the appearance of appliqué.

No. 14.—DARNED INITIAL.

A PARTICULARLY easy and effective way of managing a simply-designed initial is given here. We say "simply-designed" advisedly, for, unless the letter is bold in character and legible, the main effect of the embroidery is lost. In the original example, the background was of bright blue linen, but with the exception, of

No. 15.—Embroid

course, of the part occupied by the letter, it was entirely covered with horizontal rows of darning worked with soft white thread. In executing such a background as this, there is no necessity for the stitches to be mathematically exact in length, for it is often the shading produced by a broken surface in such grounding that is one of its chief beauties. The first thing to do is to sketch the initial, then darn over all the ground excepting that marked out for the letter. After the darning is completed, the letter itself must be clearly and accurately outlined with small stem stitches, chain, or back stitch, according to convenience, and thus the initial becomes, as it were, "silhouetted" in colour against a broken background of white, with a very charming and uncommon effect. If desired, the colours of the original may be reversed, and the background may be white or cream, darned with a colour.

Such a letter is always most satisfactory when it is embroidered within a shape of some kind—perhaps an oval medallion, a shield, heart, star, or some other fanciful form as we have selected, the edge of the medallion being finished with some fancy stitch. Among the many fanciful stitches appropriate for such a purpose are coral, feather, herringbone, buttonhole stitch in all its variety, and many known to Mountmellick workers.

Our sketch shows first an outlining of crewel stitch beyond which

No. 15.—EMBROIDERED INITIALS FOR CUSHION.

THIS handsome arrangement of letters can be executed upon a foundation of silk, satin, cloth, &c., and is suitable for placing down the side of a cushion cover, or at the end of any slip that is used upon a narrow table or sideboard. It is well adapted also for the decoration of a large book cover, cushion, or a fancy portfolio, that may be designed for the reception of engravings, photographs, or water-colour drawings. Upon a smaller scale it would be extremely pretty if worked in the middle of a double pillow sham, that is, one which extends completely across the width of a double bed. Letters grouped in this simple fashion, too, may be worked in white cords and braids or coloured flax threads upon coloured linen, holland, or damask. When this is the case they would form a really beautiful ornament for the centre of a bedspread.

There are several ways in which the letters may be worked, but there can scarcely be any more effective style of managing the willow leaves than that shown in the illustration. Rope silk is employed for them in several shades of willow green, and they are carried out in Oriental stitch, which is

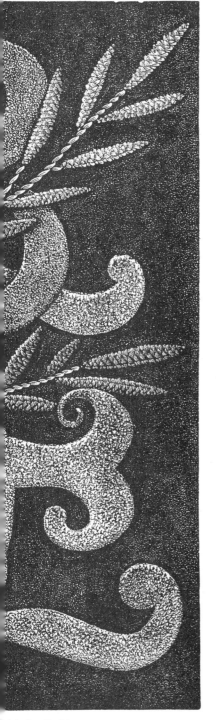

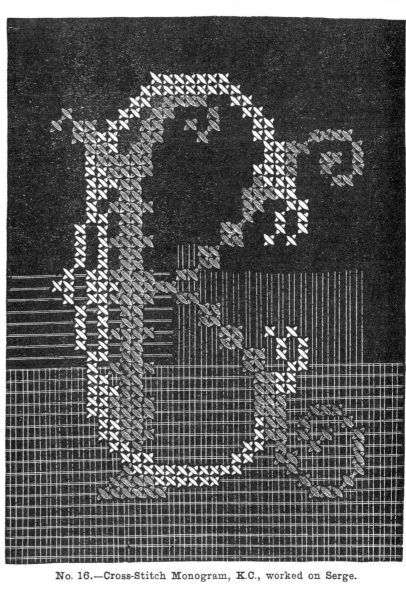

No. 16.—Cross-Stitch Monogram, K.C., worked on Serge.

is worked ordinary herringbone stitch. This style of embroidery is very effective for book covers, sachets, &c., when made in linen or more elaborate materials, as the darning can be done with cotton or silk. A cushion darned over, leaving a space in centre forming an initial, a spray of flowers, a griffin, &c., has an excellent effect. Cushions in blue, gold, old rose, and other coloured linens darned in white are particularly pretty.

particularly effective. It is merely a form of herringbone stitch, but a tiny piece only of the material is taken up with each stitch, and all are placed very closely together. This Oriental stitch is very effective when worked with coarse twisted silk. There is no shading to be done, but the leaves are embroidered each in one particular tone, and grow darker as they are near the lower part of the stems. All the stems are made in rope or stem stitch, with the lightest shade silk as was used for the leaves.

In the original, from which our illustration is taken, the letters are worked with closely-set rows of tinsel, that used for the E being blue, and gold serving for the B, and the crinkled tinsels fill up quickly, and have a very rich appearance almost as if appliqué to the foundation. Also it is of little consequence what coloured silk is employed for sewing down the tinsel, as the stitches become buried among the crinkled metal.

When such large initials as these are to be worked upon a material such as silk or satin, they may well be cut out of velvet and appliqué to the back-

tials for Cushion.

ground. It is a good plan to draw the shape of the letter upon the wrong side of the velvet, remembering, of course, that the shape of the initial must be reversed here so as to set in the right direction when it comes to be seen from the right side. The velvet should be rubbed over on the wrong side with embroidery paste, and which, when dry, will give a slight stiffness and prevent the velvet ravelling when cut.

The velvet letters should then be placed in the desired position upon the serge or satin background, and should be secured with straight overcast stitches made all round the edge and so arranged as to take up as little as possible of the velvet. Most people find it far easier to work such letters in a frame than over the hand. When the initials are placed, due attention, of course, having been paid to the way in which they are passed over and under one another, the edging must be decided upon. If the letters are small, two rows of gold thread will probably be enough to hold down the edge of the velvet and hide the overcast stitches. If they are, however, somewhat large,

No. 17.—Fancy Letter for Marking Handkerchiefs.

fine gold or fancy cord will be found more useful, or gold braid, or a couching of several strands of coarse silk caught down with silk of some contrasting colour. Chenille, too, of a totally different tint to the velvet, has a charming effect, and may well be secured with stitches of tinted " passing "—a tinsel thread fine enough to " pass " through the eye of an ordinary embroidery needle and any material that is tolerably soft.

After such an important piece of work has been finished, it may be found to be slightly puckered, and if such be the case, it should be strained out taut and straight upon a drawing-board, and held with tiny tacks or pins round the edges. The wrong side should be uppermost, and this must be spread evenly all over with embroidery paste, no great quantity being used, but such as there is being thoroughly well rubbed into material and in and out the stitches. This is enough for all ordinary cases, but where there is a large amount of tinsel, besides perhaps spangles, beads, and bullion, a sheet of tissue paper should now be laid as flat as possible over the paste, and this,

No. 18.—Embroidered Signature.

in its turn, must be pressed—not rubbed—until it adheres evenly to every part of the back of the work, then allowed to gradually dry, after which, remove the work from the board or frame, and it will be found smooth.

No. 16.—CROSS-STITCH MONOGRAM UPON SERGE.

THE illustration shows K. C. in cross stitch partially worked upon art serge with the help of ordinary Penelope canvas. This is tacked carefully upon the serge, the straight threads of the canvas being arranged so as to run equally with the length and width of the serge. Particular attention must be paid to this, or the result, when the work is finished, will be that the letters set slanting and puckered instead of straight and regular.

The monogram is then worked in cross stitch, for which the canvas is used as a guide, otherwise it is so difficult to work even stitches on a plain fabric, the stitches being taken through the serge, but on no account being allowed to pass

through any of the lines of the canvas. After the work is all finished, the canvas has to be carefully pulled away from under the stitches thread by thread, and will come out quite easily, first in one direction and then in the other.

In the illustration all stages are shown. At the bottom of the monogram the canvas is still intact : above this on the right-hand side, the widthway threads are seen removed ; while on the left-hand side the lengthway threads are removed, then at the top all are taken away, and the upper parts of the letters are shown as distinctly as though they had been worked directly upon the serge.

No. 17.—FANCY LETTER FOR MARKING HANDKERCHIEFS.

THE letter given here is a very good example of the style of fancy initial suitable for placing in the corner of a pocket handkerchief, and the article to be embroidered should be arranged in a round drum frame. White or coloured embroidery cotton is suitable, also silk, the size of which would vary according to the material upon which the letter is to be worked. The whole of the letter must be filled in with padding stitches first, and then the satin stitches are to be taken evenly and regularly across them.

There are several tiny leaves about this design, and these are each worked in two sections, so that there is a line down the middle, which represents the mid-rib of the leaf. In the centre of each leaf is a wee eyelet-hole which greatly adds to the daintiness of the embroidery. The fine upstrokes of the letter are worked very delicately in overcast stitch over a single thread run along the outline as a padding.

No. 19.—Knotted Monogram.

No. 18.—EMBROIDERED SIGNATURE.

THIS engraving shows a pretty method of marking for handkerchiefs, under-linen, &c., being in fact a facsimile of one's signature, which first should be written in pencil upon the material to be ornamented, then the pencil lines are gone over with tiny but evenly made back stitches, worked either with white or coloured cotton or silk. Simply one's initials look well done so ; and such articles as time table, photo, or album covers can be ornamented in this style.

No. 19.—KNOTTED MONOGRAM.

A CHARMINGLY arranged monogram of two letters, G. N., worked with crewel stitch and French knots. It can be executed in cottons or silks, according to the article it is to adorn, the engraving being the natural size of letters, but which can be enlarged or decreased as desired. Pale green and coral pink cottons were employed in the original, the G being of the latter tint.

The design is in no place quite as much as half an inch in width, and at each end of the G it runs off into small scrolls, which serve to prevent it being mistaken for a C. With the exception of the scrolls, the whole of the space between the outlines is covered with tiny and closely set French knots, no vestige of the material being allowed to show between them. The case is similar with the N, but here the last stroke of the letter requires finer treatment, and so is followed first with a series of tiny outline stitches, worked with green, to form the centre, on either side of which are coral pink stitches. Both letters are outlined with the same small stitches, the green knots being defined with pink outlines and *vice versâ*. The extreme ends of the letter N open out into small bosses composed of a group of French knots worked to correspond with those in the main body of the letter, while the scrolls at each end of the G are added in back stitch, worked with the rose pink.

There are many variations to be made in these knotted letters. A novelty is the "rainbow" initial. Here the tints of which the rainbow is made up are used in sequence down the letter, but there are too many to be employed within such a narrow space as that in the example before us. They are, as most people know, red, orange, yellow, green, blue, indigo, and violet, and where the space is small it is better to employ lines of outline stitch set closely together than the knots. Where the letter becomes narrower still, as in

No. 20.—Easily Worked Initials.

the last stroke of the N, the two outside colours should be carried over it side by side.

Another very good way of working such letters is with the help of silks all of the same colour, but of as many shades as the width will allow. The darkest tint should be kept at the right-hand side of the letter, the lightest being, of course, at the left-hand side. The fine parts of the initials should be worked with the lightest, middle, and darkest shades. When such letters as these are placed upon non-washing materials, a fine line of gold thread forms a better finish for the edges than do the lines of outline stitch, as these are a little apt to interfere with the effect of the rainbow and shaded effect.

No. 20.—EASILY-WORKED INITIALS.

THERE are many things about a house that it is advisable to mark, but upon which it is not worth while expending any very great amount of time or trouble. For such, the style of letters and figures shown in No. 20 is very suitable, and they may be carried out either in white or coloured threads, according to fancy. It is easy enough to write the letters and figures needed with a lead pencil upon the article to be marked, then all that is necessary is to follow the lines with back stitch, using very fine marking cotton. When the letters are extremely minute, sewing cotton gives a sharper and clearer result than do

No. 22.—Satin-Stitch Letters for Handkerchiefs.

No. 21.—MONOGRAM, G.R.

A BOLD and prettily arranged monogram for marking household linen, book covers, portfolios, cushions, quilts, &c. It can be executed in satin stitch after the style of No. 3, or could be done in appliqué work.

No. 21.—Monogram, G. R.

the more fluffy and softer makes. The strands of hair used in days gone by for such a purpose were by no means without their advantages, and there are some few ladies still left who can find nothing better when their embroidery is to be of microscopic dimensions.

When the letters are even a trifle larger than those illustrated, it is a very good plan to work them with small running stitches. These should not pass over more than three threads of the material, and one thread only should be taken up between each one. This style of marking, either in colours or in plain white thread, answers very well for everyday handkerchiefs, or, as before said, for such purpose as is not worth while to expend a large amount of time and trouble over.

No. 23.—Initial formed with Braid or Soutache.

No. 22.—SATIN STITCH LETTERS FOR HANDKERCHIEFS.

FOR everyday use many ladies prefer that their handkerchiefs should be marked in as plain and legible a fashion as possible, and for them the letters shown by Illustration No. 22 are to be recommended, for they are easily read and yet are sufficiently ornamental. For working them a drum-head frame is almost a necessity, and the Moravian thread sold for the purpose produces a more even result than do the popular flax threads. The outlines, after they have been pencilled upon the corner of the handkerchief, should be carefully filled in with padding stitches, so arranged as to be higher in the centre than at the sides, where one layer of threads is, in most cases, all sufficient. As in the larger letters, some skill is necessary to get the ends of the satin stitches perfectly even; but beginners, who cannot accomplish this successfully, will find that many imperfections may be hidden beneath a line of back stitch carried along each side of the outline of the letter. A very good effect may be gained, where there is no objection to the use of a little colour, by making these stitches with red or blue cotton, care being taken to choose a make that is guaranteed to be ingrain.

There is a fancy among some ladies for working such letters as these in coloured silks, more especially when there is a tinted border round the edge of the handkerchief. The effect of this is often very charming, more especially when pink or pale blue are the colours selected.

for beauty and regularity with that undertaken by our grandmothers. Cross-stitch marking is very useful for kitchen towels, &c., socks, stockings, and flannel goods, and is usually worked with red ingrain marking cotton, the size of which will vary with the texture of the article that is to be marked. Illustration No. 24 shows a set of capital letters, small letters, and figures done in ordinary cross stitch, such as used to be worked on a sampler, and done over two threads each way, and which are so clearly defined in our engraving as to be readily copied. Some people mark so that on the wrong side each cross stitch forms a decided square. We will suppose that for the sake of practice the marking is to be worked upon single-thread or Congress canvas, and that each cross stitch is to cover a square of two threads in each direction. It is obvious, therefore, that in order to form squares on the reverse side one must pick up all the pairs of threads for the cross stitches either in a horizontal or perpendicular direction. In making a single cross stitch, the first thing to do is to bring the thread up from the wrong side at the lower left-hand corner of the material or canvas. It is then carried across two lengthwise and two horizontal threads, and the needle picks up two threads in the usual way, thus completing the first half of an ordinary cross stitch on the right-hand side of the work and a single horizontal stitch on the wrong side. The needle is then taken across the slanting stitch in the usual way, but instead of being brought out in position for making another cross, it is drawn out through the same hole through which it came when the work was first begun.

The first stitch is then repeated, but this time the third stitch to be picked

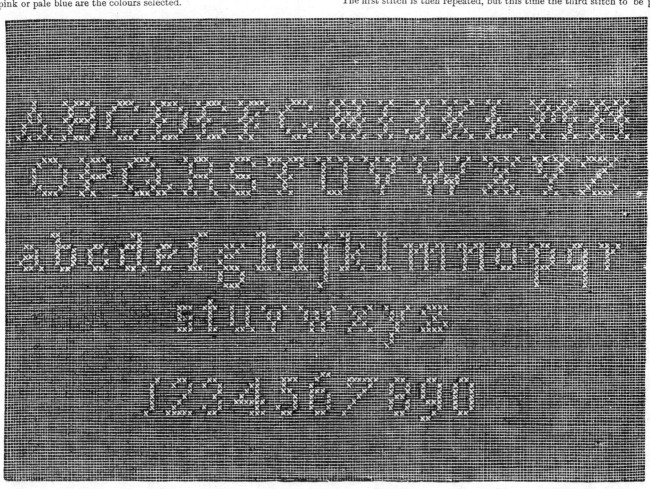

No. 24.—Cross-Stitch **Alphabets** and **Figures**.

This style of embroidered letter is very suitable for marking gentlemen's neck squares, tobacco pouches, shaving tidies, &c., worked in coloured cotton or silk.

No. 23.—INITIAL FORMED WITH BRAID OR SOUTACHE.

INITIALS so arranged are useful for marking such materials that do not repay one to spend much time upon ; also when an article is braided, such as a brush and comb bag, nightdress case, tea cosy, &c., the initial or monogram should also be done in braid. This specimen letter F will give an idea how to arrange other letters, and the method of working is to first trace out the design with pen or pencil upon the material, and go over the outline with narrow braid, either cotton or silk, according to the material being worked, and at the corners and bends the braid is folded over carefully, as the illustration indicates. The braid is sewn down with fine cotton to match the colour of braid.

No. 24.—CROSS-STITCH ALPHABETS AND FIGURES.

FORMERLY cross stitch was most general for marking purposes, and although it is still employed for certain things, the execution, as a rule, will not compare

up on the wrong side is horizontal, the needle pointing back from right to left at the top of the cross. The needle is then ready to make a second cross stitch above the first. By taking the first half stitch in the reverse direction— that is, with the first vertical stitch at the left-hand side of the square, and pointing from below upwards, the series of cross stitches may be made from above downwards instead of beginning with the lowest stitch, as in the way above described.

Of course, no knots at the end of the needlefuls of thread must be tolerated and, if eyesight will permit, the thread may be so run in and out among the meshes of the material as to be quite invisible. Also, the worker will observe that in some places the crosses are double ; that is, one stitch is laid exactly above another. This will not interfere with the general work in the least, provided that very fine thread is employed, and, indeed, it is not possible to manage the double appearance of the work without thus sometimes going over the ground twice.

No 25.—FANCY LETTERS FOR CROSS STITCH.

HERE are given capital and small letters, also a set of figures, in fancy designs, suitable for marking linen, household goods, handkerchiefs, &c., and are intended for working in red ingrain cotton. They are worked over two threads each way of the material, and can be easily copied from our engraving

No. 26.—MONOGRAM, L. A. B.

AN effective arrangement of interlaced letters suitable for working in white or coloured cotton, silk, &c., and is effective for marking sachets, bags, cloths, covers, household linen, &c. They can be executed in satin stitch, as shown by No. 3, or they can be outlined in back, crewel, or overcast stitch, and centred or filled in solid with French knots. They can also be outlined with fine cord, or even with fine braid known as soutache, or they could be pencilled out and the groundwork darned in as No. 14 shows.

They look well worked in solid satin stitch, as No. 27 illustrates, and can be enlarged or decreased to suit the purpose for which they are required.

No. 27.—MEDALLION WITH INITIAL.

THIS medallion is well adapted for insertion in the middle of a border about four inches wide, such as is often carried round the edges of the tea-cloth or across the front of a sideboard cloth. With the addition of a few scrolls it can be arranged so as to fit into the corner if this position for it is preferred. Another situation for which it is admirably adapted is on the flap of a letter case, or nightdress or handkerchief sachet.

The initial here is of a very simple description, being merely a plain E, worked in solid slightly raised satin stitch, with rose-coloured embroidery thread, the background material being ordinary white linen such as is often

themselves being worked with fine white flax thread. The medallion, in such a case may be bordered with lace braid, the kind known as antimacassar braid looking better than any other. Whatever the filling of the medallion, the letter should always be worked first, as it is easier then to fit the stitches of the background neatly in and out the curves.

Another and totally different method of executing such a letter upon coloured linen has at least the merit of novelty. Here the letter should be very distinctly sketched with pen and ink. The medallion should then be covered with coarse meshed Brussels net, or with mosquito net, if the circle is desired larger and more boldly worked than in the illustration. It may be embroidered with satin stitch, as in the illustration No. 27, or it can be outlined with overcast stitch, the net cut away from between the outlines and the space filled with seed or dot stitch. The edge of the medallion will look well if covered with buttonhole stitches raised into high relief over a padding, the net being cut away beyond the outer edge.

No. 28.—FANCY MONOGRAM.

A PRETTILY arranged monogram of three letters, S. L. B., tied together with a bow, which would be worked in satin stitch and the under part of each bow filled in with French knots. The letters are suited to satin stitch, or each can be worked in different stitches, outlined for instance, then centred

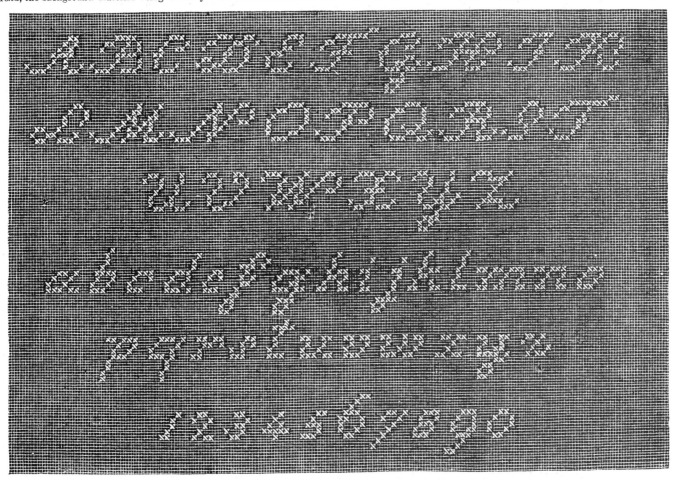

No. 25.—Fancy Letters worked in Cross Stitch.

used for tea-cloths and fancy house linen, but it can be executed on any fabric desired. The letter is surrounded with a series of tiny scrolls, all of which branch off one from the other so as to form a continuous pattern. These scrolls recall the stitched backgrounds so often found upon old English embroidery, and like them they are worked in tiny back stitches with very fine olive-green thread.

Round the outside of the scrolls runs a narrow bordering of coral or feather stitching outlined on each side with a series of back stitches worked with olive-green thread, or pale blue thread combines well with the green and rose colour already employed. The coral or feather stitch, such as is employed for ornamenting underlinen, repeats the rose-pink colour of the initial, and it should be worked neatly and evenly, and the stitches set rather closely together, so as to follow the curves of the circle without any awkward angles.

If the initial is to be employed in any position that will admit of this, it is a good plan to edge the medallion with a line of French knots worked with the green thread. These should be placed about an eighth of an inch apart, and should be worked so evenly and tightly as to look like beads, and hence to be able to stand washing successfully and without coming untwisted as badly-made knots are apt to do. Yet another way of executing this letter is to fill in the background of the medallion with open lace stitches instead of making the scrolls. These look particularly well when the linen is coloured, they

with French knots. Such a monogram could be employed for the decoration of household linen, for book covers, sachets, cushions, &c.

No. 29.—OLD ENGLISH ALPHABET.

PERHAPS few of the fanciful letters are more generally useful than those known as being in "old English" style, as our illustration gives, and it is almost a necessity to work such an alphabet in satin stitch, after the style of No. 22, for there is nothing else that gives the letters their characteristic crispness and sharpness of appearance. They should be rather highly padded too, in order that there may be sufficient contrast between the thick lines and the hair lines that appear in most of the letters. The fine lines are usually worked with very tiny overcast stitches, a single strand of thread being laid first upon the material to serve by way of padding. Some workers execute these strokes in back stitch, others in stem stitch; but there is not the compactness about either of these that is given by an unbroken series of overcast stitches.

Such letters as these must always be employed singly, no attempt being ever made to combine them into monograms. Also they should never be combined with other letters of a totally different style, for they belong so decidedly to one particular date that there would be something incongruous in mixing them with letters of a purely fanciful type, though this is occasionally done by inexperienced designers.

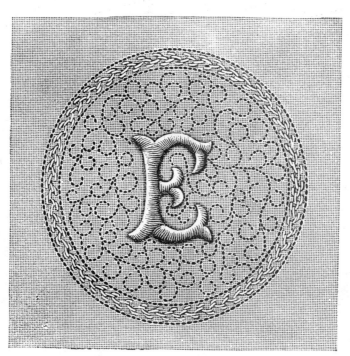

No. 26.—Monogram, L. A. B.   No. 27.—Medallion with Initial.   No. 28.—Fancy Monogram.

No. 29.—Old English Alphabet.

WELDON'S PRACTICAL
JEWELLED EMBROIDERY.

(FIRST SERIES.)

HOW TO USE JEWELS WITH EMBROIDERY SILKS FOR PERSONAL AND HOME DECORATION.

THIRTY-TWO ILLUSTRATIONS.

JEWELLED EMBROIDERY.

WHETHER the fancy will last remains to be proved, but certain it is that fashionable dresses and popular fancy-work glitter with a display of tinsel, gold thread, and gems, which more resembles the descriptions of Eastern splendour given in the "Arabian Nights" than anything we are accustomed to in these more prosaic times. It is probable that the use of such magnificent materials will be discontinued, as far as dress is concerned, long before we are weary of making them up into various dainty and pretty knick-knacks, or before our eyes become too much dazzled for us to consider them appropriate for mixing in with silk embroidery. Needless to say, the gems employed are artificial, but so perfectly are the real stones imitated that the effect given is almost the same, and is equally good for the purpose in view. At the same time, however, no worker should be tempted to utilise the jewels upon any material that is not good and durable, as they are practically everlasting, hence are appropriately placed only upon rich fabrics, such as satin, velvet, plush, or brocade. Cotton materials are occasionally used, as will be shown presently. Net, muslin, gauze, both tinsel and silk, are also often employed as backgrounds for this style of embroidery.

The jewels themselves are of many kinds, and are foiled at the back, which has the effect of greatly increasing their brilliancy. They are mostly cut exactly like the real stones, and while some are used without any setting, others are mounted in gilt claws which are provided with holes, through which the needle must be passed to form the stitches which hold the jewel down to the foundation.

The unset stones have two tiny holes pierced through them to answer the same purpose. These holes are not unfrequently too small to admit of the passage even of the finest needle, and the worker must beware how she endeavours to push it through, for the slightest force will split the gem, and so render it useless. When the holes are thus minute, the end of silk must be itself passed through them, just as through the eye of a needle, after which the needle is threaded on the silk and sews the gem down to the stuff. Gems may be had to imitate diamonds, rubies, opals, topazes, sapphires, aqua-marines, and emeralds, while pearls and turquoises are usually represented by beads. The diamonds, topazes, and aqua-marines are specially beautiful. Some of the gems are round and rose-cut, some are lozenge-shaped, some sexagonal, others square, the lozenge-shaped crystals being often known as "fish-tails." The unset stones are the most generally useful, as they do not stand up so prominently above the surface of the material as those with the metal settings. Some of the gems are smooth and uncut,

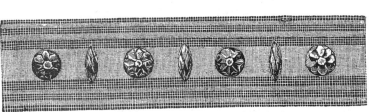

No. 1.—Jewelled Gauze for Millinery.

No. 2.—Six Ways of Sewing on the Jewels.

and these are to be had in particularly beautiful colours, while they are more suitable for use upon cotton materials than the cut stones. There are two qualities of jewels, the cheaper of which cost about twopence-halfpenny a dozen. These are very good in their way, but are not to be compared for brilliancy and neatness of make with those of the first quality, which cost about fivepence per dozen.

Jewelled embroidery is not merely confined to the use of these gems, for there are small pierced pieces of mother-o'-pearl, which are especially prepared for use in this work, and which are either lozenge-shaped, round, or square. Scraps of coral are sometimes employed, also iridescent sequins, spangles, and beetles'-wings. Spangles are to be had in a great variety of shapes and colours, but the main thing to be avoided is to employ them too scantily. To be truly effective they require massing, and indeed never look better than when they are arranged so that they overlap like the scales of a fish.

Beads of all kinds are admissible in this jewelled embroidery, and may be used in many different ways. There are the plain gold, silver, and steel beads, which are always to be had, while very useful for such work are the metal coloured ones, to be procured in shades of olive, blue, coral-pink, bronze, peacock-blue, brown, violet, old gold, crimson, &c. Moonlight and sunlight beads are not to be omitted, and small bugles often tone in well with tinsel. Sometimes the beads are merely scattered over a layer of closely set gold threads, so that they look like minute jewels; very often they are placed in the middle of a spangle, and serve to hold it down to the material. At other times they are strung and used as an outlining for some prominent part of a design. They are also largely employed with the jewels upon such materials as gauze, lace or net. Other purposes for which they are adapted will be detailed later on.

The many different kinds of gold thread may all be suitably employed in embroidery of this kind. Every one is familiar with the ordinary Japanese gold threads, but of these there are several shades of colour, one make in particular giving a warm look to the work, owing to its being twisted over a core of bright red silk instead of over yellow or white. More variety still may be given by sewing down the threads with silks of different colours instead of with silk to match the gold in tint. The use of red silk for this purpose gives a rich, coppery glow, while blue tends to increase the metallic lustre of the tinsel.

Purl or Bullion, as it is sometimes called, is invaluable. In make it is of two kinds, plain and crinkled. It consists of the finest metal wire, which is compactly twisted into a series of rings. It is very elastic, and may, if desired, be pulled out so that the rings set further apart, or may be sewn down so that they lie more closely together. The ordinary way of using bullion is to cut it up into the lengths required, which vary from one-sixteenth to three-quarters of an inch.

No. 3.—Small Linen Square.

The needle is passed through the middle of the rings, and the bullion is then sewn down exactly like a bead. Other ways of using it will be detailed by-and-by. It varies greatly in colour, and is to be had in gold and silver, and in either of these tints mixed with green, red, or blue. It is also made in either of these metallic colours with no gold or silver in it at all.

Gold cord and braid may both be very effectively used with jewels, especially when trimmings are required for bonnets or dresses. It is often far cheaper to buy an inexpensive plain passementerie, and to sew the gems on for oneself, than to purchase it already jewelled.

Gold Passing is a special make of gold thread, so extremely fine that it can be passed easily through the eye of an ordinary needle. It is, owing to its excessive fineness, only suitable for the most delicate work, and for this reason cannot be recommended where a bold and brilliant effect is required. It answers well for working chain-stitch on net round and between coloured stones.

Besides those named here, there are many kinds of fancy tinsel, some of which look as if they are studded with tiny jewels. They are scarcely so durable as the better qualities of plain gold thread, but for all that they give a very excellent effect when the work is only required perhaps for three or four evenings' wear. Sometimes very little tinsel at all is used, and the gems are surrounded and embedded in fancy cord. This way of managing the work often gives a good result, as the very dulness of the setting causes the jewels to show to better advantage.

The silks with which the gems are secured to the foundation material should be as strong as is consistent with fineness and evenness of texture. When the jewels are simply caught down without any setting or frame, the silk which holds them should match them in colour as nearly as possible, but when they are surrounded with gold thread, the same silk which sews this down may be used also for the gems. There is a particularly fine make called "horsetail" silk, which is closely twisted and very strong; it may be had in skeins or reels to match any shade of gold thread. Some of the beads and gems are rather troublesome to put on, owing to their sharp edges, which have the unfortunate faculty of cutting the silk as it is drawn through them. Beads, however, may often be sewn on with strong cotton, black or white, but this, of course, cannot be used when there is any fear of its being visible.

The embroidery itself may be executed with Messrs. Baylis, Gilles, and Co.'s Floss Filoselle (Pure China Silk), fine wools, or flax threads. Messrs. Faudel's English-made filoselles can be recommended also, as they appear to contain a greater proportion of silk than is found in ordinary silks of this kind. Faudel's Indian Silk Chenille is very largely used in jewel work.

The uses of jewelled embroidery are as varied as the gems themselves. It is just now largely employed for millinery and for dress trimmings; in fact, jewels appear as often upon gowns intended for day wear in the streets as upon evening dresses. Charming little sachets, pincushions, book-covers, work and opera-glass bags, and wall-pockets also may be thus ornamented; indeed, the pretty sparkling toys may be introduced somewhere into almost all the silk, satin, or velvet articles that are sold at the fancy shops, traced ready for ladies to work.

The amateur will do well to avoid using them so lavishly as to give her work a theatrical appearance, and in most cases it will be found that a mixture of two, or at most, three kinds of gems will give a more satisfactory result than when they are mixed in pell-mell, with little regard to harmony of tint. Also, it is a good plan to use the jewels to correspond with the colour of the foundation material, thus: few more beautiful effects can be found than that given by aqua-marines or sapphires upon blue velvet or satin, yellow topazes upon gold or brown, diamonds on white or cream, rubies upon dark red or pink. Pearls and diamonds, of course, look well upon everything, and almost every kind of gem looks admirable upon a background of cream or white satin, or black velvet. Upon light blue satin, pale pink topazes give a truly beautiful effect.

A favourite mixture is turquoise and jet. The turquoises are always represented by beads, but in the jet there are many varieties. It can be had in the form of beads, or of flat *appliqués*, either round, lozenge-shaped, or square, or in more fanciful shapes still. This combination of jewels and jet is one to which we are hardly accustomed at present, but it is largely used in Paris upon woollen dresses and jackets. Another mixture that is fashionable just now is jet and emeralds. This is somewhat peculiar, but the mere fact of its being the fashion, will recommend it to many people. Turquoises and pearls form an uncommon but beautiful mixture.

and, in short, it may be said that the more frequently a worker handles the gems the greater the number of charming combinations she will find herself able to make of them.

No. I—JEWELLED GAUZE FOR MILLINERY.

THE easiest way of utilising jewels for trimming hats, bonnets, or caps, is to sew them down to transparent tinsel gauze in the manner shown in this illustration. Here an opal and an emerald alternately are sewn on the middle stripe, each about an inch apart. Between each of these is an oval yellow topaz. When trimming a hat or bonnet, the easiest plan is to cut off the ribbon or gauze into lengths ready for the loops and to fold each piece in half. Sew the gems on the first half only, unless the back of the loop is likely to be seen when the bow is made up. This plan not only economises the jewels, but prevents the trimming from being so weighty as it might otherwise be. The worker must remember that when she is sewing gems on a transparent material, each stone must be finished off at the back and the thread cut off. If the thread is carried across from jewel to jewel in the ordinary manner, it will spoil the look of the embroidery by being visible on the right side.

No. 2.—SIX WAYS OF SEWING ON JEWELS.

THIS illustration shows six of the most common ways in which the jewels may be held down to the material. The first gem, beginning at the right-hand side, is simply caught down with a couple of stitches made by bringing the needle through one of the holes in the stone and passing it through the satin as closely as can be to the edge of the jewel. The hole in this may be large enough to allow the needle to be passed through twice or even three times more, but one stitch too many and any attempt to push the needle through after the hole is full will cause the stone to split. Jewelled embroidery is rarely subjected to hard wear, so two stitches in each hole should be sufficient to hold the gem down firmly. A similar set of stitches is made through the second hole in the gem and the work is securely fastened off with a few stitches at the back of the stone. Opal or lozenge-shaped jewels require to be sewn down with two stitches taken across them at each end, or they are apt to become tilted up when the work is in use. This is shown in the second example in the illustration. Except on tulle or gauze and similar transparent materials, the jewels are rarely sewn down to the foundation without an encircling line of gold thread or something of

the kind. The small square opal which is third in the row is sewn down in the usual way and is then surrounded with four little pieces of very pale pink and tinsel purl. Each of these pieces is cut the exact length of the side of the opal and is sewn down like a bead, so that it sets flat upon the surface of the material. The jewels which are mounted in a gilt setting may either be sewn down in the way above described or may have a wee piece of bullion or a bead placed over the hole in the setting to hide the stitches. First, make a stitch or two in the usual way, then bring the needle up through the hole, snip off a piece of gold bullion about the size of a pin's head, thread it on the needle like a bead, and when it has nearly slipped down to the gem, pass the needle back through the same hole. Work thus at each hole. A pretty effect may sometimes be given by using coloured purl, which looks much as if the gems themselves were framed with tiny jewels.

Small beads form an appropriate setting for the larger gems, and the ring of tiny silver beads surrounding the fifth (a sapphire) in the illustration is particularly pretty. The easiest way of arranging these is to bring the needle up from the wrong side about the distance of half the width of a bead from the gem, then thread enough beads to make a ring to fit exactly round the stone. Put the needle back to the wrong side where it came up and draw the thread up, holding the ring down so that it sets evenly round the jewel. Make a stitch here and there over the thread which holds the beads to keep it from slipping out of place. If the thread has been drawn up too tightly the worker will find that there will be no room for these stitches between the beads, and therefore they will not set perfectly.

The last jewel in the row is encircled with four rounds of fine gold thread. A little skill is needed to get these sufficiently even.

No. 4.—Felt Wall-Pocket with Jewels and Jet.

Choose a gem that is as nearly circular as can be (some of the cheaper ones are apt to be irregular) and sew it down, then begin to lay the gold thread quite close to the edge of the gem, pushing the end through to the wrong side in the usual way; keep the first row of tinsel close to the gem. Much of the success of the whole setting will depend upon the first round, as the remaining three have to be laid quite close together, and must follow each other exactly. The gold thread must be fastened off on a line with the place at which it was begun, or the number of rounds will be uneven. It is as well not to let the setting be wider than the diameter of the gem in the middle of it, or it will look too heavy and the brilliancy of the jewel will be overpowered by that of the gold.

6

No. 3.—SMALL LINEN SQUARE.

AN example of the use of gems upon linen fabrics is shown here, in a small square of fine linen worked with cream-coloured filo-floss and sprinkled with pink topazes. The materials are simple enough, but the effect gained is very pretty and sparkling. The flowers are worked in satin-stitch, the leaves and stems in outlining, and the scrolls in back-stitch. The jewels are sewn down with silk which matches them exactly, so that seen from a little distance they look as if they are only thrown down hap-hazard on the embroidery. Such a square as this is often used with other and plainer pieces

No. 5.—Powdering for Fancy Articles.

joined with narrow bands of lace insertion for a tea-cloth or chair-back. For a tea-cloth, those squares which lie flat on the table should not be jewelled, as the raised surface of the stones would be likely to prevent the things placed on the table from standing steadily. It is a good plan to jewel the corner squares plentifully, and to work the others far more simply. A little square of this sort is very suitable for a pincushion top, and would be pretty if laid cornerwise on a handkerchief sachet made of puffed satin or silk to match the gems in colour.

No. 4.—FELT WALL-POCKET WITH JEWELS AND JET.

THIS is very elaborately worked, and is a combination of several kinds of jewels with jet appliqués, plates of mother-o'-pearl and spangles. It is much the fashion just now to utilise fanciful pieces of jet with jewels on articles of this kind, but they are easily replaced by something lighter in appearance, should the worker not happen to care for their effect. The foundation material of the pocket illustrated is a dull shade of terra-cotta, the principal colours used upon it being pale greyish green, rich gold, very pale blue, and two shades of terra-cotta. Some of the gems are uncut, and are greenish-blue and yellow. A few cut ones are mixed in with the work and small plain spangles are added in places. A little gold thread is used for outlinings, and is sewn on double instead of single.

Five greenish lozenge-shaped pieces of mother-o'-pearl are used to form a sort of spray, centring a leaf worked with pale blue silk, at the base of which are three jewels, the middle one being blue, with a jet one on either side. The scroll issuing from beneath is worked in

outline stitch with old gold silk, as will be clearly seen on reference to the right-hand side of our illustration. Yellow uncut stones are placed at the base of each group of three old-gold stitches, which form the filling-in of the background.

No. 5.—POWDERING FOR FANCY ARTICLES.

LINEN is the material chosen for this simple but thoroughly effective little design; it is, however, quite as elegant upon a background of satin or of very fine serge, or thin flannel of an extra well-finished quality, such as has been largely employed of late for fancy articles. The colours and style of work are both simple, but the worker must not be led away on that account with the idea that poor execution will prove satisfactory. The satin-stitch leaves and the rings of buttonhole need to be worked regularly and closely, and the linen must not be allowed to become in the least degree puckered. The colours used in the model were a greyish shade of blue for the satin-stitch leaves, and a salmon shade of pink for the rings. The silk employed should be washing filoselle, of which three strands are necessary for each needleful. In the middle of the star is a small buttonholed circle of the pink, in the centre of which is sewn an uncut pink topaz. The small circles between the satin-stitch leaves are worked with the pink, then outlined with gold thread. This starts from the circle in the centre of the star, is carried down between the leaves, taken round the buttonholed disc, crossed and carried up to the centre alongside the first line of gold thread. A jewel is then sewn in the middle of each circle; in every alternate one being an uncut sapphire of a rich tone of blue, in the other a square yellow topaz. In working such stars as these over a large surface, it is advisable to leave a space equal to that occupied by two stars between each, or the work is likely to look too much crowded. It is a pretty idea, too, to counterchange the colours.

No. 6.—Cloth Tea Cosy.

Thus, every alternate star only, should be like the one given here; the others should have the leaves of the pale pink, the roundels being blue and the tints of the gems being changed to correspond. In this case, the yellow topazes would remain as they are in the first star, a single blue one should be placed in the middle, and the remaining four spaces filled with the uncut pink topazes. If something still more elaborate be required, a ring of French knots, with the space of one-eighth of an inch left between each, may be worked round the buttonholed circles. It is well to use silk of the same colour as the circles themselves for these knots, or they will be apt to be confused in effect with the leaves. Another plan is to arrange these knots down each side of the double line of gold thread, or both sets may be put in, if something very handsome indeed is required. It is the ingenuity which suggests such little variations as these which marks the difference between a worker who truly loves her task and one who has no notion of doing anything but follow a given pattern mechanically, without bestowing upon it a moment's thought.

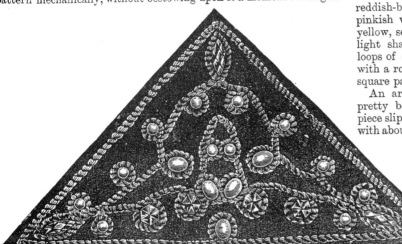

No. 7.—Corner for Book-Cover. Plush worked with Moss Chenille and Turquoises.

No. 6.—CLOTH TEA COSY.

THIS cosy is of olive green cloth worked with a bold conventional pattern in shades of green silk. The centre of the flower-like part of the design is filled in with a lattice of gold thread, caught down with cross-stitches worked in dark green silk. Many of the outlines are raised by being worked with an entire thickness of light green filoselle couched down with small stitches of the same colour. The shades of green vary from dark olive to nearly white, but the jewels are of two kinds only, garnets for the tips of the stamens and yellow topazes in the centres of the leaves. The leaves are outlined with short satin-stitches, which are placed so as to keep the edges quite clear and distinct. Most of the stems are put in with a double strand of gold thread, sewn down with fine gold silk.

No. 7.—CORNER FOR BOOK-COVER.

THE amateur always finds a certain amount of difficulty in working effectively upon piled materials such as plush or velvet. Chenilles, both plain and fancy, seem to have been specially invented to help her out of this difficulty, and by using these no stitches whatever are required beyond those which hold them down to the plush background. The corner for a book-cover given here is worked with old-gold moss chenille upon brownish plush and is plentifully studded with turquoises of different shapes. It is a good plan to draw or trace the design upon tissue paper, to tack this down upon the plush and to work over it, pulling it away when the design has been entirely worked. This will remind many people of the old method of braiding before any plan was invented for marking the pattern directly upon the material. The moss chenille will be found very easy to use, for it is twisted so as to form a series of close, but silky little loops, which set on the plush something like French knots and quite hide the stitches with which the chenille is held down. Any simple braiding pattern may be worked in this way, and if it includes a number of twists and loops, these may be very appropriately studded with jewels. Turquoises in particular, settle down very closely within this fluffy setting, but it is possible, of course, to use any other stone preferred.

No. 8.—COVER FOR HANDKERCHIEF SACHET.

THIS is another example of the many fabrics upon which it is possible to introduce jewels, for the material of which this cover is made is nothing more expensive than art serge. It is worked in a very novel and artistic fashion. In the middle of the cover, which is golden-brown in tint, is a fancy design arranged with dark green crewel wool, which is couched down with wool of a paler shade of the same colour, this being outlined with French knots, worked with maize-coloured wool, while the inner side is finished with a double row of gold thread, which naturally must be sewn down with fine silk to match. Each of the four loops is centred with a pale green jewel, while in the centre is a yellow gem. The interlaced patterns round this are worked in two different ways. The inner one is square, and is outlined with a couching of reddish-brown wool, sewn down with a darker shade, and filled with pinkish wool in coral stitch; the outer one is outlined with pale yellow, sewn down with brown, and centred with French knots in a light shade of greyish green. In the open corners are rings or loops of double strands of gold thread, each of which is filled in with a round blue stone, an oval one resting below this close to the square part of the design.

An arrangement of intertwined squares of this kind makes a pretty border for an open work-basket cover, or for a mantel-piece slip. The squares should not be laid quite close together, but with about half an inch between them. This space may be filled in with a row of French knots, a few spangles, or a line of fancy stitching.

No. 9.—CORAL EMBROIDERY.

CORAL embroidery may really be considered as a variety of jewelled work, although in point of fact no jewels except pearls are used in it. It is extremely rich and handsome in appearance, but the pearls being very brittle, oblige one to use the work only for such articles as have no rough treatment to undergo. For this reason it is usually employed for photograph frames, trinket caskets, *vide-poches*, and wall-pockets of all kinds, book-covers, and small portfolios for holding Christmas cards or loose photographs. One great advantage possessed by coral embroidery will recommend it to

No. 8.—Cover for Handkerchief Sachet.

the worker who dislikes trouble. This is the fact of its needing no formally traced pattern. With average care and some small amount of foresight in arranging the various details, the design may be planned as the work progresses. The spray illustrated here was thus executed, and was begun with the flower towards the left-hand side of the design. The very first thing to be done was the sewing down of the scrap of coral which forms the centre of the flower.

Round this was then placed a ring of steel beads; beyond these a similar ring of small pearls. As the piece of coral in the middle did not lend itself well to the formation of an exact circle, the pearls and steel beads arranged themselves naturally in a somewhat square pattern, but in this convenient style of work this is of no consequence whatever. Round the pearls were next placed four loops of gold thread to mark the petals of the flower. These loops were of such a size as to be filled in compactly with a spike of coral and two or three steel beads. Six lines of gold thread altogether were used for each petal, and they set as closely as possible, so as to render the work quite compact and solid. Between these four thick petals are placed four half-petals, shaped merely like small scallops. They are composed of two strands of gold thread instead of six, and they are filled with a scrap of coral, two small pearls, and as many steel beads as each will hold. Finally, a fragment of coral is sewn at the tip of each section, and thus the first flower is completed. Now bring four strands of gold thread laid closely side by side in a slightly curved direction from the flowers for the distance of about three inches, then bend them upward and slanting towards the right till this branch of the stem is about two inches long. The end of it should be about three inches nearer the right than the end of the first stem; this will allow sufficient space for another flower and for a tendril or short branch between them. The second flower is worked quite differently to the first one, although the centre is the same. Sew down a sprig of coral, as nearly round as possible, surround it with a ring of steel beads, put a ring of small pearls round this, and finally

bent about at the worker's fancy, and with care to avoid touching those upon the first stem. If the embroidery is desired very handsome indeed, these leaves can quite easily be worked solid instead of open in the middle. The point at which they spring from the stem is covered with a large, rough piece of coral encircled with a ring of gold beads. Pearls may be substituted for the corals here, if desired. A cluster of pearls and corals, all surrounded by beads, is now added exactly below the place where the first four strands of gold were turned upwards to form the second flower-stem. In the original a large pearl was arranged in the middle and surrounded with a ring of steel beads in the usual way. At the sides of this and close up against the curve of the stem, are two rough pieces of coral, chosen to make as good a pair as possible. A half ring of

No. 9.—Coral Embroidery, showing two ways of working the Flowers.

No. 10—Jewelle

add a second circle of steel or silver beads. Round this centre must be placed nine double loops of gold thread to form the petals of the flower. As these are more thinly worked than in the first flower, more space is gained for the beads and corals within the tinsel. A long, narrow scrap of coral is first of all sewn down between the lines of gold thread, this is encircled with steel beads, and as this does not entirely fill the space, a small pearl is added at the top of each petal. This fills up the scallop entirely. Four small slender leaves are now arranged about half-way down the stem supporting the first flower. These are made of two strands of gold thread, arranged as a sort of long, thin loop, which is curved in form to accommodate the small portion of material that lies between the two stems. Five leaves are worked on the second stem, and these are

gold beads is placed round these. Below this group is carried down a stem made of four strands of gold; it is arranged so as to curve slightly towards the left, and half-way down on the left-hand edge is worked a tendril or leaf corresponding with those already placed in the upper stems. This completes the spray illustrated here. There are very few variations to be made in coral embroidery beyond those gained by the disposal of the stems, sprays, tendrils, and leaves. If the worker should feel unequal to the task of forming her own designs, she can utilise any of the patterns sold ready traced for working, or can procure some of Messrs. Briggs' transfers, which are equally suitable. This, however, does away with much of the informality, which is one of the charms of the work, the very roughness of the scraps of coral themselves being an obstacle to extremely regular treatment, which cannot be overcome. Further richness may be given to the embroidery by sprinkling stray corals here and there hap-hazard over the ground between the other sections of the design. The pearls can scarcely be too small when they are to be used as rings of beads, but the large ones are more suitable for centres and for placing half-way down long stretches of stems and similar places. The kind of gold thread used must in great measure depend upon the colour of the foundation material. Nothing looks better with the scarlet corals than the Chinese thread, which is the same as the Japanese, except that it is twisted over a core of red silk instead of over yellow or white. This gives a coppery glow to the thread, which is eminently suited for this work. The original spray, from which the illustration was prepared, was worked

ut-Work.

No. 10.—JEWELLED CUT-WORK.

THE square shown here is of pale pink linen, worked with somewhat elaborate pattern in cut-work. The design is outlined with fine buttonhole stitch, the material being cut away beyond this, and the various portions, which would otherwise fall to pieces, are held together with bands, bars, or wheels. Some of the round spaces in the design lend themselves well to the use of jewels. In the centre of the square is a pale pink topaz; the leaves round this are each tipped with a turquoise, some of which are six-sided, others oval and more raised. Besides these, pale green, pink, and blue stones are sewn round the border in suitable places. This square would lend itself well to mixing in with plainer ones of the same material for a chair-back, or by itself would mount very prettily on a sachet, pincushion, or a case for holding cards or photographs.

No. 11.—SMALL D'OYLEY ORNAMENTED WITH GEMS AND METALLIC PAINTS.

PAINTING nowadays frequently appears on the same piece of work with embroidery, and gives an opportunity for the display of considerable variety both in colour and in general effect. An example of this is shown in the small d'oyley given here. It is made of dark red velvet, on which has been traced, in the ordinary manner, a wreath of ivy leaves similar to those to be obtained amongst Messrs. Briggs and Co.'s Transfer Patterns. This design is clearly marked out with gold paint, the veins and stems being put in

No. 11.—Small D'Oyley ornamented with Gems and Metallic Paints.

upon écru tussore silk. It is advisable not to use any embroidery stitches upon the work, as the colours of the silks are apt to detract from, rather than add to the beauty of the whole. The corals employed are those tiny rough pieces used for children's necklaces and sleeve ties. They are to be had at most fancy shops for about 1s. 6d. or 1s. 8d. a string, this being sufficient for two small pieces, such as the above, or for one large piece of the work. It will probably be found that the better the quality of the coral the smaller are the holes in it, and it will often be necessary to pass the thread itself through the holes, no needle being sufficiently fine. There are several kinds of beads to be had, which are at first sight a sufficiently good imitation of the real thing, but no one who has once tried the genuine coral will ever be satisfied with the sham, however good.

with the same. The group of ivy leaves in the middle is not only outlined with gold, but is filled in with green lustre paints. The leaves at the corners are traced round, within the gold, with a row of French knots made with dark old-gold coloured silk, and a single green stone is sewn at the base of each. The smaller leaves between these are entirely filled with knots worked in a paler shade of yellow silk. At the tip of four of the short branches is sewn a ruby, which accords well with the rich red of the velvet. The edges of the d'oyley are cut out into points, each of which is painted round with the gold paint and finished with a pearl at the base of each vandyke. It will be noticed that a d'oyley cannot be so plentifully jewelled as some other things, as, if it is to be really useful, nothing so raised as are the gems should be placed in the middle.

No. 12.—JEWELLED NET WORKED WITH CHENILLE.

THE sides of bonnets and the brims of hats are often bound with a fanciful embroidery worked upon net, which is frequently studded with jewels, coloured according to the bonnet upon which it is to be employed. The preparation of a little piece of trimming such as is needed for a fashionable bonnet is a really pleasant task, and one which requires a small amount of skill only. The piece illustrated is of a very simple pattern, which is repeated all along the net. The net is dark brown in colour, and the design is outlined with gold beads and filled in with golden-brown chenille, the jewels being pale green in tint. The pattern must be first drawn with pen and ink very distinctly on a strong piece of white paper, or upon a piece of white or pink glazed calico. It is advisable, when so short a length as that for the sides of a bonnet is needed, to draw the whole of the pattern on the paper so as to obviate having to shift the net until the trimming is finished. This cannot, of course, be done when a long piece is to be made. The worker must be very careful to tack the net by giving it a snip with a sharply pointed pair of scissors. Sometimes, the chenille is used in the same way as the Japanese gold thread and is laid on the surface of the material and caught down with stitches, as in couching, instead of being taken through and through in the ordinary way. Very elegant fronts for dresses may be worked in a similar manner to the trimming given here, the chenille having much the effect of an *appliqué* of velvet.

No. 13.—JEWELS ON JAPANESE LEATHER-PAPER.

AN exceedingly good and quaint effect may be gained by utilising the jewels upon Japanese leather paper, and in this way may be made a great many antique-looking little articles which would have the rare quality of novelty to recommend them. A little penwiper is given here to show how the jewels may thus be employed. The paper is of a golden-bronze colour, and is embossed in a formal pattern somewhat resembling tiles. In the middle of the

No. 12.—Jewelled Net worked with Chenille

No. 13.—Jewels on Japanese. Leather-Paper.

No. 14.—Spray of Mistletoe.

No. 15.—Jewelled and Beaded Net.

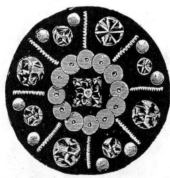

No. 16.—Jewelled Button

No. 17.—Jewels used as a Powdering.

net down quite straight upon the pattern and yet not to pull it at all out of shape, or her design will be all aslant when removed from the background. The chenille part of the embroidery should be worked first, the whole of the little leaves being covered with stitches taken in a slanting direction across and across the design. When all this part of the work is done, the embroidery is outlined with fine gold beads and finally the gems are sewn on; in the middle of each large cluster of leaves is a round stone, an oval one being placed at the base of each group of three leaves. A very pretty trimming of this sort may be made on black net by the use of black chenille, steel beads and diamonds or, if something ultra-fashionable be required, emeralds may be substituted for the diamonds. In using chenille upon such a material as net, the worker must be careful to use a needle that has an amply large eye, for the smallest amount of pulling will be likely to tear the net. If it seems at all difficult to get the needle through when the stitches become rather crowded, it is easy to enlarge any particular mesh of

squares is a small eight-rayed star, which has a deep blue sapphire in the centre. The framework which runs round this has a ruby in each corner. This penwiper is, of course, very small and there is only space for this set of five gems, but it is sufficient to show how pretty the various colours look upon a metallic background. Good imitations of antique jewel-caskets may be made by covering cardboard boxes of various shapes with this metal paper, upon which the jewels have been sewn, or upon which they can be cemented after the paper is pasted down. Any jeweller will procure the gems without any holes in them, and these are, of course, better suited for any purpose in which they are to be glued on instead of being sewn in the usual way.

No. 14.—SPRAY OF MISTLETOE.

SOME of the prettiest sprays made of gems represent small flowers or fruits, and one of these, a spray of mistletoe, is given here as an example. The background is a very dark brown plush. The stems of the spray are worked with dull old-gold coloured silk, the small buds, which are found where the branches fork, being represented by crinkled gold beads. The leaves are made of oval pale green stones, the berries with round white uncut gems. Another idea is to make the berries of a cluster of seed pearls. A little thought will soon suggest other pretty floral sprays that may be made with the gems, many of which lend themselves admirably to the representation of clusters of berries and sprays of flowers, such as daisies, forget-me-nots, or jasmine. In the same way wheat-ears may be imitated by arranging some of the oval yellow stones on each side of a centre stem and working the "beards" in yellow silk. Oats, too, look pretty worked in a similar manner.

No. 15.—JEWELLED AND BEADED NET.

NET plentifully sprinkled with beads and jewels is largely used for softly falling vests to black faille or satin dresses. The net is

are often encrusted with jewels, and as they are somewhat expensive to buy, many ladies contrive them for themselves out of scraps of velvet or satin to match their dresses. A simple, yet effective button of this kind is given here. The foundation material is dark crimson velvet. The first thing to do is to draw on it with white chalk a circle about the size of a half-crown. Make a dot in the exact middle of this circle and draw two lines crossing each other in the middle. Make two more lines also crossing in the middle, thus dividing the circle into eight sections. In the centre, sew on a sapphire mounted in a claw setting and held down with scraps of gold purl. Round this arrange a ring of spangles. If the eye is not sufficiently good to do without a guide, rule a circle with chalk, using a sixpence or the bottom of a thimble for the purpose. Use either plain or fancy spangles of rather a large size. Sew each one down in the following way : bring the needle up, thread a spangle, then a bead, and pass the needle back through the hole in the spangle and into the wrong side of the work. Bring the needle

No. 18.—Four Ways of Grouping the Jewels.

No. 19.—Jewelled Butterfly.

No. 20.—Jewelled Bow for Shoes.

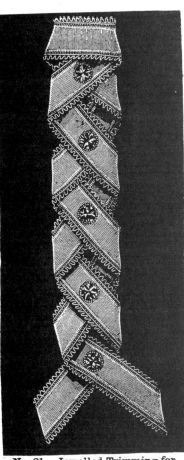

No. 21.—Jewelled Trimming for Fancy Articles.

ornamented first with tiny sprays, which are followed with a tracery of very small cut jet beads. These are threaded on the working thread in groups of two or three, and are then caught down according to the pattern. This is a less laborious task than when each one has to be put on separately. When all the sprays are finished, a jewel (a pink topaz in the original), is sewn down in the space left between each jet spray. The thread which fastens each of these stones must be finished off firmly at the back, not taken from place to place across the material as in any other fabric, or the stitches will be very unsightly. Pretty effects can also be gained by using yellow topazes, diamonds, aqua-marines, or emeralds, instead of the pink gems, but the selection, of course, must depend upon the colours in the dress with which the net is to be worn.

No. 16.—JEWELLED BUTTON.

WITH the present style of dress, large fanciful buttons are much used, and, indeed, are necessary for the proper carrying out of some of the fashionable gowns. For dinner and fête dresses these buttons

up on the circle again and close to the edge of the first spangle, sew down another in the same way. It should overlap the first one for about half its width. Continue thus till the circle is entirely covered. Now cut eight pieces of crinkled gold purl, long enough to reach from the spangles to the edge of the button, thread each one separately on the needle like a long bead and sew it down on one of the lines which divided the circle into eight. Fill the spaces thus made alternately with one large diamond and a group of three gems, two small turquoises and one ruby, or any others preferred. This completes the embroidery of the button. Run a strong gathering thread round the edge of the velvet and draw it up over a large button mould, over which has been laid a piece of thin wadding or cotton wool. Fasten the thread off very strongly on the wrong side and the button is ready to be sewn on to the dress. Large ornamental buttons are often used to give the effect of holding up draperies on screens, easels, and wall-pockets, and when these are made of soft silk or gauze, the cluster of jewels adds greatly to the appearance of the draperies.

No. 17.—JEWELS USED AS A POWDERING.

THIS is one of the most dainty ways of employing jewels for the decoration of small articles. Nothing could be prettier for the cover of a fancy note-book or letter-case, and the design is one which recommends itself to an amateur from its requiring no tracing, that is, provided the worker has a good eye and can measure distances. It would also form a pretty design for bordering a dress, for the cuffs, collar, plastron, &c. To work the stars, make first a series of dots on the material, each about an inch apart, then measure the same distance below this first row of dots and make a similar set exactly below them. When a sufficient number is made, or the material quite covered, mark another row of dots between those already made, and alternating with them instead of being exactly beneath them. These dots mark the centre of each star. To work

No. 22.—Ornamentation for Work Bags or Handkerchief Cases.

the stars, bring the needle up from the wrong side on the dot, put it back at the distance of a quarter of an inch above the dot, thus making an upright stitch a quarter of an inch long, make another vertical stitch below the dot, and two horizontal ones to the left and right; this completes a cross of four stitches. Make four more stitches slanting between those already worked, thus finishing the star of eight stitches. Finally, sew a gem in the middle of each. When a material woven in even lines is used, the straight threads of the silk will serve as a guide for placing the straight stitches, and when two or three stars have been made, they will serve to show where the stitches belonging to other stars should be worked. The material used in the original was tussore silk, the stars were executed with greyish-blue filoselle, the entire twelve strands being used for each needleful. The jewel in the middle of each star matched the filoselle exactly, but an equally good effect can be obtained by the use of rose-coloured silk and pink topazes, or gold-coloured silk and yellow topazes. Emeralds on white silk are pretty, or pale pink topazes on light blue.

No. 18.—FOUR WAYS OF GROUPING THE JEWELS.

UPON some articles it is better to use the jewels in clusters or groups than to mix them in with embroidery, beads, or gold thread, and four out of the many ways in which they may thus be arranged are shown in the above engraving. At the top of the engraving is shown a six-rayed star composed of six lozenge-shaped pieces of mother-o'-pearl arranged round a single and rather large pink topaz. Next to this is a group of six pink moonstones arranged round a sapphire. Beyond this is a cluster of four square stones, the good effect of which is greatly dependent upon the colours that are employed for them. The two stones at the sides should be alike, and those at the top and bottom should also correspond. The last group in the row has a slight resemblance to a pansy, and is made up of five yellow topazes, two small round ones and three oval ones, and

two amethysts at the right ride, a small round diamond being placed in the middle. Clusters of gems, such as these, are very useful when an embroidered design occupies only a small proportion of the field of any large article, such as a screen or mantel-border. The ornamentation of these is not unfrequently rather mean in appearance, unless it is balanced, as it were, by something on the rest of the material, and a small unimportant cluster of gems placed at certain intervals is often quite sufficient to fill the vacancy.

No. 19.—JEWELLED BUTTERFLY.

HANDKERCHIEF sachets, photograph frames and similar knick-knacks are now frequently ornamented with a spray of artificial flowers or fruit, or one or two gaily coloured insects or birds. These are, as it were, thrown carelessly down upon the silk or other material, not sewn down closely, but allowed to set freely and quite loose from the background. A butterfly to be used for such a purpose is illustrated here, and the task of making such a one will be found by no means difficult. The first thing to do is to trace the shape of a butterfly upon a piece of linen, or in fact almost any material, as it is to be entirely covered with stitches. Then embroider the insect, using any colours that happen to be convenient. Work in satin-stitch and work in rows from the outer edge towards the body, which is, of course, worked across and across. Set the rows of stitches quite closely together and when the insect is entirely covered, rub some paste, in which a little resin has been boiled, all

No. 23.—Jewelled Quilting.

over the back of the work, and set it by to get perfectly dry. Then take a sharp pair of scissors and cut out the butterfly all round the edges. Be very careful not to snip the embroidery or to allow any of the linen to remain beyond the stitches. Get some fine wire and sew this on the wrong side of the work round the edges of the wings and run a double row down the body of the insect. The feelers should have a single row of wire unless, as is often the case, they are too slender to allow of its being sewn at the back of them. The jewels are then put on. They should be cut and un-set, and may be placed almost anywhere on the wings. On the body they should be put close together so that it is entirely covered. When the insect is sewn on the article for which it is intended, the wings should be curved and bent about to look as naturally placed as possible, but the underside should not be allowed to become visible, as the stitches and wire do not add to its ornament.

No. 20.—JEWELLED BOW FOR SHOES.

With the introduction of gilded and silvered leather, the bows for the shoes have become more and more elaborate, and they are frequently sprinkled with gems and beads and enriched with embroidery, which renders them worthy of closer inspection than they can possibly receive when in wear. A favourite occupation of ladies who go out a great deal is that of decorating the bows for their shoes, and the one given here is an example of a good effect easily obtained. The strap across the centre only is decorated, this being outlined with small pearls, which are sewn in two lines down the sides, and carried across in two places. This divides the band into

No. 24.—Tinsel Ribbon decorated with Jewels and Chain Stitch in Silk.

three divisions. In the middle one is sewn a large diamond which is enclosed in a claw setting, thus raising this stone rather high in the centre of the strap. Round the outside of the setting are arranged four short lengths of greenish bullion, thus filling the middle of the three spaces. The remaining two are each occupied by a six-sided diamond, each of which is surrounded with pieces of the same bullion as that used in the middle space. This completes the bow as illustrated here. The tint of the bullion used should depend upon the colour of the dress with which the shoes are to be worn, and the stones, it is needless to say, may be infinitely varied as to colour, size, shape, and style of arrangement. Many ladies embroider a small spray on the satin of which they intend their shoes to be made before they send it to their shoemaker to be mounted. The stems, &c., of a little spray of flowers are thus often followed with tiny gold or silver beads, the little flowers themselves being put in with gems of appropriate shapes. These are extremely brilliant when the shoes are in use, for they gleam brightly according to the frequent changes of the light upon them.

No. 21.—JEWELLED TRIMMING FOR FANCY ARTICLES.

It is often a difficulty to find something more novel and less commonplace than cord for finishing off the edges of sachets, pincushions, and various other fancy articles. The pleated ribbon shown here forms a very pretty trimming. Two lengths of ribbon are required, or one folded in half. The two pieces are folded down the sides and are brought alternately over and under each other, a gem being sewn in the middle of each fold and surrounded with a ring of tiny silver beads.

No. 22.—ORNAMENTATION FOR WORK-BAGS OR HANDKERCHIEF CASES.

This style of decoration is both novel and effective, and is to be recommended to those ladies who have neither time nor skill for the execution of elaborate embroideries. The work consists of a lattice work of narrow ribbon of two colours, the straps of which are placed at some distance apart, so as to show the background in between the interlacing. The bands of ribbon are passed alternately over and under each other, and are held down where they cross with a single jewel, which gives much the effect of a stud. In the original these studs were diamonds, the ribbons being greyish-blue and pale pink. There are many other colours which blend very prettily, such as light blue and pale terra-cotta, sage green and pale salmon-pink, rose colour and a certain dull shade of brown. Ribbons having a fancy edge are more effective than those with a plain finish.

No. 25.—Jewels used in Anglo-Indian Embroidery.

The velvet background should be kept very subdued in tint, as this increases the effect of the fancy ribbons. Sometimes a linen or cotton material is selected for the foundation, and in such a case the ribbons are laid quite close together, so that the background is hidden by them. The foundation should be cut of the size required before the ribbons are laid in place, and it is a good plan to tack some of these down firmly at the edges of the foundation before beginning to weave them over and under each other. When all the plaiting is done the ribbons must be arranged so that all set equally tight across the background, and they are then secured round the edges with a few stitches. The jewels are sewn on next, and these help to keep the bands in place. The work is then ready to be made up. It can be adapted to charming little photograph cases, made like enormous envelopes, and quilted. scented, and edged round with cord or with one of the ribbon trimmings already described. Handkerchief sachets can be made in a similar fashion, but the shape, of course, is slightly different. The thickness of the work itself renders it more appropriate to such articles as have to be lined with quilted satin than to those which are to be made up quite flat.

No. 23.—JEWELLED QUILTING.

In many old portraits of the beauties of bygone days, we find quilting largely employed for petticoats and fronts of dresses, and this is rarely the plain, unornamented quilting that we now use, to the exclusion of every other kind. Jewels or beads were sewn down at the places where the lines of stitching crossed, and this stitching itself was often executed fancifully, sometimes even with a number of minutely worked sprays of embroidery. Jewels are admirably suited for this ornamental quilting, and a very good specimen is that given here, which would make a pretty covering for a handkerchief sachet, a glove box or nightdress case. It is also well suited for a cover to an open work-basket. In the original, the satin was old-gold colour, and two kinds of jewels alone were used, these being pink topazes and sapphires. They are alternated and are sewn down exactly where each line of stitching meets. Beyond the jewels are placed four crinkled gold beads, each of which rests upon a line of stitching. Many varieties may be made in this fancy quilting, according to the way in which the jewels are sewn down and surrounded. Any of the four methods shown on page 11 would be appropriate. The gems in a claw setting look especially well upon quilted satin, but if rounds of gold thread are used, two will be sufficient, a larger number being likely to flatten the quilting.

No. 24.—TINSEL RIBBON DECORATED WITH JEWELS, &c.

Amongst the very attractive novelties lately brought out in the way of ribbons are some in which gold or silver tinsel is woven into more or less elaborate designs. These are largely used as trimmings for evening dresses, or for streamers to bouquets, while if a long length be taken and gathered up with a silver tassel at each end, nothing can be prettier as a girdle for a young lady's white ball dress. The effect of some of these ribbons is greatly improved by the addition of a little colour, and this suggestion can be recommended to any one who has worn such a ribbon two or three times and finds it requires freshening up. In our engraving it will be seen that the wavy line down the centre has been followed with a single row of chain-stitch worked with pale pink silk. The circles are worked round with pale blue, also in chain-stitch, and have a pink topaz in the middle of each. Other and smaller circles are filled with a yellow moonstone, which though uncut is very brilliant, and the natural weaving of the ribbon forms a little ring of silver round each. Down each side of the ribbon is woven a row of round dots of white velvet which seen in certain light bear a good resemblance to pearls and are quite in keeping with the jewels added to the rest of the ribbon.

No. 25.—JEWELS IN ANGLO-INDIAN EMBROIDERY.

Anglo-Indian embroidery has been popular for a long time past, but the introduction of jewels has enabled workers to execute it far more brilliantly than hitherto. Most people know that Anglo-Indian embroidery is worked upon large-patterned and gaudy-printed cotton handkerchiefs or neck-cloths. These are, as a rule, only to be obtained in country towns, and often in the markets, but a few of a rather better quality have been brought out for the purpose, and are to be had at most fancy shops. The cotton material is first lined with soft linen, and is then almost entirely covered with stitches, worked with silks and wools of every shade of colour to blend artistically. Spangles and gold thread and every variety of stitch are admissible. In the piece of the work given here, the colours used in the two pine patterns are much the same, but pearls are used on one where turquoises appear on the other. It is one of the advantages of Anglo-Indian embroidery that any and every colour of silk or wool may be employed, it being by no means necessary that one part of the work should correspond with the same pattern found elsewhere on the material. The worker is entirely free to follow her own taste, and often produces very excellent results. The newest way of managing the work is to embroider, perhaps, a pine such as one of those given here, then to cut it out and *appliqué* it to plush, velvet, or some other rich material. It can then be made up into sofa cushions, blotting-books, or anything of the kind.

No. 26.—BRAIDED TRIMMING, WITH TURQUOISES AND JET.

The mixture of jet and turquoises is very popular, and is used even upon bands made of worsted braid for outdoor jackets and mantle trimming. These braided garnitures are rarely executed directly upon the material, but are made up and ornamented before being applied to the garment they are to decorate. Worsted braid is used, and this is generally tubular instead of flat, thus giving a slightly raised effect. The braiding pattern is either bought ready printed on glazed linen or may be transferred to a similar material by the worker herself. The outlines of the design are then covered with braid, and this is tacked down with large stitches of coloured or white cotton. These need not be very carefully made, as they will be removed when the work is finished. When the strip is all braided some strong black sewing silk is taken and the edges of the braid are caught together wherever they overlap or set sufficiently close to enable this to be done. The stitches must be strong and neat, and it must be borne in mind

No. 26.—Braided Trimming with Jet and Turquoises.

No. 27.—Gold Braiding and Jewels.

that the right side of the braiding is that which at present lies next to the pattern on the glazed linen. When all the loose sections of the pattern have thus been sewn together, the tacking threads are removed and the turquoises and jet are placed on the trimming. In the pattern shown here the flat round *appliqués* are jet, the turquoises being oval and raised. The oval stones are faceted, the round ones are perfectly smooth like beads. The trimming will be found effective either on black or dark blue cloth, while on a dull green material emeralds may be substituted for the turquoises, and another fashionable mixture will be thereby obtained.

No. 27.—GOLD BRAIDING AND JEWELS.

This simple braiding is quite as effective for a dress trimming as are some of the more elaborate designs and embroideries sold for the purpose. It may be managed in two ways, either with narrow gold braid, or with a double row of gold cord, as shown in the illustration. The former plan is perhaps the easier of the two, but the effect is very similar to that given by braid, except that the cord is slightly more raised. The jewels are sewn on the foundation material in the middle of the various little loops of which the pattern consists. Almost any easy braiding design lends itself to an admixture of jewels in this simple style, and such embroidery may be executed for a gown made of any material, from cloth or serge to plush or velvet.

WELDON'S
PRACTICAL KNICK-KNACKS.

(FIRST SERIES.)

How to Make Pretty Things for Home Decoration, Gifts, or Bazaars.

TWENTY-SIX ILLUSTRATIONS.

WELDON'S PRACTICAL KNICK-KNACKS.

The heart hath its own memory, like the mind,
And in it are enshrined
The precious keepsakes into which is wrought
The giver's loving thought."

LADIES who have lots of leisure and with a taste for fancy work will, we are sure, welcome with pleasure this issue, which will be found replete with many a novelty in the way of dainty knick-knacks both for presentation and personal use.

Birthdays and festivals are always coming round, and ladies who have lots of loved ones on the *qui vive* of expectancy will be glad to know how to fashion useful and fanciful tokens, which not only cost a mere nothing and thus save a ruthless raiding of resources at command, but render all the more pleasing their presents from the fact of their being a part of their personality as well as their purses.

Those in need of suggestions for bazaar work cannot do better than follow out a few of the ideas herein presented, and which we have endeavoured to fully and clearly explain how to make.

HEART - SHAPE BOX FOR TRINKETS.

A CHARMING little receptacle for brooches, or the small fancy pins so much used just now for fastening down the frills of chiffons worn on dress bodices. It makes an ornamental addition to the toilet table, and may be made of almost any odds and ends of pretty, thin materials. It is very easily and quickly made, but requires a little care owing to its curved shape. The top and bottom of the box must be cut out of cardboard according to the full-sized diagram given on page 7. This will make a small box, but it is easy to cut it rather larger if preferred. One of these pieces is to serve as the bottom, the other as the lid of the box. Cover the bottom piece on both sides with satin or silk. These two sides need not be alike, but the prettiest colour must be arranged to be inside, as the bottom scarcely ever shows when the box is in use. The top must be covered rather more elaborately. Get some pongée silk of any delicate shade of colour, cut it into the shape of the heart, but much larger than the cardboard. Lay this on the cardboard and tack it here and there to form series of tiny puffs. Do not let the stitches show which hold down these fullings, but use cotton or silk that matches the covering exactly. A pretty effect is gained by sewing on a little metal bead wherever a stitch is made, or better still, the jewelled beads now so fashionable.

When the cardboard is covered, tack the silk just over the edge of the heart, then cut off any that may set beyond it. These stitches are hidden beneath a band of ornamental gold or fancy galon which is sewn down flat all round the heart, one edge projecting just about a sixteenth of an inch beyond the card

Heart-Shape Box for Trinkets.

board, or you could use gold braid or ribbon, which dot along with jewels This done, line the other side very neatly with a piece of the same silk or sateen that was used for the inside of the bottom of the box. Sew it round the edges to the edge of the galon that was arranged to set beyond the cardboard. In the tip of the heart is sewn a dainty bow of narrow ribbon which serves as a handle to raise the lid by. Add a full bow of wider ribbon to the upper end of the heart. This is all that can be done to the lid at present. For the side cut a narrow band of upholsterer's buckram or stiffened canvas such as tailors use for lining collars. This must be about an inch and a half wide, and must be covered on both sides; on one with the silk to match the inside lining, and on the other with plush, velvet, or any suitable material that looks well with the puffed silk top. This band must be long enough to fit exactly round the lower part of the box, the two ends meeting at the back. It must be sewn on with very small stitches matching the colour of the velvet.

If velvet or plush be used, the stitches will probably be hidden beneath the pile of the material, but if satin, brocade, or silk be employed, it will be necessary to hide the seam with a slender line of gold thread or fine silk cord. The lid is now joined to the bottom of the box with a tiny strap of the same ribbon of which the larger bow was made. Sew one end of this over the join at the back of the box for neatness, but it must be sewn slightly slack; so that when the lid is opened it will fold right back and the tip of the heart rest on the table, thus preventing the lid from overbalancing the bottom of the box.

When a larger sized box is made, it is as well to cover the cardboard with flannel, or with a thin layer of wadding. This makes the thin silk covering set far better than when it is stretched directly over the cardboard. Instead of the puffed top, a small piece of embroidery or painting may be used, or the lid may be covered partially with brocade and partially with velvet or satin; yet another plan is to cover the top with satin and to stretch a band of fancy galon or bullion braid slantwise over it. There is an infinite number of ways in which a dainty little receptacle of this kind may be varied and a dozen such may be made without costing the worker more than a few pence, for surely everybody possesses the little scraps necessary for these small boxes.

By covering two pieces of cardboard to the shape of the diagram and sewing same together, a very pretty pincushion could be formed, while this design would serve as a watch-holder if a fancy hook were sewn from beneath the bows.

BOOK COVER.

THERE is always an unlimited demand at bazaars for book covers of all kinds, made in all sizes, and trimmed and ornamented in every conceivable manner, while they make very pretty presents at all times. Such a one as that given here costs very little to make even if the worker has to buy all the materials. Two pieces of stout card are needed for the sides, a piece of linen for the back, moiré, plush, or brocade for the cover, with a broad band of ribbon which can be embroidered and laid diagonally across the front. Gold thread, silks, satin for the inside, and several other odds and ends will be required as the work progresses.

The first thing to do is to prepare the cardboard foundation of the cover. Cut the two cards the necessary size, lay them on a piece of board, leaving a space between them equal to the width of the back of the book they are to cover, pin them down to the board with a few drawing-pins along the top and bottom edges, measuring the space between them very carefully to be sure they are quite even. Cut a strip of linen or calico the length of the covers, and two inches wider. Glue this over the space between the covers, allowing the extra width to lay firmly over the edges of the cards. Put a pile of heavy books or anything weighty over the cover till the glue is perfectly dry, and meanwhile get on with the outside. Cut a piece of moiré one inch larger all

Book-Cover.

round than the covers, and in two of the corners embroider a spray of flowers, arranging one in the upper left-hand corner, the other in the lower right-hand corner. Across the middle is arranged a band of ribbon, on which should be embroidered a running pattern in conventional style, bordered on either edge with a gold braid. A few jewels may be mixed in with the embroidery with very good effect. By this time the covers will probably be dry and ready for the trimming. Lay the moiré on the table wrong side uppermost, then place the cards upon it, fold the edges of the moiré over and glue them down firmly to the cards inside and allow to dry. The lining must next be made ready. Cut a piece of stiff muslin the exact size of the cards and cover it with thin satin or silk. Cut two more pieces of muslin, each one inch and a half wide and the length of the cover, and cover with silk also; these two pieces are used as a pocket at either end. Fold down the edge along one of the long sides of the pocket, then lay it in its proper place on the lining, fold the raw edges over to the wrong side of this, and fasten them down securely. The lining is now ready to be placed inside the cover. Place a thin layer of glue all over the back of the lining, which now place over the cards, press it well down, then leave it to dry. Make next a smart little bookmarker of fine gold cord. Cut a length of cord about three inches longer than the cover, make a loop at one end and sew it inside just below the upper edge in the centre of the cover. Finish the other end of the cord with a little tassel made by cutting a number of strands, folding them in half, and tying them in the usual way. If preferred the bookmarker may be made of a strip of narrow ribbon finished at the end with a tassel or with a small rosette-like bow.

When working for a bazaar it is advisable to make a series of covers for well-known volumes, so that the purchaser need not run the risk of taking them on the chance of their fitting some favourite volume. *Bradshaw* and *A.B.C.* railway guides, *Academy Notes*, *The Queen*, *Punch*, *Weldon's Journal*, and many other publications may have covers specially made for them with the title embroidered outside as part of the ornamentation. The shallow pockets inside the lining are intended to hold the covers of the book, but the width in which they are to be made must, of course, depend upon the size of the volume. The inch and a half mentioned above is appropriate for octavo books, but it is never advisable to make the pockets narrower than an inch wide even in the case of very tiny books indeed.

CASE FOR CREWEL SILKS.

EVERY lady who does much embroidery appreciates the comfort of being able to keep her silks tidily and conveniently arranged. No better form of case for this purpose could be desired than that illustrated here, which is most compact and neat, yet simple and easy to make. Workers for bazaars will find

that these cases sell well, while as there is generally either very little or no embroidery at all about them, they are quickly put together, and will prove a welcome suggestion to those ladies who are more skilled in the execution of plain work than fancy work. Unlike many such things, cases for holding silks are more convenient when made of cotton or linen material than when a richer fabric is chosen for them. Sateen, cream or écru twill, jean, or cretonne are suitable, brown holland also making up very attractively for the purpose.

The case illustrated here is made of a piece of material measuring eleven inches wide and twenty-five inches long. Each end is turned up to the depth of four inches to form the pocket. The top edge of each of these pockets must be bound either with coloured braid or ribbon. The pocket is then tacked all round to keep it from slipping out of place. Cut next a piece of the material measuring six inches in depth and thirteen and a half inches long. Lay this across the middle of the case so that an equal space is left between it and the top of each pocket; tack it down and make ten lines of stitching across it an inch apart, thus dividing it into eleven sections. Be careful to get these lines quite straight and all at equal distances one from the other. The best plan is to mark the case itself at every inch, then divide the piece of linen (thirteen and a half inches long) into ten equal parts, and place each of these divisions over the corresponding line on case, where they would be stitched together. The piece of linen laid on case is obliged to be a trifle longer than case is wide to form the pockets through which the skeins of silk are drawn. The case is next bound all round with the binding that was used for the pockets. It is an improvement also to bind the edges of the piece of material laid across to form the receptacle for the skeins of silk. Two ends of braid or ribbon should now be sewn in the middle of the case outside to serve as strings.

Similar cases may be made for holding wools. The casings in these must however, be made to run across the case instead of down its length, as since the wool is more bulky than the silk, the case could be more easily rolled up. It is also advisable to add a flap at each end of the divisions which hold the wools, so that this may fold over into the inside of the case and keep the ends of the wools tidy. Another plan is to arrange a pocket at one end only of the case and at the other to make a rounded flap with a buttonhole in the point to fasten over a button placed upon the body of the case. A little embroidery may be worked upon this flap if desired, but all that is really necessary is the word "Silks" or "Wools" worked in ornamental letters with perhaps a tiny spray of flowers, or a scroll or two of gold thread at either end.

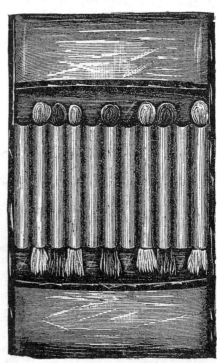

Case for Crewel Silks.

The greater part of the stitching required in making these cases may be executed far more neatly with the sewing machine than by hand, and thus both time and labour are saved.

TRIPLE WALL-POCKET.

A WALL-POCKET of quite a novel shape, resembling a colossal shamrock leaf. It is both pretty and convenient, and is well adapted for bazaars, as several can be prepared each of different colours and materials. Half the shape in the full working size is given in the diagram on page 7, the line marked with stars indicating the middle of the back of the wall-pocket, and where a seam must be avoided. The tip of the middle leaf has, in the diagram, been simply folded back to allow the design to fit the page. This shape must be cut out of cardboard and covered smoothly first with flannel, which greatly adds to the appearance of the vide-poche when made up. This covering must be caught down with long stitches carried across at the back from edge to edge of the flannel. The worker must be careful to keep the material as flat as possible, even on the wrong side. It will be as well to gather the material round the three large curves of the pocket, and to snip pieces out wherever the flannel can be removed without interfering with the set of the front.

This done the ornamental cover should be placed in position. It may be made of some material decorated with embroidery, or with brocade, or even cretonne or printed sateen. This must be stretched over the flannel, the snippings being made in the same way. The flat pockets for the two sides of the vide-poche must now be made. These are quite flat, and therefore are useful for holding letters, cards, and such things, the bag in the middle division serving for handkerchiefs, work, and similar articles. For the two side pockets two pieces of cardboard are required, cut of the shape shown by the darkened portion of the diagram. These are covered on one side with flannel and with plush to correspond in colour with that of the brocade used for the foundation. They should be lined with plain silk, then sewn neatly into place, as shown in the sketch. The worker must, in making these, be careful to prepare one to fit the left-hand side, the other to fit the right-hand

Triple Wall Pocket.

side. It is advisable to lay the pieces of card on the foundation before covering them, and to make a pencil mark on that side which is to be covered with the plush. This will save the possible trouble of having to take the covering off and transferring it to the other side of the card, a matter which is sure to damage the material more or less. The bag for the lower division is made of silk the colour of the plush. It is cut three inches wider than the depth of the lower part, about two inches larger than the lowest edge, and from the height of about three inches it must widen out till it is four inches wider on each side than the foundation measured just an inch below the beginning of the side pieces. An inch and a half is turned over at the top to form a hem with a casing, into which is run a narrow elastic. This should draw up the mouth of the pocket till it is about an inch wider than the brocade-covered foundation.

The pocket is then sewn into place. The best way of doing this is to turn the edges over to the wrong side, and to sew them down firmly. The silk will need easing here and there to use up the extra fulness, and to give plenty of space in the pocket. An ornamental brass hook for a watch must now be firmly sewn to the front just where the handle or stem meets the leaves. At the end of the stem will be needed a brass ring by which the pocket can be hung up. Line the back next very neatly with sateen, satin, or sarcenet. Finally pass a band of ribbon round the upper part of the stem, and tie it into a smart bow in the front. This band and bow will probably require fixing with a few stitches, but these need not be taken through to the wrong side and so spoil its neat appearance.

FLOWER-POT COVER.

THIS is a particularly convenient shape of cover for a flower-pot, as it is suitable for more than one size, being expansive both in width and height. Either velvet or soft silk may be used for the cover, but the prettiest are composed of a mixture of these materials, velveteen or velvet being used for the outside, and soft silk for the inside. The base of the cover is made of cardboard. This is cut round in shape and rather larger than the bottom of an ordinary flower-pot. Cover the outside of this circle with the velvet or other material chosen for the bag. For the cover cut a strip of the velvet, measuring three inches wider than the height of a flower-pot and long enough to set full round the broadest part. Join the two short sides together, of course, on the wrong side. Cut a similar piece of silk for the lining, join the two short sides together, then lay the top edge of the velvet and the top edge

of the silk together, running them along on the wrong side, then turn them over so that the silk sets as a lining to the velvet and the upper edge is quite neat and tidy. Make a gathering round the lower edges of these two materials, draw up to the size of the circle and sew the velvet and silk to the wrong side of the circle, so that the raw edges set towards the inside. Line this inner side of the circle with the silk, thus making all neat. Make a casing about an inch wide and three inches below the top edge of the cover and into this run drawstrings of ribbon about an inch wide. Instead of joining the ends into a loop, in the usual way, they should be left free and each one finished at the end with a dainty bow. When the pot is inside the case, these ribbons are drawn up closely and tied so that the cover fits the pot exactly. Should the case be found too large for any particular pot it is to contain, the ribbons can be drawn up so that it will fit closely round it, while should it be too tall, the case is easily pulled out round the middle of the pot so as to lower the frill round the upper edge. These pot-covers may easily be adapted to other purposes; for example, they make excellent work-bags, while, if a small jar be slipped inside, they form pretty receptacles for cut flowers and ferns. Made in more slender shapes they may contain a glass flower vase and thus form a very fashionable style of dinner-table ornament. The vase need not be of a particularly good quality, but should have a fancifully crumpled wide-spreading mouth, to show slightly above the frill of the covers. When the covers are used for this purpose, silk of two colours is more suitable for them than velvet, as being less bulky.

SHOPPING OR BOOK BAG.

SMALL receptacles for parcels always compel a ready sale at bazaars, as people are often glad to have something in which to carry their numerous purchases. The bag illustrated here is a very convenient shape, as it holds a good deal, the two sides folding quite flatly together when it is empty. The most effective materials to use for such a bag are linens of various colours. For instance, two shades of blue form a pretty covering, the darker being used inside, the paler outside. The diagrams for one side and end of the bag are given half their full size, the line in the pattern marked with stars showing the middle of the piece of cardboard and the linen for the cover and which should be placed to a fold in the material to avoid a seam. The wedge-shaped gussets for the ends do not require a cardboard foundation, simply two pieces of linen being necessary, which would be laid over one another, the raw edges turned in and neatly sewn together. The piece of linen for the front of the bag can either have one's Christian name embroidered upon it, or some pretty design, using flax threads to harmonise with the colour of the linen.

The linen should be drawn quite smoothly and tightly over the cardboard, and secured with stitches of very strong thread taken in lacing-fashion across and across the linen at back. The lining should then be put in. This need not reach quite to the edge of the outside cover except along the upper edge, where it would be slip-stitched neatly down to meet the outer cover. When

Flower-Pot Cover.

the four pieces are ready, they should be neatly but very strongly sewn together. The seams may be improved in appearance by laying over them about six strands of coloured flax thread, and catching this down at quarter-inch intervals with a stitch of thread of a different colour. Round the upper edge of the basket outside should be sewn a band of either cotton or woollen ball fringe. This should be chosen, if possible, with a wide and ornamental heading, and if this has a row of loops along the upper edge, as is frequently the case, these should be allowed to stand up above the top of the bag.

For the handles, cut two pieces of ordinary rope each about twelve inches long. Tie a piece of fine twine tightly round each end to prevent the rope from becoming untwisted, and cover these pieces with dark braid to match the linen used for the inside. Lay the rope upon the braid, and sew the two edges firmly together. This done, sew the two handles on the basket very strongly in the manner shown in the sketch, hiding where they are secured with two full rosettes of braid or ribbon to match the outer part of the basket.

6

Fold the soft sides of the bag into pleats so that these will not project beyond the basket when it is not in use. The manner of doing this will be easily understood by examining the pockets in a purse, writing-case, or pocket-book. The success of a bag of this kind depends upon the colours chosen for the covering and lining. Shades of blue always look well, or dark blue and red, brown and gold, or cream and pale blue. A more uncommon combination is faded green with salmon pink, or terra cotta and light blue. A full ruche of one of the two materials, or of ribbon, may be used instead of the ball fringe should there be any difficulty in procuring this to match the materials used for the bag.

BUTTERFLY WATCH-HOLDER AND PINCUSHION.

THIS pretty little novelty is composed of small scraps of material, such as satin and velvet, while wire, narrow ribbon, gold thread, and embroidery silks are all needed. As usual with these fancy articles the first thing is to cut the foundation of the holder out in cardboard, which can be done from the diagram on page 10, which shows the full working size.

Having accomplished this, take a piece of satin—very pale blue or green would be pretty—lay it on the table right side uppermost, place the cardboard upon it, hold it down firmly with the left hand, and draw a pencil or chalk line all round it. Trace also on the satin the shape of the body of the insect, as shown in the diagram. The wings have to be embroidered with lines of fine gold thread, then jewels are sewn on outlined with satin stitch worked with coloured silk. The part where the body comes need not, of course, be worked upon. Work a row of spaced buttonholes round the edges of the wings to form double wings as it were, and the lower portion can be curved away from the body, as illustrated, or be left as in the diagram. Stretch the satin very smoothly over the cardboard shape, snipping it at the edges wherever necessary in order to get it to set satisfactorily. Prepare the body next, cut

Shopping or Book Bag.

a piece of cardboard to the shape of the body shown in the diagram, cover it with black velvet, having previously put a tiny bit of wadding over the cardboard to give a slight roundness. Glue it down in its proper place on the butterfly, and add a few invisible stitches to make it quite secure. Procure an ornamental watch-hook, pierced with holes, and sew it firmly to the body of the butterfly just below the head of the insect. Add the feelers next. Make these of a piece of wire about two inches and half long, pushed through the velvet at the top of the head. Thread a small bead at the end of each piece of wire, turn over the wire just beyond the bead, and twist the end two or three times round to prevent the bead from falling off. Take the narrow ribbon, make a loop to hold the watch-holder up by, sew it firmly at the back of the cardboard, and add a smart little bow at the top of the loop, as shown in the sketch.

A second piece of cardboard (of thinner make) should now be cut to the same pattern, and covered with sateen or sarcenet, matching the satin in colour, to serve as lining, and which would be sewn all round the edges to the first piece of cardboard, thus completing the watch-holder. The pins are pushed in round the edges between the two layers of cardboard.

Another way of making a watch-holder of this kind, but without the pincushion, is to cut the wings out in stiff muslin, and to sew a fine wire round them. The satin is laid over these in the usual way, the advantage of the wire being that the wings may be bent about according to fancy. Large butterflies, such as illustrated, may be utilised for bazaar purposes. They can be sewn at the top of two or three pieces of cloth to serve as penwipers, or above leaves of flannel to serve as needlebooks. Made of gigantic size they can be placed on the side of a handkerchief sachet, while, if composed of gold gauze and wired round the edges, they may be perched on the edges of photograph frames or of fancy baskets, their appearance being greatly enhanced if the gauze is sprinkled with jewels or spangles. They are often made, too, of the cheap silk squares now sold and used as chairbacks for small chairs, or as supports for curtains.

DIAGRAMS.

ON page 7 will be found diagrams for cutting out the Triple Wall-Pocket, Thermometer Holder, Heart-shape Box, Powder Puff, and Shopping Bag, each of which is denoted by a distinct line, as shown by the diagram keys.

NEWSPAPER HOLDER.

NEWSPAPER and magazine holders of every conceivable shape and size find a ready sale at bazaars nowadays, when it is so much the custom to crowd the walls of a room with as many such knick-knacks as can possibly find a place there. The holder sketched here may be made very ornamental, but much will depend upon the colours used for it. The large piece of cardboard needed for the back must be cut out first. The shape is clearly shown in miniature on the diagram given on page 10. From A to B it must measure nine inches in width, then gradually widen out at each side till from the points C to D it is eleven inches across. The middle scallop is about five inches wide at the bottom and narrows to three inches in width at the top. The extreme length of the back from E to F is eighteen inches. A pretty material for covering the front of this piece of cardboard is moiré, pale pink or old gold looking well with an embroidered design representing peacocks' feathers. Before covering the foundation of the holder, however, it is necessary to make the actual case which is to contain the newspapers. This consists of a piece of cardboard the shape of the smaller diagram on page 10, two narrow pieces for the sides, a strip for the bottom, and a piece for the back. This back piece must measure five inches in width and nine inches in length. The division for the front should be cut exactly the same size as this, but the upper edge must be hollowed out in the manner shown in the diagram, the depth of the slope in the middle being about two inches. The front piece is covered with some of the same moiré as that used for the back,

Butterfly Watch-Holder and Pincushion.

ornamented with embroidery executed in the same way. The moiré is laid over the card and the edges are glued down on the wrong side, being carefully snipped so that the silk sets quite smoothly over the upper and curved edge. The wrong side should be lined either with plain silk or sateen, the edges of this, of course, are turned in and the material either sewn or glued into place. A narrow band of fancy or gold galon should be fastened as a finish along the upper and curved edge. The straight piece for the back of the pocket is covered on both sides with sateen, those for the sides being covered with moiré and lined with the cheaper material. These narrower pieces should measure about two inches in width and nine inches in length. The four pieces are sewn together down the sides so that they make a rather flat case like a post-card case on a large scale. The piece for the bottom is made last. The cardboard should measure two inches in width like the side pieces, and five inches in length. It also is covered outside with moiré, inside with sateen, and is then sewn into place, thus completing the shape of the box. A novel way of hiding the stitches which joined the sections of the holder consists in working a row of buttonhole stitch with coarse twist along the edge of the moiré, placing them so that the straight edges of the stitches set over the seam. A similar row of buttonholing should be worked down each seam, the straight edges pointing always in the same direction. The double row of stitches should completely hide those of the seam below them. A variation may be made by laying two or three strands of gold thread over the seam and catching them down at half-inch intervals with an overcast stitch of coarse coloured twist, this being taken through one of the buttonhole stitches on each side of the seam alternately.

The next thing to be done is to fasten the holder to the piece of moiré already prepared for covering the large piece of cardboard. Get some paste and spread a little at the back of the holder, laying it on thinly, but so that it is all covered. Lay the holder in position on the moiré and let it dry. Smooth and pull it into place with the hands so that it does not become at all shrunken or puckered. When quite dry take a needle threaded with some strong cotton and further fasten the holder to the moiré by making a line of

7

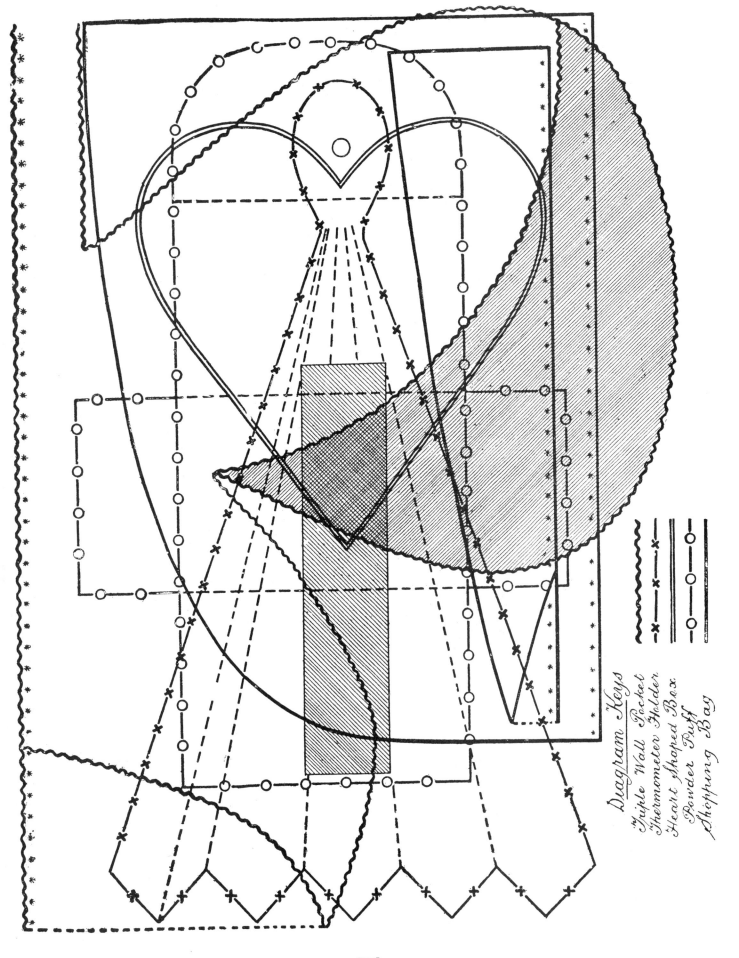

Diagram Keys

Triple Wall Pocket
Thermometer Holder
Heart Shaped Box
Powder Puff
Shopping Bag

[89]

stitches through the moiré and through the sateen cover of the case. Of course this must be done on the wrong side. Again be careful to avoid drawing the moiré out of place.

This satisfactorily done, the moiré is laid over the cardboard back and the edges glued down firmly to the wrong side. The lower edge of the holder must set along the lower edge of the back, and the worker must see that the whole thing is not spoilt by this setting crooked upon the card. When the glue is dry it is as well to make all doubly secure by taking a series of stitches completely through the card and moiré all round about a quarter of an inch from the edge. These stitches may easily be hidden beneath a band of ornamental gold braid, the look of which is often greatly improved by being woven in a series of little loops or picots either on one or both sides. Four small brass rings are next sewn at the back of the holder to hang it up by. Four bows of ribbon are next arranged in the manner shown in the sketch. The colours of the ribbon should be very mixed. Some of the loops should match the moiré, one at least in each bow should be gold or tinsel, the others should correspond with he tints of the embroidery. The loops at the right and left sides of the lower bows should be long enough to enable them to be brought up the sides of the holder and to set slightly over the front, where they can easily be held down with a stitch. The last thing to do is to line the back of the holder with sateen, sewing it neatly to the moiré just below the edge of the gold galon, which should completely prevent the stitches from being visible from the front.

TABLE SCREEN for PHOTOGRAPHS.

THIS is a very convenient holder for photographs, and may be made to take either three or six. In the screen illustrated three photographs only can be placed, and two of the divisions are covered in a simpler way than is the third. This is newer than when all the sections are made exactly alike. Cut out three pieces of stout cardboard, each measuring eight inches and a half long and six inches and a half wide. Cut another set of three pieces the same size, but in the exact middle of these cut out an oblong opening measuring five inches and a half long and three inches and a half wide. If the screen is to have three divisions and yet hold six photographs, all six of these cards must be cut with the opening in the middle. The screen may be made with five or even seven sections if preferred, but it will then be rather more bulky when folded up. If several screens are to be made, it will save the amateur a deal of time and trouble in measuring if she gets a professional mount-cutter to prepare the cards, which will add very little to the cost. Brocade, velvet, satin,

Newspaper Holder.

or any other rich material should be chosen for the covering. This must be laid with the right side downwards on the table, the cardboard placed upon it and the edges folded over to the wrong side of the cardboard, and laced across and across with stitches of strong thread. The material must be snipped at the corners of the opening or it will not set smoothly upon the card. The ornamentation in the middle division consists of bands of fancy gold trimming, coarse lace or embroidery, laid slantwise upon the frame, but this is only appropriate for use with a plain material such as velvet or satin.

When all the cards are covered, they are firmly glued together, one side either at the top or bottom (the former is generally found most convenient) being left free to enable the photograph being slipped in. It can be readily understood that if the screen is open all through each division so as to hold six photographs, these are put in in pairs, back to back, so that the screen is exactly the same at the back as in the front. The divisions are very simply joined together with a few stitches of silk taken across from division to division, but left loose instead of being drawn up tightly. This arrangement it must be noted enables the screen to be folded up, and the worker must be careful to see that she has left the stitches sufficiently loose to enable this to be done easily and without undue strain. Two sets of stitches must be placed between every two divisions, one set just about half an inch below the top, the other at the same distance above the bottom. Bows of ribbon are placed here and there upon the frames, and a very great improvement to the general look of the screen may be effected by pushing a pin with a large ornamental head into each corner of the divisions. Those for the bottom should be chosen with flat heads to serve as feet for the screen to stand upon.

When the screen is made with three divisions and to hold only three photographs, the pieces of cardboard that have no openings in the middle should be covered on both sides, or they will look very unsightly should the owner have occasion to remove any of the photographs; more especially is this necessary when making the frames for sale at a bazaar, as most probably they would be shown without photographs. The divisions which are outermost when the screen is folded up may be ornamented with a spray of artificial flowers, laid across the corner and arranged with a bow of ribbon over the stalks to look as if the ribbon held them in place. All kinds and shapes of table screens may be made on this principle, and especially pretty are those which hold two photographs in each division, one above the other. The frames in this case must be left free at the bottom as well as at the top to allow of the pair of portraits being slipped in.

MAGAZINE HOLDER.

THIS elaborate holder calls for a variety of materials, but for the consolation of an economical worker it may be stated that a very small quantity only of each is required. Procure quarter yard of satin, half a yard of moiré, and half a yard of sateen; a sufficient quantity of satin ribbon two inches wide to make one large full rosette and two small bows, half a yard of ribbon one inch wide and a yard of ribbon the same width but of a different colour; about two dozen artificial marguerites, fancy galon with a double picot edge; cardboard and

Table Scre

buckram or stiff muslin for the foundation of the holder, while scraps of gold thread and stray needlefuls of silk will also be useful.

The first thing to do is to cut the foundation for the back and front of the holder out of cardboard. The former should measure twelve inches in width, its greatest length being eighteen inches. As will be seen from the diagram, which is in miniature and merely given as a guide to the shape, it is quite straight till a depth of nine inches from the bottom is reached, and then is curved round very gradually, finished in the middle with a deep but narrow point, only two inches wide, which, as will be seen from the sketch of the completed holder, serves as a support for the rosette and also holds a ring at the back by which the holder can be suspended from a convenient knob or nail. The piece of card for the front measures twelve inches one way and seven inches the other and is quite straight, as seen from the diagram. The gussets for the sides of the holder are cut out in stiff muslin the shape given in the diagram. They are each covered on the outside with moiré and lined with sateen. The satin is used for the front of the holder; it should first have a really good piece of embroidery executed upon it, but if the worker is not able to manage this, a good effect may be gained by the use of the crewel appliqués to be had now in such a great variety at almost every fancy shop. The worker should not be satisfied by merely pasting these down upon the material, but should work a few stitches round the edges with silk, matching the appliqué as exactly as possible. Failing this, a line of gold thread may be carried round them. This will be a great improvement and will do much to disguise the fact that they are not really worked directly upon the material. When the satin is ready, it is stretched tightly and smoothly over the cardboard, this having first been covered with a layer of flannel or other woolly material. The satin may be held down either with lacing stitches or with touches of gum or glue on the wrong side. The daisies are then sewn on all round the edges of the front. They are set so that they just touch, but do not overlap one another. The two lower corners are left free so that there is room for a bow of ribbon in each. These are sewn on next and the front piece is then lined with sateen.

The back piece is covered on one side with moiré, on the other with sateen. The moiré is arranged on the side which will be the front, the upper edge where it shows above the pocket being edged with the gold galon. At the lower edge is sewn a series of ribbon streamers, alternately long and short. The short strands are three inches long, the longer ones about four inches. Each of these is mitred at the end, and finished alternately with a small pompon and a little gilt sequin. The rosette is made for the top next and duly sewn into place. The sateen lining is then sewn on, and should cover all imperfections, even the raw edges of the ribbons setting between the sateen and the cardboard.

The front and back sections of the holder can now be joined; sew the lower edges of these together, so that when the front is turned up in its proper place the stitches will not be visible, after which the gussets should be sewn in, the stitches down the front seam being hidden by the daisies on the front piece.

This completes the holder as sketched here. It will be found a very convenient and capacious shape, and may be made in a great variety of

must be cut out with a sharp penknife as it is not easy to cut them cleanly with a pair of scissors. The right side of the card must be covered first. For this, either satin, silk, plush, velvet, brocade, or even linen or cretonne may be used. If a plain material be selected, it should be ornamented with embroidery or painting, but a fancy fabric needs only a few lines across it to represent some of the folds of the fan, according to the dotted lines in the diagram. These lines can be of gold thread or very fine fancy cord, and on each side should be sewn a few small gold beads, about a quarter of an inch being left between each one.

It will be noticed from the diagram that a free space must be left in the middle of the fan to hold the thermometer. The easiest way of managing this is to lay the thermometer on the foundation, and, holding it in a perfectly straight position, draw a chalk or pencil line all round it. When the covering is thus far ready, it must be stretched very tightly upon the cardboard. Any difficulty found in getting it to set smoothly over the vandykes at the lower edge may be obviated by snipping it between each one, and it will most likely be easier to glue down the raw edges on the wrong side than to sew them. Should the snippings be at all unsightly when the work is finished, they can easily be hidden beneath a line of gold thread or cord. Make the bow of ribbon next for the lower right-hand corner and sew it firmly into place. The covering for the back of the fan can be of sateen or any suitable material, as it will be completely hidden when the fan is hanging against the wall, and it is managed just in the same way as the front side, turning in the lower edge of the vandykes and glueing them neatly down. The round hole may now be made in the handle of the fan, and it should be rather larger than actually desired, as the oversewing will fill it up slightly. Coarse twist should be used for this and buttonhole stitches set very closely together. A line of gold cord is then taken round the outside of the stitches and finally a band of ribbon and a bow are arranged just below the handle of the fan. This holder is now ready for the thermometer, which must be glued into the place that was marked out with chalk during an earlier stage of the proceedings. Should there be, as is often the case, a ring on the thermometer to hang it up by, it is as well to pass a few stitches through this and through the cardboard to make it additionally secure.

GLOVE-BOX.

THERE is really scarcely any limit to the number of pretty things that may be made out of cardboard boxes. Even if these are slit and damaged at the corners it is of no consequence, for they can be easily repaired in the making up; they should, however, not be used if the flat part of the card at the sides, top, or bottom is at all bent or broken. The glove case sketched here is made

Photographs

Magazine Holder.

materials, such for instance as cretonne, sateen, plush, velvet, velveteen, brocade or tapestry. Ball fringe may take the place of the ribbons if preferred. If a very plain and economical wall-pocket be desired, it may be made of Turkey twill, embroidered in white and trimmed with ruchings of white braid. Linen of any colour may be used and would look well if trimmed with quillings of very narrow strips of the material cut on the cross and fringed at each side, while a cross-stitch design could ornament the part shown for embroidery in the illustration.

DIAGRAMS.

ON page 10, diagrams for cutting out the Brush and Comb Holder, Newspaper Holder, Opera-Glass Bag, Magazine Holder, and Butterfly Watch-Holder are given, and which can easily be distinguished on reference to the diagram keys at side.

THERMOMETER HOLDER.

THIS holder is a pretty novelty that is sure to meet with a ready sale at a bazaar, and it is by no means difficult to make half-a-dozen, each ornamented in a different style. The easiest plan is that shown in the sketch. The foundation is of moderately firm white cardboard cut into the shape of a partially opened fan, as shown in the diagram on page 7. The points at the lower end

of nothing more elaborate than an old corset-box. The material used for the cover is art serge of any pretty, soft colour. The lid, if attached to the bottom part of the box, must be taken off and the sides removed, thus leaving only a flat oblong piece of card. Cover with a layer of wadding, and over this stretch a piece of the serge upon which has been worked a pretty trailing embroidery design. Line it by cutting a piece of thin card or stout paper exactly the same size, covering this with satin or sarcenet, laying the two together and sewing them very neatly round the edges. Border the lid with a fancy chenille cord mixed with a little tinsel wool, which twist into loops at each corner and in the exact middle of what is intended to be the front of the lid sew a smart ribbon bow to serve as a handle. A gauze butterfly or a spray of art ficial flowers may be laid on the lid for additional ornamentation.

Now take the bottom of the box. Cut a strip of the material long enough to fit exactly round the sides when the ends are seamed together. This should be embroidered along the front to match the lid, then stretch this strip over the box, fold the raw edges to the bottom and over the edge of the inside of the box, holding them down with a few touches of glue. To make the lining, cut four pieces of thin card or paper such as was used for the lid lining and to correspond in size with the sides of the box, cover each piece with wadding, then with sarcenet or sateen, and sew them together down the sides on the wrong side. Glue them on the wrong side, and slip them into the inside of the box, pressing them down well with the hands till they set closely and evenly against the sides. Cut another piece of card for the bottom of the box about one-eighth of an inch smaller all round than the original. Cover this also with wadding and sarcenet and push it well down into the inside. If it has been

10

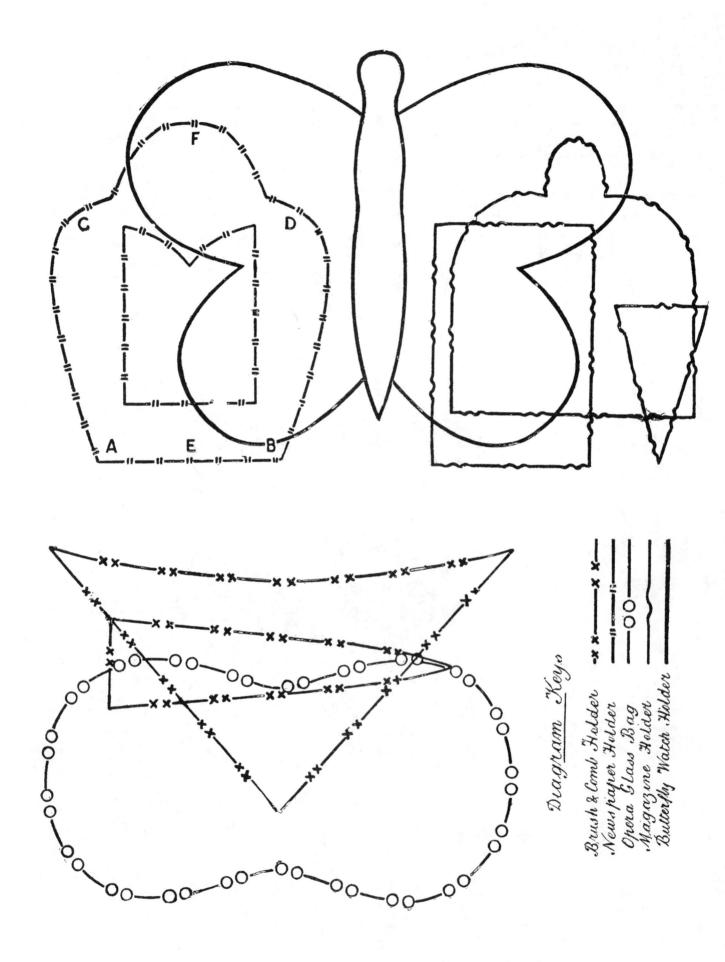

Diagram Keys

Brush & Comb Holder
Newspaper Holder
Opera Glass Bag
Magazine Holder
Butterfly Watch Holder

properly made, it should fit perfectly without any fixing. Finally, cover the bottom of the box outside with sateen or any other suitable material.

The covering of the box is now complete, and it remains only to trim it down the sides and along the edges with cord to match the lid and to push four pins with very large fancy heads into the bottom of the lower corners to serve as feet upon which the box may stand. Now fasten on the lid by sewing the back edge to the back edge of the box. Add two small hinges of ribbon to prevent the case from overbalancing and the glove-box is finished.

Other boxes may be covered exactly on this principle, and are useful for handkerchiefs, photographs, Christmas cards, letters, lace, trinkets, and other things. In some, the lid may be stuffed to serve as a pincushion, but for these a wooden box is better as being rather more substantial, and therefore better able to hold the weight of the cushion. Others may be fitted up as work cases to stand on a toilet table, and bottles of perfume may be stowed away in those of other shapes. Some may have a sheet of glass arranged as a lid. This can be cut by any glazier or picture frame-maker for a few pence, and should be bound all round with ribbon firmly glued on. Scent powder may be sprinkled into those that are lined with wadding or quilted satin. There is immense variety to be made also in the style of covering. Puffed satin makes a pretty cover, so does brocade with plush corners, or velvet with diagonal bands of gold gimp. Some can have a frill round the lower part, others a puff or a full ruche; others again may be left quite plain. Quilted satin may be used for the outside as well as for the inside, and looks especially well if studded with jewels. The smaller the box, the less puffing and draping will there be room for, so it is better to make these up with brocade trimmed with flat bands of gimp. Adorned in this way, the ordinary round collar boxes make really elegant receptacles for a ball of string, and their value is doubled if a tiny pair of scissors be slipped into a little sheath at the side of the box.

sachet may be made quite straight at the ends and may be simply ornamented with a set of very tiny pompons or tassels, or tiny, half-closed, drooping daisies, or other small flowers. These sachets look pretty, too, in fanciful shapes, such as triangular, or star-shaped; as butterflies or various flowers. The latter forms need touching-up with oil-paints to represent the various markings and spots. Of course any pretty little pattern may be worked on the silk instead of the lavender design suggested above, and dozens of such are to be found amongst Briggs' transfers.

WORK-BAG.

THIS dainty work-bag can be recommended as a means of using a number of lengths of ribbon, which may be either of two colours or each one different. It is more convenient to have the ribbons all the same width, but even this is not absolutely essential. The number of strips of ribbon must of course depend upon the size the bag is to be and upon the width of the ribbons. They must all be cut the same length and be neatly seamed together, then their lower edge mitred and finished with a tiny ball, pompon, tassel, or even a small bell or sequin could be employed as a finish. After having pressed open each little seam with the finger and thimble, they can be hidden with rows of feather stitching, worked in rather coarse silk. The next proceeding is to line the bag with soft silk, choosing a colour that will harmonise well with the ribbons. This inner bag should be made a trifle less deep than the ribbons, as it would look ugly if showing between the points, and at the top would be made a hem about three inches deep, twice stitched, so that a double draw-string may be run in, by means of which the mouth of the bag can be closed.

Thermometer Holder.

Glove-Box.

Lavender Sachet.

LAVENDER SACHET.

A SACHET filled with lavender flowers is appreciated by every one who loves this sweet country scent, as indeed, who does not? Those who own a garden with lavender bushes in it, may, in the proper season, make up a dozen or twenty sachets out of odds and ends of ribbon and lace, while spare beads and spangles, scraps of embroidery silks, and gold thread can all be utilised. The flat-shaped sachet in the sketch is made simply of two pieces of ribbon, each measuring about two inches and a half in width and seven inches in length. Turn down each end of the ribbon to make a point, and catch the raw edges down very lightly with a few stitches. Sew the ribbons together on the wrong side down the edges. Trim one of the ends of the sachet with lace; gather this slightly, push it into the open end of the sachet, so that the edge of the lace appears just beyond the tip of the point, then close the end by taking a line of small stitches round the end of the ribbon, a quarter of an inch below the edge. Finish off the end by working a line of feather stitches along the edge, and add a few beads or spangles at intervals. Now put in the lavender flowers; not too many, but just enough to allow of their being shaken about freely inside the case, and remember to remove every scrap of hard stem.

Now, the second end of the sachet can be closed in the way already described for the first end. The silk or ribbon may be ornamented in different ways; a pretty idea being to embroider upon it sprays of lavender; of course, if it will contrast nicely with the ribbons employed. One's name may be worked across the sachet if desired, and should be traced with gold thread twined in and out amongst the embroidery. There are innumerable other ways in which such a sachet may be made. Soft silk, or even art muslin, can be used instead of ribbon, and fringe substituted for the frills of lace. The

It is easy to make a number of these bags in different styles and colours, at a very small cost; some may be multi-coloured and ticketed "Harlequin" bags; others of two colours only or of two shades of the same tint. Another pretty idea is to use alternate bands of black velvet and coloured ribbon, while yet another style of bag may be composed of alternate stripes of black or coloured velvet or ribbon and stripes of net or lace. Through the holes in the net would be run narrow bébé ribbon finished off in a small cluster of loops at the lower end. A full rosette of the same ribbon added to each loop of the ribbon which draws up the mouth of the bag would be a pretty finish. Of course any shape of bag may be made in this fashion, especially choice being those which are gathered round a circle of silk stretched over cardboard. Others may be made on the principle of an enormous envelope, some again, drawn up in jelly-bag style at each end.

BRUSH AND COMB HOLDER.

THIS is a novel and pretty little holder, and it can be made very quickly. It consists of two triangular pieces of card and two tiny gussets, the shapes for which are given in the diagram, on page 10, but the size of the case will depend, of course, upon whether it is to contain more than one brush and comb. The upper or longest side of the triangles should, if a medium-sized holder is required, measure from eight to ten inches, and be sloped off proportionately into a point at the bottom. It is very easy to cut out the shape from a piece of newspaper, folding it in half first across and then downwards to make quite sure that the form is straight and true. This paper pattern should then be pasted down to the cardboard, and cut round with a sharp penknife. The gussets should be two inches wide at the top, and must slope gradually down to a point, the entire length being equal to that of one of the sides of the triangle against which they are to be placed. Having cut two pieces of card for the front and back and two pieces for the gussets, cover these neatly with any material preferred, such as velvet, brocade, &c., turning the raw edges over, and pasting them down, or else lacing them neatly together with sewing cotton. Now join the pieces all round, having previously, however, lined each piece with sateen or any plain material that can be appropriately used with that employed for the outside. If the worker is especially anxious to be economical, the card which hangs against the wall may be covered with the same material as the lining instead of with that used for the front. Linen embroidered tastefully is very suitable for covering such a holder as this, and a pretty effect may be gained by the use of terra-cotta linen worked with ox-eye daisies and grass, using white, yellow, and dull green shades of flax-threads or silks. Pale blue linen is equally satisfactory, or white or fawn may be employed if preferred, but of course due regard must be given to the tinting of the wall paper against which the holder will hang. The artistic cretonnes and printed sateens now shown, and which are so inexpensive, are quite appropriate for such a purpose as this, and can be recommended to those workers who do not care for the trouble of executing the embroidery.

Work Bag.

After the holder is made up the pompons are sewn on. They are rather large, and silken or woollen, according to taste. One inch is left between each one, and they are sewn along the seam which joins the front to the gussets. Along the lower end of the gussets is arranged a strap or loop of the ribbon, which is finished at the point of the holder with a smart bow. This ribbon can be so arranged as to hide any imperfections made in joining the points of the gusset in. Another, but much larger loop of ribbon, is sewn to the two upper ends of the holder, and serves for hanging it to the wall, handles of the dressing-table, or other suitable place.

If made of handsome pieces this holder is really suitable for the drawing-room, where it would be useful for small books, letters, cards, and other odds and ends.

POCKET POWDER PUFF.

By many ladies a slight dusting of face powder is considered a comfort to the skin in hot weather, or when spending an evening in an overheated ball-room. A soft holder for the powder, too, is far more convenient to carry in the pocket than the pretty, but unyielding boxes generally sold for the purpose. The pocket powder puff shown in the sketches is made of wash-leather, four pieces of this being needed. The largest piece is cut to the shape of the diagram on page 7, the dotted lines showing where it is folded up. The two flaps at the side are cut separately, and the fourth piece is cut half an inch wider than the space between the first and second dotted lines on the diagram. A number of small holes must be cut in this piece of washleather, and each long side must be cut into tiny vandykes. It will be seen that this part forms the front of the puff itself, and the holes must therefore only be large enough to enable the powder to work through lightly when dabbed over the face. If they are too large, this will sift through in lumps. Lay the piece of wash-leather on the large piece between the first and second rows of dots on the diagram, and stitch it firmly down just below the vandykes. Bind the case, as it were, round with ribbon, running it along on the right side, turning it over and hemming it down on the wrong side. Leave the ribbon unsewn for the present along one end of the puff, so that the powder can be poured in through the opening. Make the flaps next, binding them all round with ribbon, sew one edge of each flap to the side of the puff, setting the stitches very closely together. Add two ribbon strings to the middle of the rounded end of the case, making them long enough to pass round it and tie in a bow.

If the puff is intended for a present, the initials of the owner should be embroidered upon the flap, but if for a bazaar, these may be superseded by a tiny spray of flowers—violets, for instance, or some similar device. The last thing to do is to sew up the opening after putting in the powder. It is a good plan to make these few stitches of a different colour to the rest so that they can be easily undone when the puff requires refilling.

PACKET-OF-TEA PINCUSHION.

A NOVELTY in the way of pincushions is here given, our design resembling a packet of tea. The main part of the work connected with it lies in the pincushion itself rather than in the cover for the outside. Cut six pieces of soft linen or calico, two measuring two inches wide by four inches long, two the same length but only an inch and a half wide, and the remaining two measuring an inch and a half by two inches. These must be sewn together so that the two widest pieces set opposite to one another and form the back and front of the packet; the two narrower pieces are at the sides and the smallest pieces form the ends. It is necessary to leave the last three seams open so that the case can be turned right side outermost. Now fill this linen case with bran, pushing it well into the corners, then sew up the open seams, and when only a few more stitches are required to close the opening, pour in more bran till the case is absolutely tightly packed and quite firm and solid through; then finish the pincushion.

Now prepare the cover: This consists merely of a piece of silk or satin resembling grocers' paper, silver, blue, or white, as nearly as possible. It must be cut eleven inches long and six inches wide exclusive of half an inch all round, which should be turned over and invisibly caught down with a few stitches. The packet is then neatly wrapped up in the silk or satin, exactly as any other parcel would be covered with brown paper. A stitch or two may be made here and there to keep the cover in place. The two edges of the satin should be arranged so that they set on the under side of the packet

Brush and Comb Holder.

exactly down the middle. The ends are folded up smoothly and neatly and are also tacked lightly here and there. Finally the packet is bound round length-wise with ribbon or gold cord, which is tied in a bow at the top. Put a stitch or two through this bow to prevent it from becoming untied. The resemblance to a packet of tea may be further increased by painting or drawing with pen and ink upon one of the broad sides of the pincushion the name of some superfine tea.

CHÂTELAINE.

THIS is a handy little article for those ladies who do much work, and it is especially appreciated by such as are in the habit of attending sewing or Dorcas meetings. Such châtelaines are very inexpensive to make, and the worker can purchase odd remnants of three or four yards of ribbon which will do well for the purpose.

The first thing to do is to cut six lengths of the ribbon, which should be about an inch and a half wide. Two of these should be fifteen inches long, two thirteen inches, and the remaining two eleven inches in length. One end of each ribbon is turned up and neatly hemmed, a line of strong gathering thread being run in near the edge and drawn up as tightly as possible. At the other end, which is to be used at the top of the châtelaine, the ribbon is gathered up closely without being hemmed. The ends are joined and hidden beneath a smart bow, at the back of which is sewn a large hook—a stay hook answers very well—for attaching the châtelaine to the waist of the dress. Sew the ribbons, the bow, and the hook to a square piece of stiff net or muslin, which will keep them all firmly in place. For the other ends of the ribbon must be prepared the various work requisites; two reels of cotton, a pincushion, needlebook, pair of scissors, and a thimble case.

The reels of cotton are fastened to the two longest bands of ribbon. Get a yard of sarcenet ribbon about half an inch wide, and matching the broader ribbon first used. Cut this length of ribbon in half, sew one piece firmly to the gathered end of the broad ribbon, pass the free ends of the narrow ribbon through the hole in the reel of cotton, and sew a small flat button on the

the edges of the calico scraps all round and sew them together so as to make a sort of square box. There will be no less than twelve tiny seams to be made. Leave the last one open and push in the bran till the little case is quite full, corners and all, and quite tight and firm. Sew up the last seam, and if possible, push in more bran. Make the outside cover in the same way; sew all the seams on the wrong side except the last three, which must be left open so that the pincushion may be pushed in. Then sew these up as neatly as possible and add a loop of ribbon at one of the corners, by which to fasten the pincushion to the châtelaine. This is a particularly useful shape, as there are no fewer than six sides ready for pins.

The thimble case is necessarily rather troublesome to make, as it is so very small. First cut a strip of cardboard exactly the depth of the thimble and long enough to meet round it. This must be curved into a round, tube-like shape and the two ends fastened together, either with flat stitches or with a strip of gummed paper on each side of the seam, that is, both inside and outside. The thimble should fit in the little tube quite easily, or when this is covered with velvet it will be too tight. The velvet for the lining must be cut about half an inch wider than the case and so long that when the two short ends are seamed together on the wrong side, it will fit exactly into the tube. Put it into place inside, fold the raw edges over to the outside, and glue them down securely. For the outside of the thimble case make a similar tube of cardboard which, when covered with satin, is just the right size to contain the velvet lining. Before putting this in, however, sew a strap of narrow ribbon to each side of the lined tube to form a kind of handle. Then glue the tube and fix it firmly into the one that is covered with satin. The

Packet-of-Tea Pincushion.

Pocket Powder Puff (closed).

Pocket Powder Puff (open).

ribbon close to the reel so that it is prevented from slipping through the holes in the reel. Make the ribbon into a cluster of small loops round the button, and arrange the second reel in the same way. When a fresh reel is wanted, all that is necessary is to loosen the narrow ribbon where it is joined to the broad, take off the reel, replacing it with the new one, and again sewing the ribbon to the end of the broader band. A simpler way perhaps of managing the reels is to take a piece of the narrow ribbon about an inch longer than double the depth of the reel. Pass one end of this through the middle of the reel, then bring this end back outside it and sew the two very firmly to the châtelaine.

The pincushion and thimble-case are fastened to the next two bands. The pincushion is made by cutting two circles of card about the size of a five-shilling piece, and covering each of these with satin or silk to match or contrast with the ribbon. The satin is cut about half an inch larger all round than the card, a gathering thread is run in about a quarter of an inch from the edge, the card is laid on the satin and the gathering thread drawn up tightly. When both cards are covered, they are laid together, of course with the right side outermost, and are sewn together round the edge. These stitches must be neatly made, but not set so closely together that there is no room for the pins to be pushed in between them. When the cards are nearly joined, a tiny loop of the narrow ribbon must be pushed in between them and sewn in firmly. By this loop the pincushion is tightly sewn to the broad ribbon.

If a plump cushion is thought more convenient than a flat one, the worker may easily make one by taking six pieces of satin each about an inch and a half square and also six pieces of soft calico for the inside cover. Turn in

bottom of the case has next to be thought of. Cut a circle of cardboard exactly the size of the base of the case, cover it on one side with satin and on the other with velvet. Sew it into place so that the velvet is inside and the thimble case is ready to be sewn by the ribbon strap to the end of the broad ribbon band.

The needle-case is next to be considered. For this take a piece of card about five inches long and three wide—an ordinary post-card will answer the purpose capitally—and fold it exactly in half. Cover the outside with satin to match or contrast with the ribbons, gluing the ends down inside the card. Line it with a piece of silk, moiré, or even thin flannel. The best way of managing this is to gum the material over a thin piece of card or stout paper the size required, and then to glue it into position inside the cover. Add about four leaves of thin flannel, or cashmere, either pinked or buttonholed round the edge. Secure these by passing a length of narrow ribbon through them and through the cover. Tie the ends of ribbon into a knot very firmly, then into a bow, which stitch lightly to prevent it from coming untied, and sew one or two of the loops to the end of the ribbon band intended for the needle-book. If desired an end of ribbon may be sewn on each front of the book to tie in a bow, and so prevent the covers from opening.

The scissors are fastened to the ribbon simply by passing a length of ribbon through both handles, leaving it loose enough to allow the scissors free play when in use. A sheath can be made for the scissors as follows: Cut two pieces of card the shape and size of the points of the scissors when these are closed. Cut the points off straight, then cover these cards on one side with satin to match the other articles, on the other with thin flannel. Lay the flannel-covered sides together, and sew the two divisions neatly but strongly round the edges. Now sew one end of a piece of narrow black elastic to the tip of the sheath. Put the sheath on the scissors and draw the elastic down the length of the scissors to the end of the ribbon of the châtelaine, allow another inch or inch and a half of the elastic, so that the sheath has sufficient play, and sew it neatly but securely to the end of the ribbon.

This completes the châtelaine, which although requiring so much space to describe, is indeed easily and quickly made. It is by no means essential that silk ribbon alone should be used for a châtelaine of this kind. Exceedingly pretty ones may be made of bands of black velvet, or the ribbon may be of some fancy kind, such as tartan or brocade. Another way of making them is to cut the bands out of brown holland and to bind each one with coloured ribbon. This, however, takes rather more time, and most people prefer the appearance of the ribbon. Very attractive-looking châtelaines can be made of bands of cross-stitched linen, or canvas, prettily embroidered, bound and lined with ribbon. When the bands are made of material other than velvet or ribbon, ribbon must, all the same, be used for the bow at the top as a thicker material would be too clumsy. Sometimes chatelaines are provided with a note-book, pencil, penholder, ink-eraser, and penknife, instead of with needle-work necessaries, and these form suitable presents for those of a literary turn of mind.

OPERA-GLASS BAG.

SMART little bags for holding the opera-glasses are now looked upon as

Opera-Glass Bag.

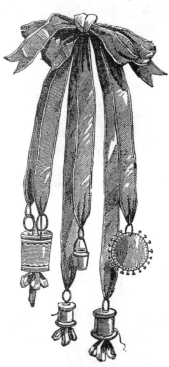

Châtelaine.

indispensable to the comfort of every theatre-goer, and while they make useful presents, there is never any difficulty in disposing of a large number of them at bazaars. One thing with regard to them is very essential, and this is that they shall be made only of the richest materials and ornamented with tasteful embroidery made still more resplendent with jewels, beads, or spangles. A good idea is to choose some small but rather distinct pattern brocade for the lower part, and to outline the design with a double line of gold thread. If this is not considered too much trouble a larger pattern may be chosen and worked over thickly with coloured silks. An immense variety is always to be had in gold braids and galons, with or without picots, and which are exactly suitable for trimming and finishing these elegant little articles. There are two ways of making them, the most customary being that illustrated here, and which will be described first.

The shape for cutting the cardboard base of the opera-glass bag is shown in full working size in the diagram on page 10, but in making them for bazaars it is well to vary the size a little, as opera-glasses are not all exactly alike. The foundation is covered on one side with some of the brocade that is to be used for the sides, but of course it need not be embroidered; the other side is lined with sarcenet, silk, satin, moiré, or anything else that happens to be convenient.

Now cut a band of buckram about two to three inches wide and long enough to fit exactly round the base; join the two short ends. Cut a similar strip of the embroidered material, join the ends, and slip it over the buckram. Turn the raw edges over to the wrong side and hold them down with lacing stitches carried across and across. Line the circle with silk to match that used for the bottom of the bag, then sew it round the edge of the base. Make the bag itself next, using satin of a colour that will contrast nicely with the

brocade. Cut the satin about twice the depth of the embroidered band, and wide enough to allow of easing it on, allowing an extra three or four inches to the depth to turn over at the top to make a hem and a running to hold the ribbons or cord and tassels with which to close the mouth. Join the satin to form a circle, then sew it to the lower part. The easiest way of managing this is to hem down the satin edge to the upper part of the brocade-covered band, easing the satin on to make it fit nicely. Any stitches may be hidden beneath a band of gold braid, and a similar band should be sewn round the lower edge of the embroidered band. This completes the bag as shown in the sketch.

The second way of making an opera bag does away with the stiff sides, the bag itself springing directly from the cardboard base. This, of course, gives a smaller space for embroidery, and only one material can conveniently be used. Cases for the small collapsible glasses are usually made thus, but the weightier glasses require the more substantial bag.

FEATHER BRUSH HOLDER.

THIS dainty little holder consists of nothing more elaborate than a tube or cylinder of cardboard, and which may be contrived out of a tall, narrow box, such as chocolate, cocoa and baking powder are often packed in, while brushes may be bought as cheaply as 4½d. each. The cardboard, if the worker is obliged to make her own tube, should measure about seven inches in depth and be sufficiently wide to fold closely round the thickest part of the brush; about five inches will probably be needed, but feather dusters vary considerably

Feather Brush Holder.

both in length and thickness. The two longest sides of the cardboard are joined together, either with a band of glued calico or paper laid down them both inside and outside, or by overlapping them slightly and either gluing or sewing them together.

The inside of the holder is finished off first. A piece of material is chosen an inch deeper and wider than the cardboard; the two longest edges are seamed together on the wrong side so that the lining thus made fits exactly into the inside of the tube. The edges are folded over to the outside and are held down with a few touches of glue. The cover must be cut an inch narrower than the depth of the tube and must be made to fit tightly and smoothly over it when the two ends are seamed together. A band of fancy braid should be glued round the top and bottom edges of the holder. It will be better to join the two ends of this with stitches rather than with glue. Now a loop of ribbon should be made, sewing one end to the top and one to the bottom edge of the holder, and finish it with a dainty bow.

This explains the general make of the holder, but as yet nothing has been said respecting the materials or ornamentation required. The worker is absolutely free to use any material for the outside that suits her own convenience best; silk, satin, moiré, plush, velvet, brocade, cretonne, sateen, or even art muslin, all look well. The inside lining may well be of sateen, plain silk, art muslin, or cretonne. Embroidery may be employed for the further ornamentation of the outside of the holder, or it may be decorated somewhat in the style of the one shown in the sketch. Here two bands of ribbon velvet with a picot edge are stretched round the tube, each band being ornamented with a few stitches of light coloured chenille, or tiny jewels would be effective. Bands of jewelled trimming look admirable on these fancy articles, or ornamental galon such as is often sold for ladies' dresses.